Radio Programming

Radio Programming
Consultancy and Formatics

MICHAEL C. KEITH

Focal Press
Boston   London

Focal Press is an imprint of Butterworth Publishers.

Copyright © 1987 by Michael C. Keith.
All rights reserved.

No part of this publication may be reproduced, stored in a retrieval system, or transmitted, in any form or by any means, electronic, mechanical, photocopying, recording, or otherwise, without the prior written permission of the publisher.

Library of Congress Cataloging-in-Publication Data
Keith, Michael C., date
  Radio programming.

  Bibliography: p.
  Includes index.
  1. Radio programs—Planning. 2. Radio programming—consultants. I. Title.
PN1991.55.K45 1987   791.44′0236   87-417
ISBN 0-240-51792-X

Butterworth Publishers
80 Montvale Avenue
Stoneham, MA 02180

10 9 8 7 6 5 4 3 2 1

Printed in the United States of America

To Claudia and Pamela

Contents

Foreword by Kent Burkhart   xiii
Preface   xv

1 RADIO PROGRAMMING AND THE CONSULTANT   1
   The Emergence of Radio Consultants   1
      Proliferation and Innovation   2
      Restoration through Adjustment   3
      Explosive Growth   3
   Types of Radio Consultants   7
      Full-Service Consultancy   7
      Programming Consultancy   11
   The Future of Radio Consultancy   11

2 CONSULTANCY AND FORMATICS   13
   Selecting a Format   13
      Case Study   15
      Targeting the Audience   18
      Radio's Popularity   18
      Generating Income   19
      Cost Considerations   20
      Going Head-to-Head   20
   Elements of Programming   21
      Music   21

       News   23
       Public Affairs   25
       Sports   25
       Weather   26
       Announcing   26
       Spots   27
       Contests and Promotions   29
       Jingles   30
       Call Letters   30
       Features   31
    Critiquing Time: Methods and Procedures   31
       Research Techniques   33
       Consulting Obstacles   36
    Industry Notes   38

3   ADULT CONTEMPORARY   45
    Format Characteristics   46
       Music   46
       Announcing   48
       News   49
       Contests and Promotions   52
       Public Affairs   52
       Commercials   52
    Competition   53
    Future   53
    Industry Notes   54

4   CONTEMPORARY HIT RADIO   59
    Format Characteristics   61
       Music   61
       Announcing   66
       News   67
       Features   67
       Contests and Promotions   67
       Public Affairs   68
       Commercials   68
       Jingles   69
    Competition   69
    Future   69
    Industry Notes   70

5   EASY LISTENING   77
    Format Characteristics   78
       Music   78
       Announcing   80
       News   81
       Features   81
       Contests and Promotions   81
       Public Affairs   82
       Commercials   82

CONTENTS

    Competition   84
    Future   85
    Industry Notes   85

6 ALBUM-ORIENTED ROCK   89
    Format Characteristics   91
        Music   91
        Announcing   91
        News   92
        Features   93
        Commercials   94
        Jingles, Contests, and Promotions   94
    Competition   95
    Future   95
    Industry Notes   96

7 NEWS AND TALK   99
    News Characteristics   100
        Features   101
        Commercials   102
    Talk Characteristics   102
        Announcing   102
        News   104
        Features   104
        Contests and Promotions   104
        Commercials   105
        Jingles   105
    News/Talk and News Plus Characteristics   105
    Competition   107
    Future   107
    Industry Notes   108

8 CLASSICAL   113
    Format Characteristics   114
        Music   114
        Announcing   116
        News   117
        Features   118
        Contests and Promotions   119
        Public Affairs   119
        Commercials   119
    Competition   119
    Future   120
    Industry Notes   120

9 COUNTRY   123
    Format Characteristics   124
        Music   124
        Announcing   128
        News   128

CONTENTS

    Contests and Promotions *130*
    Commercials *130*
    Jingles *130*
   Competition 130
   Future 131
   Industry Notes 132

10 VINTAGE 135
   Format Characteristics 137
    Music *137*
    Announcing *137*
    News *139*
    Features *140*
    Contests and Promotions *140*
    Public Affairs *142*
    Commercials *142*
    Jingles *142*
   Competition 142
   Future 143
   Industry Notes 144

11 URBAN CONTEMPORARY 147
   Format Characteristics 148
    Music *148*
    Announcing *148*
    News *149*
    Features and Public Affairs *150*
    Commercials *150*
   Competition 150
   Future 150
   Industry Notes 151

12 MIDDLE-OF-THE-ROAD 155
   Format Characteristics 156
    Middle-of-the-Road *156*
    Full-Service *158*
    Block/Variety *160*
   Industry Notes 162

13 ETHNIC AND RELIGIOUS 165
   Ethnic 165
    Black *165*
    Hispanic *166*
    Other Ethnic *169*
   Religious 172
   Industry Notes 174

14 PUBLIC AND NONCOMMERCIAL   177
   Public Radio Programming   179
   College (Educational) Radio Programming   180
   Community Radio Programming   181
   Industry Notes   183

Suggested Reading   189
Index   191

Foreword
Kent Burkhart

Mr. Burkhart is chairman of the Atlanta-based Burkhart/Abrams/ Douglas/Elliot and Associates, Inc., one of the top radio consultancy firms in the world.

A programmer is a programmer regardless of format. I have been hired numerous times to program a variety of formats, including News, Talk, Contemporary Hit, Album Rock, Country, Classical, Urban, Black, and Hispanic. I have found that there is not a vast difference in the skills needed to program a News or Contemporary Hits format. The bottom line is that they both require heavy repetition, announcer communication, community awareness, and all the other elements that add up to producing a great radio station.

We all have marveled at the stories of ten-year-old children who are able to play the piano like seasoned musical veterans. We also have marveled at eight-year-olds who paint as well as those who have been studying art for decades. Some people are more talented at a younger age than others. This is called natural talent. This natural talent applies to radio programmers. There are good programmers, and then there are great programmers. The great programmers seem to have an immediate sense for the commercialism of audio presentation. In short, good programmers study for decades, and even though they do an acceptable job, they never quite achieve greatness.

FOREWORD

If you aspire to greatness in radio programming, you will find much inspiration in this unique book written by Michael Keith with the assistance of some of the best programmers in the United States. The more you read this book, the better you will understand the challenge of blending science (research) and emotion in a manner designed to increase ratings. After all, ratings (audience popularity) state whether we as programmers have done a good job or a great job.

Preface

This text is designed to convey the realities, the so-called "facts" or "insider's perspective," on an important aspect of a truly unique business. To this end, I have enlisted the aid of select consultants and programmers, who have generously contributed insights and opinions pertaining to radio station programming.

The book's approach to the subject of modern radio programming is somewhat unusual in that it closely examines the role of the programming consultant. I believe this to be an appropriate strategy given the significant involvement of the consultant in the medium. It would be a mistake to underreport the contribution of the consultant, since many of the nation's most successful stations are guided by outside advisers. To date, the relationship between station and programming consultant has been only casually assessed. This study seeks to rectify that.

Therefore, the perspectives of both station programmers and consultants (every station has a program director, and one out of three uses a consultant) serve as the post and lintel of this text, which focuses on the elements and ingredients that constitute particular radio formats and make them work.

After a brief retrospective on the evolution of programming consultancy (Chapter 1), I examine the practices and methods employed by consultants (Chapter 2). The rest of the book (Chapters 3–14) is divided into twelve chapters, each devoted to the unique programming considerations of a different radio format. The twelve formats surveyed have been chosen because of their widespread application and popularity.

Chapters 2–14 conclude with a section called Industry Notes. Here the reader will find actual consultant critiques, program monitors, articles, essays, and memos to client stations relevant to the format covered by the chapter.

Due to the extraordinarily complex and dynamic nature of modern radio programming, a book of this length can only partially examine the subject. If this text has shed some light on the vast and intricate fabric that is radio programming, then my goal has been realized.

Without the input of those broadcasters and consultants whose comments appear within these covers, there would be no book. Thus, it is only fitting that this work also be dedicated to them.

A further expression of gratitude is owed Lou Emond, Roger Crosley, David Guenette, and Philip Sutherland for their considerable assistance and suggestions.

Radio—The transmission of intelligence by means of electromagnetic waves through the ether.

—*S. Gernsback*
Radio Encyclopedia, 1927

1
Radio Programming and the Consultant

Television changed the course of radio forever. Ironically, it was the new home screen, "sight radio," that eventually gave rise to the radio station consultancy profession. Before 1950 radio programming was primarily the province of network executives and advertising agencies. Most of the nation's stations (97 percent in 1947) depended on the major networks (NBC, CBS, MBS, and ABC) for the programming they aired. Stations not affiliated with the networks (independents) usually relied on local talent, community events, and phonograph records to fill their broadcast schedules. Competition, especially outside the major metropolitan areas, was relatively light. Prior to World War II fewer than one thousand stations were authorized to broadcast. In 1947 there were twelve hundred radio outlets. Today nearly ten thousand stations beam signals into the ether—an increase of nearly 800 percent since the time when many media observers were predicting the demise of radio as the consequence of television's auspicious arrival.

THE EMERGENCE OF RADIO CONSULTANTS

The market for radio consultant services manifested as the medium shifted its programming approach. During their heyday, prior to television, radio stations sought to be all things to all people, offering a variety of program genres to the entire demographic spectrum. Situation comedies, soap operas, mysteries, quiz shows, and musical programs were among the more popular recurring features of the day. Prior to 1950 radio programming resembled today's television. With the exception of some Hit Parade stations, there were no specialized radio formats to speak of, so the demand for programming consultants was virtually nonexistent.

As the medium attempted to come to terms with the unpleasant reality that television presented, it realized the futility of a tit-for-tat combat strategy. Parallel or reactionary programming simply did not work. After a few years of competing program for program with television, the majority of radio broadcasters accepted the fact that the public was not interested in listening to radio when the same type of program was offered by television.

By the mid-1950s radio had all but abandoned the block (segmenting) programming approach that had won it prominence. It was the dawning of a new era, of program specialization and selectivity. Radio broadcasters began to narrow their programming to gain a share of the listening audience that would generate advertiser interest. The day when radio stations could successfully broadcast in a random fashion was coming to a close for all but a few stations.

Proliferation and Innovation

Although radio's future seemed less than promising in the early 1950s, the actual number of stations increased, partly because the Federal Communications Commission (FCC) made available an abundance of lower power frequencies. The idea was to generate more local broadcasting in nonurban areas.

In 1954 more than thirty-one hundred stations were authorized to broadcast, and competition, especially in medium and large markets, was heating up. Increased mobility resulting from the advent of the transistor and miniaturization helped market the medium. Radios became more portable. The transistor radio opened up a whole new market. Receiver sales soared, and listenership jumped. Radio was the perfect companion for a day at the beach or on a picnic.

Another innovation, this one in the field of music, contributed to the recovery effort as well. Rock 'n' roll (initially referred to by some as "race" music because of its roots in black rhythm and blues) established itself in a major way in 1955 when Bill Haley and the Comets' recording of "Rock Around the Clock" surpassed the million sales mark. A few daring stations had been airing the newest form of pop music since its emergence a year or so before, but Haley's recording opened the eyes of many broadcasters who realized that something unique had arrived.

Stations that had confined their playlists to the hits of the day soon found that rock music was dominating the top slots. Young people were purchasing millions of 45 RPMs by their favorite rock 'n' roll artists. The "doowop" sound had the nation's youth firmly in its embrace. Stations were inundated with requests for the new sound, while jukebox companies stocked their machines with the latest releases. It was out of this phenomenon that the Top 40 format found its place in the hearts of the radio listening public.

Many in radio feel that Top 40, with its emphasis on best-selling records, was the first highly targeted format to surface in the age of programming specialization. No other format at the time adhered so closely to a formula. Todd Storz and Gordon McLendon were the young program innovators who introduced the new programming strategy, and in whatever market they applied their special approach, the stations they guided soon led the competition.

Restoration through Adjustment

At the close of the same decade that had seen the medium topple from preeminence, radio returned with even greater vigor. In the late 1950s several formats, including Beautiful Music, Top 40, Middle-of-the-Road, and Country, had carved a niche for themselves and were generating substantial revenue. The old-line block programming stations were becoming extinct.

During the same period the radio programming consultancy profession was launched when a successful young station program director by the name of Mike Joseph decided to go into business for himself. His first client, WMAX-AM in Grand Rapids, Michigan, quickly achieved ratings success. Joseph immediately went on to guide the programming of WROK, Rockford, Illinois; WKZO, Kalamazoo, Michigan; KDAL, Duluth, Minnesota; and WKBW, Buffalo, New York. In each situation Joseph's stations invariably enjoyed new and larger followings.

Despite Joseph's accomplishments, the market for programming consultancy remained relatively limited at the onset. This would change in the 1960s, however, as hundreds of new stations attempted to establish themselves in an increasingly competitive environment. In major markets where radio consultants found the most fertile ground for their product, the atmosphere was charged. Numbers became the name of the game. To be number one was to be king of the hill. Stations in large cities depended on strong showings in the ratings survey to attract major advertisers. One weak book (*Ratings Survey*) could send a station into a financial tailspin. A couple of poor ratings periods could mark the beginning of the end. "Call a consultant" became a cry commonly heard when a station stood at the edge of the abyss.

In the 1960s radio rep companies and program syndicators became more actively involved in individual station programming consultation. In addition, independent consultants and consultancy firms increased as more successful station program directors and network programming executives entered the field.

Explosive Growth

Competition increased throughout the 1960s. Not only were there hundreds more AM stations, but FM began to make its presence felt. Until the mid-sixties, FM was considered the alternative band. This was another way of saying second choice. AM was radio. FM was, well, FM. It was the place to go if you wanted "good" music. The term FM was nearly synonymous with highbrow. It was radio for the cultured, condescendingly referred to by some as the egghead band. Although FM was technically superior and provided its listeners with stereophonic reception, an aura hung about the medium that

RADIO PROGRAMMING

11 Punchbowl Drive
Westport, Connecticut
06880

MICHAEL JOSEPH
Program Consultant

Phone: (203) 227-8326

STATION	CITY	FACILITY	NET	TYPE	YEAR	RESULTS
WTNS-Coshocton Tribune	Coshocton, Ohio	1000-1560	Ind.	M	50-1	---
WJEF, Fetzer	Grand Rapids (71)	250-1230	CBS	M	51-5	1st Place
WTAC, Founders	Flint (76)	1000-600	ABC	R	55-8	4th - 1st
WFBL, Founders	Syracuse (59)	5000-1390	ABC	R	56-7	4th-1st
WSMB, Founders	New Orleans (33)	5000-1350	ABC	M	56-7	6th-1st
KPOA, Founders	Honolulu (56)	10000-650	Mut.	R	57-8	1st Place
WMAX	Grand Rapids (71)	1000-1480	Ind.	R	58	6th-1st
WROK	Rockford (140)	1000-1440	ABC	R	58	2nd-1st
WIBW, Stauffer	Topeka (170)	5000-580	CBS	M	58	1st Place
WKZO, Fetzer	Kalamazoo (137)	5000-590	CBS	M	58	1st Place
KDAL, Chicago Tribune	Duluth (139)	5000-610	CBS	M	58	3rd-1st
WKBW, Capital Cities	Buffalo (30)	50000-1520	Ind.	R	58	9th-1st
WROW, Capital Cities	Albany (49)	5000-590	CBS	B	59-60	3rd-1st
WFBC, Multi Media	Greenville, SC. (73)	5000-1330	NBC	M	59	5th-1st
WPRO, Capital Cities	Providence (41)	5000-630	CBS	R	59-60	6th-1st
WORC	Worcester, Mass. (101)	5000-1390	Mut.	R	60	2nd-1st

'TYPE' Code: R = Top 40/Hot Hits
M = Pop Adult/AC
T = All Talk
B = Beautiful Music
N = All News
S = Spanish
G = Oldies

Figure 1.1 An early client list showing the results of consultant Mike Joseph's programming guidance. Courtesy Mike Joseph.

resulted in limited audiences. Consequently, most broadcasters and the majority of listeners paid homage to AM, while FM was left to the near solitude of the waiting room.

In 1965 the FCC decided that broadcasters with AM/FM licenses in cities with populations of one hundred thousand or more had to originate separate programming on their FM stations. Until then most combo licensees simulcast their AM programming on their FM outlets. The FCC regarded this practice with disdain, believing it was an inefficient use of broadcast frequencies. Not long after FM was given its citizenship papers, it began to attract a substantial following. Not until the late 1960s and early 1970s, however, did AM's former understudy begin to draw the kind of numbers that would raise eyebrows. Breaking from tradition in the quest for greater financial rewards, FM broadcasters introduced album rock music and, eventually, Top 40. As the 1970s progressed, radio listeners shifted to this sound alternative for the day's hottest music.

RADIO PROGRAMMING AND THE CONSULTANT

Station programming consultancy became a much more complex and challenging task, as the medium's reliance on survey results, namely Arbitron, grew throughout the 1970s. The ability of consultants to turn around low power stations (known as small sticks) was significantly affected. The big signal operations with wider coverage areas simply drew larger numbers in the listener surveys. Increasing the listener shares of small stations, especially AM, was a Herculean task that only a few master consultants were up to.

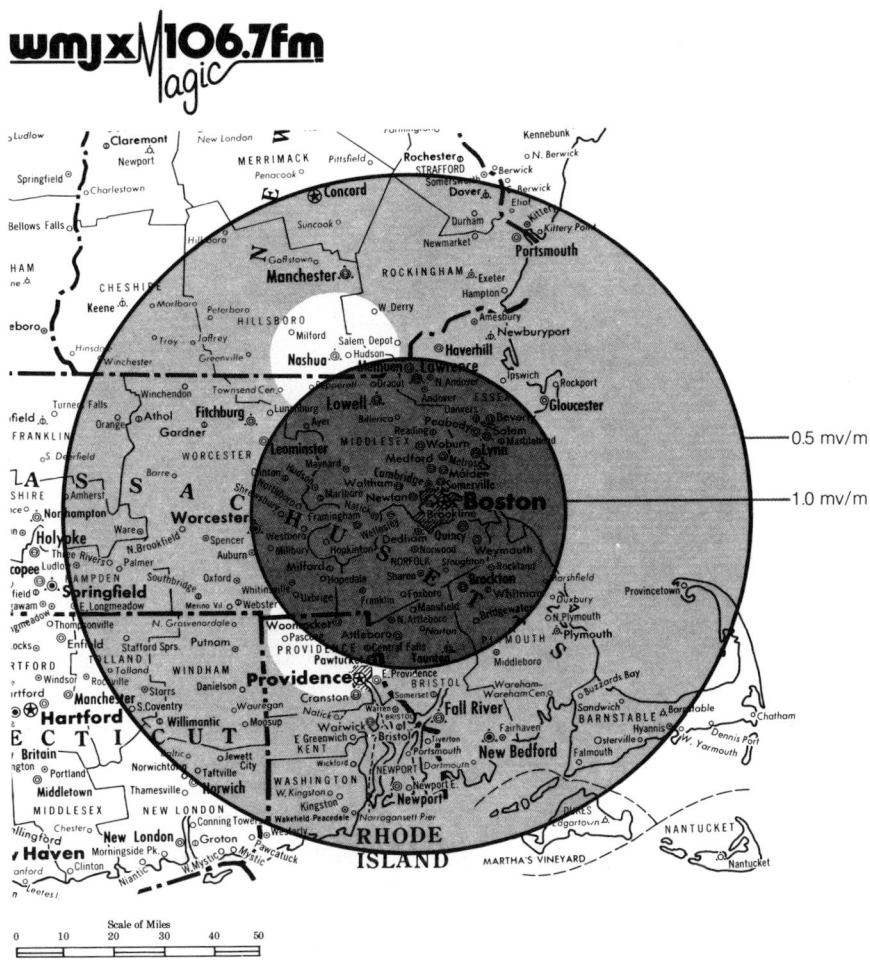

WMJX-FM, Greater Boston, Radio, Inc., Boston, Massachusetts Ch. 294B (106.7 Mhz) ERP 11.5 Kw, 900 ft. HAAT
Copyright, American Map Co., New York, NY License No. 18753

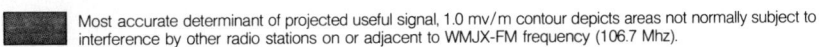 Most accurate determinant of projected useful signal, 1.0 mv/m contour depicts areas not normally subject to interference by other radio stations on or adjacent to WMJX-FM frequency (106.7 Mhz).

0.5 mv/m contour depicts areas generally receivable, though subject to interference due to terrain, obstructions or other radio stations.

Contours depict areas of possible interference due to stations on frequencies adjacent to WMJX-FM frequency (106.7 Mhz).

Figure 1.2 A greater signal coverage area means more potential listeners. Courtesy WMJX-FM.

Figure 1.3 Ratings services have actually inspired the growth of programming consultancy. Courtesy Arbitron.

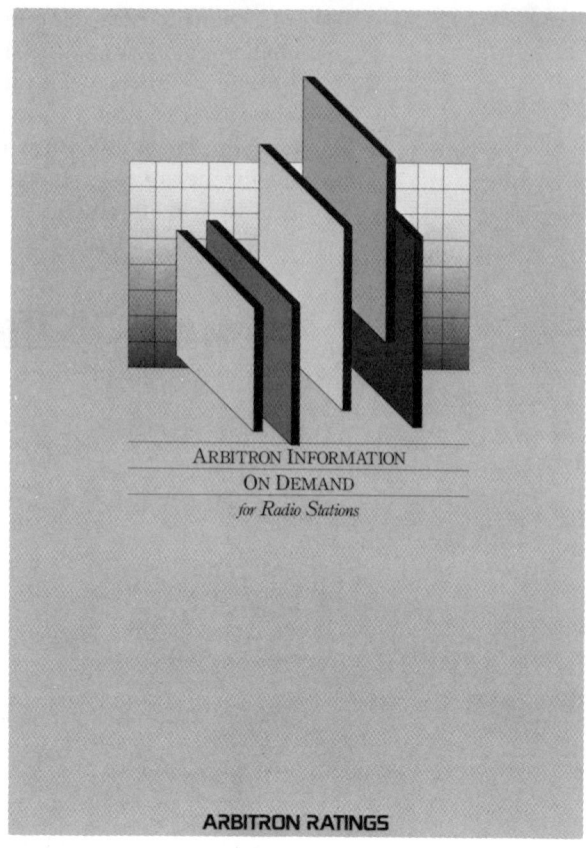

FM's tenure as second cousin to AM ended in 1978, when a listener survey concluded that it attracted 51 percent of the radio audience. By the mid-1980s AM lagged far behind FM in listenership. Nearly three-quarters of the nation's radios are tuned to FM today.

FM's ascent fanned the already raging fire of competition and, in so doing, expanded the market for radio consultancy. The number of stations doubled, as the number of formats tripled. The audience pie was sliced into many more pieces. Radio consultants, who found themselves an integral part of FM's bid for prominence in the 1960s and 1970s, worked the AM side with as much fervor in the 1980s in an attempt to reverse the misfortunes that befell the one-time ratings leader.

Figure 1.4 AM broadcasters look to stereo as one way to regain listeners. Courtesy KDES-AM Stereo.

TYPES OF RADIO CONSULTANTS

Full-Service Consultancy

While many radio consultants work exclusively in programming, others provide their clients a variety of services. Donna Halper, *Pop Music Survey*'s Radio Consultant of the Year in 1984, is called on for staff training and motivation, format changes, music research, and positioning studies. She also counsels staff who may have drug- or alcohol-related problems.

"My radio experience is not just confined to music and programming," Halper says. "It also includes news and public affairs, and I have two engineering consultants available for complicated technical problems. In addition, I do management consulting work and support station efforts in increasing their visibility in the industry or even improving record service. My critiques and positioning studies have been used by stations of all sizes and formats in all parts of the U.S., Canada, and Puerto Rico."

Rick Sklar, president of Sklar Communications and former programming vice president for ABC Radio, provides a similar list of services to his clients and also acts as negotiator. "We negotiate on behalf of clients with syndication companies, unions, music suppliers, and record companies, among others," he says. "We work very closely with station management."

Better numbers. Now.

Since opening her consulting firm in 1980, Donna Halper has earned a reputation for getting results, in markets of all sizes, and in all formats.

In 1984, Donna was named **RADIO CONSULTANT OF THE YEAR** by *Pop Music Survey,* and for good reason - over **90%** of her clients have shown ratings increases. In nearly half of these, the ratings **doubled,** and in a few cases, **tripled.** Here are some of her success stories:

☐ **WWMJ** (AC)
Bangor, Maine
5.6 to 15.4 with an 18.6 in men - 1984
#1 in 25-54 adults with a **26.9** - 1985

☐ **KQDS** (AOR)
Duluth, Minnesota
From #5 to a tie for #1 - 1982
#1 in 18-34 - 1983

☐ **WKCQ-FM** (Country)
Saginaw, Michigan
From 11.4 to 15.7 in one year (1985)
#2 in the market overall (1985)

☐ **WQKS** (Urban)
Williamsburg/Richmond, Virginia
From 1.9 to 6.7 (1983-1984)

For positioning studies, monitors, critiques, format modifications, and staff motivation, Donna Halper gets results.

No promises. Just results.

Donna Halper and Associates
Radio Programming Consultants
28 Exeter Street #611
Boston, MA 02116
(617) 266-5666

All numbers from Arbitron

Figure 1.5 Consultant promo piece boasting ratings successes for client stations. Courtesy Donna Halper and Associates.

DIRECTORY

Consultants

Harris Marketing Group, Inc. 15889 Preston Road, #1012 Dallas, TX 75248 (214) 960-8733 *Bob Harris, President*	**Landsman Media** 135 E. 54th St. New York, NY 10022 (718) 855-0444 *Dean Landsman, President*	**Ott & Snead** 300 Turner Road, Suite 514 Richmond, VA 23225 (804) 320-5223 *Rick Ott, President* *Martin Snead, Vice President*	**Ray Sasser & Associates** P.O. Box 3181 Winston-Salem, NC 27102 (919) 945-5323 *Ray Sasser, President*
Bob Hattrik Communications P.O. Box 1333 St. Petersburg, FL 33731 (813) 896-6666 *Sue Jackson-Raines, Director*	**Local Marketing Corp.** 319 Dixie Terminal Building Cincinnati, OH 45202 (513) 241-5158 *Lee Carter, President*	**Peterson Media Services** 4535 White Oak Place Encino, CA 91316 (818) 344-7014 *Al Peterson, President*	**Shane Media Services** 6405 Richmond St., Suite 311 Houston, TX 77057 (713) 952-9221 *Ed Shane, President*
Bob Henabery Associates 136 E. 55th St. New York, NY 10022 (212) 753-6513 *Bob Henabery, President*	**Jim Long Companies** 13747 Montfort Drive, #220 Dallas, TX 75240 (214) 934-2222 *Jim Long, President*	**Jeff Pollack Communications** 984 Monument Street, Suite 204 Pacific Palisades, CA 90272 (213) 459-8556 *Jeff Pollack, President*	**Barry Sherman & Associates** 1828 L Street, NW, #300 Washington, DC 20036 (202) 429-0658
Bill Hennes & Associates 1814 Catalpa Lane Mt. Prospect, IL 60056 (312) 364-6966 *Bill Hennes, President*	**Pam Lontos, Inc.** P.O. Box 741387 Dallas, TX 75374-1387 (214) 341-1670 *Pam Lontos, President*	**Programming Co-Op** Rt. 1, Box 400E Fayetteville, AR 72703 (501) 521-1435 *Steven Warren, Director*	**Jon Sinton Associates** 943 Otter Way Marietta, GA 30067 (404) 971-4647 *Jon Sinton, President*
Irv Joel & Associates 528 River Road Teaneck, NJ 07666 (201) 692-0010 *Irv Joel, President*	**The Lund Consultants To Broadcast Management, Inc.** 1330 Millbrae Ave. Millbrae, CA 94030 (415) 692-777 *John C. Lund, President*	**Radioactivity Broadcast Consultation** 3954 Peachtree Road, Suite 202 Atlanta, GA 30319 (404) 266-1977 *Dain Schult, President*	**Barry Skidelski & Associates** 132 E. 45th Street, Suite 12C New York, NY 10017 (212) 370-0130 *Barry Skidelski, President*
Johns Co./Fairwest 1250 Prospect Place, #102 La Jolla, CA 92037 (619) 454-3202 *Jim Johns, President*	**Chris Lytle & Associates** 429 Gammon Place Madison, WI 53719 (608) 833-8384 *Chris Lytle, President*	**Radio Arts, Inc.** 210 N. Pass Ave., #104 Burbank, CA 91505 (818) 841-0225 *Larry C. Vanderveen, President*	**Sklar Communications** 100 Park Ave. New York, NY 10017 (212) 370-0077 *Rick Sklar, President*
Mike Joseph 11 Punchbowl Drive Westport, CT 06880 (203) 227-8326 *Mike Joseph, President*	**Marketing Entertainment Group** 270 Lafayette Street, #901 New York, NY 10012 (212) 226-8700 *Whitten Pell, President*	**Radio Marketing Concepts** Route 4, Box 43 Warrenton, VA 22186 (703) 347-3555 *Norm Goldsmith, President*	**Clark Smidt** 85 Westbourne Terrace Brookline, MA 02146 (617) 232-1322 *Clark Smidt, President*
Paul Kagan Associates Carmel, CA 93923 (408) 624-1536 *Paul F. Kagan, President*	**McVay Media** 24650 Center Ridge Rd., #340 Westlake, OH 44145 (216) 574-2311 *Michael A. McVay, President*	**The Research Group** 2517 Eastlake Ave. East Seattle, WA 98102 (206) 328-2993 *William Moyes, President*	**Stecker-Thompson Associates** 4202 Hidden Elm Woods San Antonio, TX 78249 (512) 492-8677
E. Karl Broadcast Consulting 1665 Knoll Drive San Luis Obispo, CA 93401 (805) 543-6386 *E. Karl, President*	**Media Strategies** 30606 Squire's Trail Farmington Hills, MI 48108 (313) 626-7158 *Fred Jacobs, President*	**Reymer & Gersin Associates** 20300 Civic Center Drive, #320 Southfield, MI 48076 (313) 354-4950 *Harvey Gersin, Exec. VP*	**Mary Catherine Sneed** 5010 Spruce Bluff Drive Atlanta, GA 30360 (404) 394-8291 *Mary Sneed, President*
Don Kelly & Associates 39 Mayberry Road Chappaqua, NY 10514 (914) 666-0175 *Don Kelly, President*	**Larry Moffit, Consultant** 3900 NE Broadway Des Moines, IA 50317 (515) 265-6181 *Larry Moffit, President*	**Pete Salant Broadcast Consultants** Box 575 Cheshire, CT 06410 (203) 272-9424 *Pete Salant, President*	**Surrey Consulting & Research** 165 South Union, #606 Denver, CO 80228 (303) 989-9980 *Roger Wimmer, President* *Mike Henry, Dir./Marketing*
Klemm Media, Inc. Box 647 Kent, CT 06757 (203) 927-3581 *David R. Klemm, President*	**Only Radio Sales** 8681 South West 137th Ave. Miami, FL 33183 (305) 385-1880 *Bob Grim, President*	**SB Management** 550 Price Ave., #8 Redwood City, CA 94063 (415) 366-1781 *Mike Hesser, President*	**TM Communications, Inc.** 1349 Regal Row Dallas, TX 75247 (214) 634-8511 *Pat Shaughnessy, President*

1986 R&R RATINGS REPORT Vol. 1/57

Figure 1.6 Consultant directory excerpt as listed by *Radio and Records*. Courtesy *Radio and Records*.

Consultants often advise the business and financial side of a radio station. "We become very much involved in the sales and marketing aspect," says Jay Williams, Jr., president of Broadcasting Unlimited. "We work alongside the sales department to bring about maximum results."

Consultants provide clients research data pertaining to audience and market trends. "Everything we do is based, at least in part, on research findings," Halper notes. "We are anything but rash in our judgments. Suggestions and recommendations are invariably inspired by some type of on-the-

January 10, 1985

Mr. Rick Sklar
SKLAR Communications, Inc.
154 East 46th Street
New York, N. Y. 10017

Dear Rick:

While the memory of your visit is still fresh in my mind, I want to let you know how impressed I was with your consultation visit to WINZ and I-95.

I have had many opportunities to work with some of the finest consultants in our industry and you are head and shoulders above the pack.

Your recommendations were clear and concise, and are already being implemented. I am certain they will result in increased shares for both stations.

Regular back to basics lessons are the best education we can get, and you put us back on the right path in a very short time.

Thank you again for your expertise. We look forward to your next visit!

Sincerely,

Stanley Cohen
General Manager

SC:jl

4330 Northwest 207th Drive, Miami, Florida 33055
Dade (305) 624-6101   Broward (305) 763-7222

Figure 1.7 Letter of commendation to consultant from satisfied client. Courtesy Rick Sklar.

scene or nationally conducted research. Instincts are important in this business, and I pride myself on having some of the best, but I am also long enough on experience to know the value of careful, methodical study."

Full-service radio consultancy firms have increased since 1970. Some companies actually supply clients with programming. Dave Scott, president of Century 21 Programming Incorporated, explains: "Our clients receive comprehensive consulting services from our seasoned staff. We begin with a detailed study of their radio market. We probe demographics, psychographics, and population growth trends of a client's available audience. We analyze their competition quantitatively—through available ratings—and qualitatively—from air checks. Then a client's programming will be professionally positioned to maximize sales, ratings, and profits."

Firms that provide client stations with programming product as well as consultancy usually provide the latter service after contracting for the former. These companies also are called syndicators. Radio stations can utilize the

RADIO PROGRAMMING

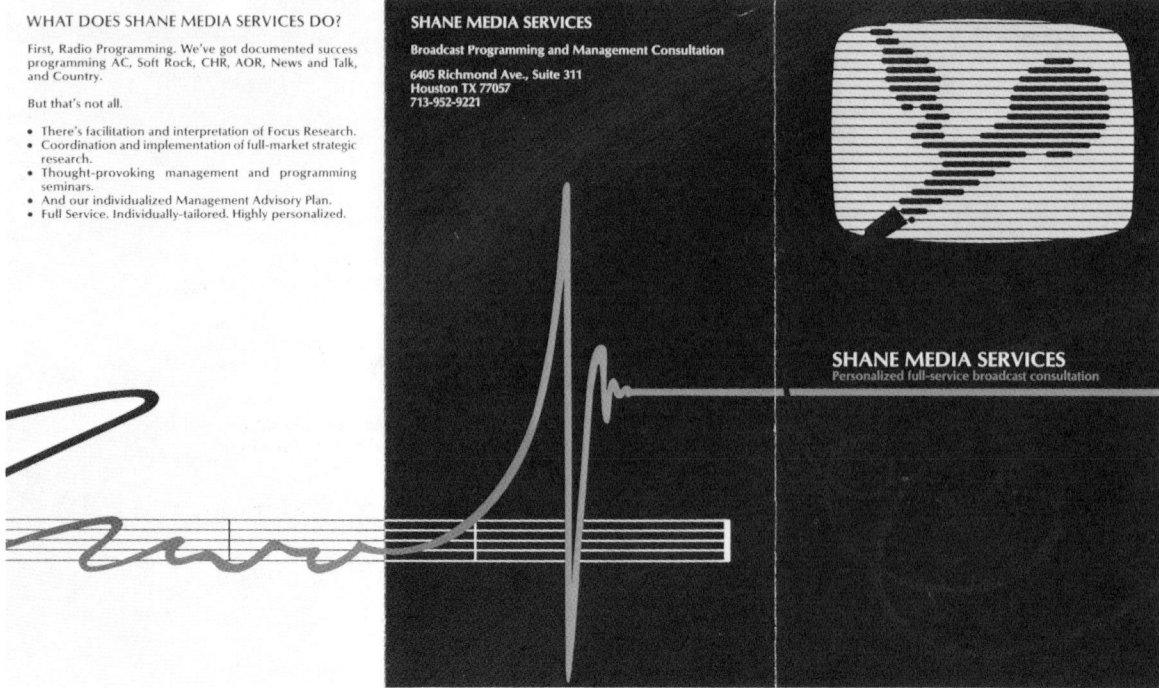

WHY DO I NEED A PROGRAMMING CONSULTANT?

We call our consulting services a "second ear" for radio managers. Shane Media Services is the doctor who offers the "second opinion." An objective, outside view.

Sometimes it's as comprehensive as a Strategic Plan including weekly music lists, talent training, performance analysis and critique, promotion outline, and research coordination.

Sometimes it's as simple as a Market Audit — a calculation of strength and vulnerability.

Most often, it's in-between. An individually-tailored program that develops a Win System for your station.

WHAT DO I GET?

We can't answer that without meeting you and your key staff face to face. We must work with *you* to define your problems.

Every station has unique concerns. We know that no two operations have the same competitive pressures. And no two stations have identical resources.

With Shane Media Services, there's no boilerplate plan. Our solution to your problem is unique to your situation. It's individually tailored to your station.

We realize that some problems can be solved quickly, so we solve them quickly. Other problems take time, so Shane Media Services provides a strategic plan to be executed over time, under our supervision.

As a Shane Media Services client, you get an intense, highly personalized service that leads to success in terms that *you* define.

WHO DO I CALL?

Call Ed Shane at 713-952-9221.

Ed has offered strategic communications consultation to an impressive list of clients since 1976. He's the author of the radio industry bestseller, *Programming Dynamics: Radio's Management Guide*.

He established Shane Media Services on three principles: COMMITMENT. INTEGRITY. SUCCESS.

Figure 1.8 Many consultancy firms provide a vast range of services. Courtesy Shane Media Services.

syndicator 100 percent (automated operation) or provide their own local announcers, while the syndicator provides the music on tape or via satellite (automated/live assist operation).

Programming Consultancy

The number of radio consultants devoted exclusively to programming has increased threefold since the mid-1960s. While some radio consultant firms have large staffs, many consist of one person who hires outside help as the need arises. For example, although Donna Halper consults with stations across the country, she is the only full-time employee of the company that bears her name. When she determines that a client station needs assistance in an area outside her field of expertise, perhaps dealing with something of a technical nature, she enlists the aid of a professional qualified to help. This person generally has worked for Halper before.

While the number of one-person consultancy operations remains fairly constant (in 1986 more than fifty were listed in various directories), the names on that list change frequently, as fates are determined to a large extent by ratings. "There are a lot of here-today gone-tomorrow radio consultants," Halper observes.

A number of station program directors work the consulting circuit when they have achieved a degree of ratings success. According to Halper, there are few really effective program directors (PDs) functioning in the role of consultant. "A couple of good books does not a consultant make," she notes. "In general, PDs usually don't fare as well when they attempt to program outside their own backyard. Of course, there are exceptions."

Statistics tend to bear out the fact that in most cases, it is the established radio consultant possessing a vast portfolio of programming successes who most consistently hits the target.

THE FUTURE OF RADIO CONSULTANCY

The number of radio stations is expected to continue increasing through the 1990s and beyond. In the early 1980s the FCC passed legislation intended to make available hundreds of new AM and FM frequencies. By extending the Standard Broadcast Band to 1705 kHz, the FCC has provided opportunities for minorities to become more actively involved in the ownership and management end of broadcasting, something not as likely to happen with the existing frequencies all but locked up. It will take time for these new stations to find an audience, since existing receivers do not extend much beyond 1600 kHz. But manufacturers are gearing up to market sets able to accommodate the new frequencies and the several hundred radio stations that may broadcast from them.

Meanwhile, Docket 80-90 (legislation designed to increase FM frequencies) has resulted in a whole new group of FM station classifications. In addition to the existing categories—Classes C, B, A, and D—the following classifications have been created:

Class C-1: Stations granted licenses to operate within this classification may be authorized to transmit up to 100 kw ERP (effective radiated power) with antennas not exceeding 984 feet. The maximum reach of stations in this class is around fifty miles.

Class C-2: The operating parameters of stations in this grouping are close to Class B's. The maximum power granted C-2 stations is 50 kw, and antennas may not exceed 492 feet. Stations in this class can reach approximately thirty miles.

Class B-1: The maximum antenna height permitted for this type of station is 328 feet, making it nearly identical to Class As. Class B-1 stations are assigned up to 25 kw ERP. Class B-1 signals carry twenty-five to thirty miles.

As of this writing, the FCC was nearing completion on legislation designed to reconstitute the FM classification system to allow for a more efficient and effective use of the much sought after spectrum space.

Of course, more stations will mean increased competition and further audience fragmentation. This will no doubt inspire the creation of new formats, or variations on existing ones, as stations attempt to secure a share of the listenership. Key broadcast trade associations have expressed concern over the continuing proliferation, fearing oversaturation of the radio marketplace. The FCC has adopted the position that increased competition fosters quality and creativity, two things some media critics claim are in short supply.

In the 1980s there are ample signs that radio is on its way to becoming hyperspecialized in its programming efforts. In metropolitan areas where there often are forty or fifty stations from which listeners can choose, specialty formats have surfaced, especially on the embattled AM band. In a growing number of large cities, listeners can tune in stations that offer round-the-clock comedy, sports, health, financial, weather, and children's formats, to mention a few.

Most consultants predict that stations are going to be peering through the cracks in hopes of finding a new program product that will generate listener interest. It will become even more of a challenge to program a station. Other media compound the problem. Music video stations and specialty channels on cable, as well as broadcast radio superstations on cable, must be added into the equation. "It's hot now, but it's going to get hotter out there," says Dave Scott of Century 21 Programming.

What this means to the radio consultancy profession is obvious. As competition increases, so will the demand for the services of the successful program consultant. It is estimated that one out of three radio stations uses consultants, and there is every indication that the time will come when the majority of stations will find operating without a consultant untenable.

2
Consultancy and Formatics

Successful radio stations do not suddenly or miraculously appear out of nowhere. They evolve slowly and gradually. There is no such thing as an overnight success. An overnight sensation, yes, but sensations die as quickly as they are born. Long-term success is much more difficult to attain.

Extensive planning goes into choosing exactly what to offer the listening public. Innumerable considerations bear on this decision. When a choice is finally made, the presentation schema (what to air and when and how to air it) must be carefully drawn.

It is the programmer's (be he or she consultant or station PD) challenge to provide a marketable segment of the listening audience with something that it desires and values. The process involved in meeting this challenge is complex.

SELECTING A FORMAT

The first thing a radio station must determine is what it will air. Numerous factors enter into this decision. The importance of each factor varies, but none is ignored by a consultant when recommending a change in format.

A consultant examines the physical plant itself. A station without a good signal, one that does not effectively cover the area, is at a significant disadvantage. "Generally speaking, when two stations offer the same format in a like manner—that is, comparative execution and performance levels—the outlet with the strongest and clearest signal will nearly always garner the largest following," consultant Jay Williams, Jr., observes.

Some formats are decidedly AM or FM, or at least have been up until now. A radio consultant with an AM client in a medium-size market probably would not be inclined to suggest a Contemporary Hits format if an FM station is offering similar programming. At the same time, suggesting that an FM client broadcast All-Talk when the market is already saturated with nonmusic AM stations might be ill-advised. Traditionally, listeners tune to FM for music and AM for news and information, although in the 1980s a small but increasing number of AM stations with stereo capacity have returned to the music programming fold. High-quality fidelity has been the reason FM has become the preferred radio band for the overwhelming majority of music listeners. Whether a station is AM or FM plays a central role in a consultant's decision concerning what should be programmed.

Many AM outlets are affected by operating constraints. More than two thousand AM stations sign off around sunset. Some sign off within a couple of hours after sunset but operate at drastically reduced power. For example, a one-thousand-watt daytimer might operate with a postsunset authorized power of thirty-six watts. This creates an obvious programming consideration. A case in point would be an AM daytimer (WXXX) in a midwestern, five-station market that also includes one AM and three FM stations, all operating on a full-time (round-the-clock) basis. The format that each station employs and their operating parameters might look like this:

WYYY-FM = Easy Listening, 20 kw, antenna 900 feet

WBBB-FM = Contemporary Hit, 10 kw, antenna 780 feet

WCCC-FM = Adult Contemporary, 3 kw, antenna 330 feet

WQQQ-AM = MOR/News, 5 kw daytime, 1 kw nighttime, antenna 150 feet

WXXX-AM = Undecided, 1 kw daytime, antenna 163 feet

At first glance a radio consultant might decide to examine the potential of a Country format, which traditionally does well in the Midwest and on the AM band. This is an obvious choice when, in actuality, arriving at a decision is seldom so simple.

Dial position also figures into the AM equation. Because of simple physics, a station located at the lower end or midpoint (550 to 1100 kHz) of the Standard Broadcast Band generally fares better than one at the high end (1300 to 1600 kHz). The lower the frequency, the greater the range of the AM signal. For example, under most circumstances, an outlet operating with one thousand watts at 570 kHz would reach farther than one transmitting five thousand watts at 1520 kHz.

Operating limitations are a point for careful consideration on FM, too, but not to the degree they are on AM. FM broadcasters are not faced with having to sign off around sunset, nor must they redirect their signals or decrease their power at night, as do a substantial number of AM stations. In the programming business, this is a prime variable.

The nature of the competition's technical facilities is a crucial element in any market assessment, as is what is being aired by the competition. For example, it was suggested that a consultant might determine that WXXX-AM could attract a segment of the listening audience by offering a Country format. The rationale was based on the facts that no other station was airing Country in this particular market, that WXXX was on the AM band, where Country has done extremely well, and that the market was located in a region particularly receptive to this type of format.

Case Study

Not all programming options are so obvious and accessible. Put WXXX-AM in a northeastern market with more than a dozen stations, and the task of positioning becomes far more complex. For the sake of illustration, Table 2.1 lists the stations in a hypothetical medium-size market.

As a daytimer, WXXX is confronted with the task of overcoming the stigma of being the only station in the market that must cease broadcasting shortly after sunset. It is also licensed in a predominantly FM market. Eight out of the fourteen stations operating are FM, and four are rated among the top five. Obviously an AM daytimer in this particular environment is confronted by many more obstacles than one in a small market. The management of WXXX must decide what can be done, given the resources it possesses, to generate an income sufficient to sustain operations. The question it must address is what can a 1 kw AM daytimer at 1520 kHz do to attract both listeners and advertisers who already have an abundance of choices? This is not an easy question to answer. Through a process of elimination, however, it might arrive at certain conclusions:

> *CHR* (Contemporary Hit Radio) is not viable. The market's number one rated outlet, WPPP-FM, programs contemporary hits. WPPP is a powerful full-time stereo facility with a sharp signal, and it invests heavily in outside promotion to retain its position. A daytime AM station could do little to attract listeners away from the rating's leader.

Table 2.1

Ranking	Station	Freq.		Format	Operating Limits
3	WDDD-AM	1270	kHz	News	5 kw full-time
2	WEEE-FM	98.1	mHz	Easy Listening	10 kw
13	WFFF-FM	90.3	mHz	Diversified	800 w
9	WGGG-FM	106.5	mHz	Adult Contemp.	3 kw
10	WHHH-AM	780	kHz	Country	5 kw day, 1 kw night
7	WIII-AM	1080	kHz	MOR	5 kw full-time
6	WJJJ-FM	101.7	mHz	AOR	20 kw
4	WKKK-FM	94.5	mHz	Adult Contemp.	6 kw
5	WLLL-FM	97.1	mHz	Urban Contemp.	10 kw
12	WMMM-AM	1410	mHz	Religious	1 kw day, 500 w night
11	WNNN-FM	89.7	mHz	Classical	20 kw
8	WOOO-AM	850	kHz	Talk	1 kw full-time
1	WPPP-FM	92.9	mHz	CHR	10 kw
—	WXXX-AM	1520	kHz	—	1 kw day

Easy Listening also is ruled out as a possible format. Both the consultant and owner feel that the more-music emphasis of the format would put a nonstereo competitor at a distinct disadvantage. WXXX lacks the finances to convert to stereo.

News and *Talk* are already aired by two AM outlets, both with signals superior to WXXX's. WMMM-AM also features extensive nonmusic programming, including a two-hour, midday talk show. Going head-to-head with the other AM talkers would serve only to fragment further an already limited nonmusic audience.

Adult Contemporary is presented effectively by WKKK-FM and WGGG-FM. Again, a nonstereo daytimer would be at a major disadvantage competing against two well-established FM outlets.

Urban Contemporary is effectively presented by WLLL-FM in a market with a fairly homogeneous population, with the exception of a large contingent of non-English-speaking Portuguese. With a format that emphasizes music, WXXX-AM would be at a disadvantage without stereo.

Country attracts only a modest share of the audience by a more powerful full-time AM station at 780 kHz. Although WHHH-AM ranks tenth, it has been a slow, uphill climb to achieve that position in this northeastern market. This is not a viable format option.

MOR (Middle-of-the-Road) has been aired by WIII-AM since the early 1960s. The "Triple Eye" air personalities have established a modest foothold in the market, and another AM station, especially a daytimer, would find it rough sailing to compete with this 5 kw outlet, whose signal is far-reaching and whose audience has remained loyal throughout the years.

AOR (Album-Oriented Rock) is a fidelity (stereo-compact disc) oriented format. While WJJJ-FM is not noted for its slick execution, it would present almost insurmountable obstacles for a lower power AM daytimer. This is equally true for the *Classical* format in this market. While there are serious shortcomings in the presentation of the college-run facility, a small, nonstereo outlet would find itself hard-pressed to compete against the more powerful and technically superior WNNN-FM. The noncommercial nature of WNNN-FM also would give it an edge over a station obliged to schedule commercials.

Religious programming was introduced into the market in the mid-1970s by WMMM-AM, which has since hovered near the bottom of the ratings. While it is known to generate a solid income, another religious station—especially a daytimer—probably would find it difficult to do so, as WMMM-AM signs off at midnight.

Block (Diversified) programming as presented by the local noncommercial community college station, WFFF-FM, would create a marketing problem for a commercial station, which must convey an image of consistency to attract the kind of listenership advertisers find attractive.

CONSULTANCY AND FORMATICS

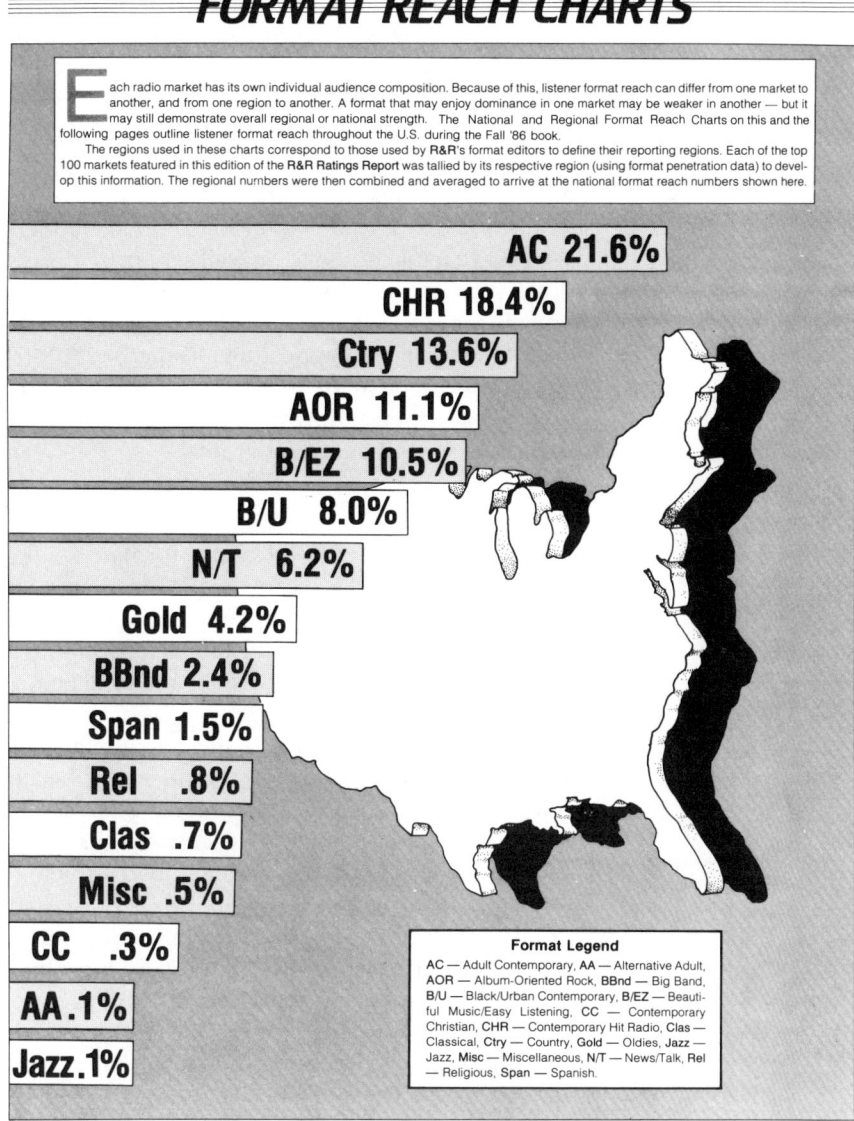

Figure 2.1 Trade publications such as *Radio and Records* provide broadcasters insight into format acceptance on the national level. Reprinted with permission from *Radio and Records*.

After a preliminary analysis of the competition, WXXX-AM has come up with two possibilities. Since 8 percent of the market's population are first-generation Portuguese, broadcasting to that audience segment might yield a marketable share. *Ethnic* does extremely well in other markets throughout the country with similar population configurations.

The other format possibility is Vintage: *Oldies* or *Nostalgia* (Big Band). While the MOR and Adult Contemporary stations occasionally program songs from the late 1950s and 1960s, rarely do they dip back as far as the

17

1940s and early 1950s. The question that WXXX-AM must consider is what Vintage audience age group would generate the greatest advertiser interest, since Oldies commonly draws 34- to 49-year-old adults, while Nostalgia is popular with the over-fifty listener. Another point to consider is how many stations already cater to these particular age groups. Adult Contemporary, News, Country, and Classical pull good numbers in the 34–49 age range, and Easy Listening and Talk do well with the over-fifty listener.

From this initial evaluation, the consultant might conclude that the 34-to 49-year-old audience is well served by the existing formats and that an Oldies station would stir only marginal interest. Alternatively, Nostalgia, with an emphasis on the Big Band sound of the 1940s, would give the over-fifty listeners an appealing alternative. Another important factor is the fact that 35 percent of the market's population is over fifty, so listening potential is substantial, while competition is somewhat less formidable than it is in the 34–49 age demographic.

Targeting the Audience

Once WXXX-AM has decided on a format, be it Ethnic or Nostalgia, it must research its proposed target audience thoroughly. It is not enough to launch a format based strictly on quantitative data. Certainly it is essential to determine that there is enough of an audience to support a particular format, but it is equally important to get to know and understand the audience expected to tune in.

A station cannot operate in a vacuum and hope to succeed. It must go into the community and observe life-styles because what people do is reflected in their listening preferences. The individual who spends a great amount of leisure time going to dance clubs serves as an illustration. In all likelihood this person is a prime candidate for what the Urban Contemporary format has to offer, since it emphasizes music with a danceable beat.

This is an obvious example of establishing a connection between audience interests and station programming. The point is that a well-programmed station takes into account external as well as internal factors. "You cannot market a product without a sense of who your market is, and knowing only gender and age is not enough," consultant Jay Williams notes. "You must look deeper to effectively determine what your target audience wants. It is based on the data derived through careful audience research that a station's programming is best constructed."

Radio's Popularity

The attitude of the listening audience regarding radio in general, and a certain format or station in particular, is another question worth investigating, contends consultant Donna Halper: "Does the radio listener like what he hears? If so, what exactly turns him on the most about the medium? If not, what does he object to or possibly tune out? 'All deejays are stupid and talk too much' may be the reaction of one person, while another may claim to be a fan of a particular station because of a certain deejay. Is it the general consensus in your market that jocks should play a less prominent role? Some stations, and even whole markets, actually suffer from jock burnout. This is something that certainly is worth finding out."

Generating Income

The socioeconomics of a community will add into the equation as well. An obvious example of weak judgment would be airing a format that typically appeals to people in an upper-income bracket in a predominantly blue-collar market. It would be a mistake to program classical music in a mill town simply because no one else is doing so. Research has long concluded that classical radio listeners typically are better-educated, white-collar professionals who earn higher incomes. That is why most Classical stations are found in metropolitan markets and in exclusive communities. Alternatively, an area with high-end demographics might be unsupportive of formats, such as Country, that generally pull from the opposite end of the socioeconomic scale.

The 18- to 49-year-old audience is most attractive to advertisers, but should WXXX-AM choose to adopt a Nostalgia format, it also would be considered worthy of spot buys because the over-fifty listener has considerable disposable income, on which restaurants and travel agencies, to mention only a couple businesses, tend to rely.

Can a Nostalgia or Ethnic format support the activities of WXXX-AM? The radio consultant and station manager survey financial statistics for the market as part of the decision-making process. The fact that 8 percent of the population is unserved by a radio station does not necessarily mean that enough advertising dollars can be generated to meet operating expenses, let alone a profit. To begin with, no station has a total hold on an entire segment of the population. If WXXX-AM programmed Portuguese, not every Portuguese radio listener would tune in. A demographic breakdown of the potential audience for this format might appear as follows:

Available audience = 39,000 (2.5% without radio)
Under 12   = 6,000 (51% female/49% male)
12 to 18   = 7,000 (53% female/47% male)
18 to 49   = 19,000 (51% female/49% male)
49 +   = 7,000 (54% female/46% male)

WXXX-AM also would have to decide toward which segment of the population it should direct its programming. Would it focus on contemporary or traditional Portuguese music? This will determine which age demographic the station draws. Is the 12- to 18-year-old Portuguese audience capable of inspiring advertiser interest? Should the station shift its programming focus throughout the day in an effort to attract as many cells (audience parts) as possible? Will this approach create problems? There are a prodigious number of variables to consider. Only a few have been discussed.

"The bottom line is revenue," consultant Donna Halper says. "A station must make money to operate. Therefore, it must select a programming formula that will most effectively do the job. Choosing a format is perhaps the single most important and complex tasking confronting a station."

Cost Considerations

Once competition and audience considerations are thoroughly analyzed, the cost of implementing and sustaining a format must be weighed. For the sake of argument, let us assume that projections reveal that the Nostalgia and Ethnic formats will yield approximately the same revenue in the market to which WXXX-AM is licensed. That is to say, both will attract a similar sum in advertiser dollars. Since this is the case, it must then be determined which programming approach will require the least amount of money to present.

To do an effective job with Nostalgia, the consultant might suggest syndicated programming, the cost of which will run in the vicinity of $1,800 a month. Automation equipment also must be purchased, since Nostalgia syndicators customarily provide client stations with taped music imprinted with cue tones designed to activate successive program elements. This alone constitutes a sizable outlay of capital, since very few state-of-the-art automation systems are available for less than $20,000.

Several syndicators also use satellites to deliver their product to client stations. This, too, can be a cost effective approach after initial money is invested for signal receiving hardware (dishes, etc.).

Of course, with automation (or satellite) in place, staffing expenses can be reduced. For example, a strong more-music emphasis can decrease the need for an elaborate announcer presence. Live (operator) assist salaries tend to be lower than straight announcer salaries. Certainly numerous other cost factors must be weighed in going the Nostalgia route, but these are among the foremost.

A foreign language (Ethnic) format, such as Portuguese, poses different budgetary problems. Personnel costs can run higher than a "canned" format. Finding experienced on-air talent can create a problem, so in-house training sometimes is necessary. Costs involved in acquiring program material suitable for an Ethnic format can be substantial, too.

Going Head-to-Head

From the preceding discussion it should be apparent that ascertaining the type of programming a station should broadcast involves more than a casual survey of market conditions. The fact that a certain format is not available in an area may be an indication that it should not be. At the same time, the fact that one station already employs a particular format does not mean that another should not do so. The demographics of a market alone might justify replication. A decision to go head-to-head with another station can be based on a variety of things. For instance, pure economics might be the deciding factor—that is, there is enough of a bankable audience for a particular format (Adult Contemporary, Easy Listening, or Album-Oriented Rock) to support another station offering comparable programming.

In market after market, stations implementing a format similar to an existing one have found ratings success, and in many cases, the new stations have surpassed their competition in listenership. The way in which a format is packaged and executed will greatly determine the level of success it will attain.

"There may be three rock stations in the same market, but the station with the best execution will lead the pack—given that the station has a good, clear signal to start with," programmer Marlin Taylor notes. "As a rule, listeners are impatient with sloppiness and mediocrity. They know what sounds good and are intolerant of what doesn't. The station that shines the brightest will attract the most attention. A good, tight sound with programming elements in the right place generally works."

ELEMENTS OF PROGRAMMING

Music

Music, news, deejay patter, commercials, public affairs features, public service announcements, contests and promotions, and jingles are among the ingredients comprising a format. Stations differ in the amount of time devoted to each of these elements, but music is accorded the bulk of the clock, except at those stations airing News and Talk formats.

Composing a music playlist is not simply a matter of grabbing a stack of recent hits, if it is a Top 40 station, and scheduling them randomly throughout the broadcast day. Trade journals, such as *Radio and Records* and *Billboard*, local record stores, and listeners are surveyed to determine which songs are in the greatest demand.

Codification Once a playlist is assembled and a station's music library is in place, a system for presentation must be designed. Programmers sensitive to listener desires know that while a song might work wonderfully at 8:00 A.M., it could be a turnoff at 8:00 P.M. Thus, separate categories are created for songs depending on their tempo, arrangement, and mood.

On Adult Contemporary stations, for example, up-tempo songs typically are scheduled in greater abundance during the morning drive time when the idea is to get the listener up and out of bed and on his or her way. Slow-tempo cuts have a calming effect, and for this reason they get greater airplay at night when listeners might be winding down and relaxing. Medium-tempo selections are aired throughout the day for balance.

In addition to categorizing a song by its tempo, its arrangement, or thickness, also is gauged. Whereas a fully orchestrated song might be labeled a 3, one with only minimal elements might earn a 1.

The mood or attitude that a song's lyrics conveys warrants another category at many stations. For this reason, a tune with a downbeat message might be given a B and one with cheerful, upbeat lyrics a Y.

Stations also categorize music according to the gender of the performer—F for female and M for male. Some programmers consider it unwise to air two female artists back-to-back. This is particularly true at Easy Listening stations.

Based on the preceding codification system, an up-tempo, upbeat tune performed by a female, backed by full orchestration, would be labeled U/3/Y/F; a soft, bluesy song performed by a male, accompanied only by a piano, would be labeled S/1/B/M.

Rotations In addition to assessing the particular production values of a song, a hierarchy must be constructed to establish rotation patterns—the

RADIO PROGRAMMING

frequency at which songs are aired. Using a Contemporary Hits format as a model, the following general rotation categories could be devised:

Power Cuts: The twenty most popular songs appearing in current surveys. Ultrarotation.

Super Cuts: Songs appearing in the remaining Top 50 slots. High rotation.

Recurrents: Thirty songs recently appearing on the charts. Moderate rotation.

Golds: Former hits of the recent rock era. Classics that never tire. Level (consistent) rotation.

Bronze: Former Top 50 and special-interest or novelty songs. Light rotation.

Consistent with the preceding categories, a slow female vocal with guitar accompaniment that is ranked number two on the music charts would be codified in the following manner: S/1/B/F/PC, which means slow/simple arrangement/downbeat mood/female/power cut.

Of course, numerous systems can be designed to help define a song's place on a station's playlist. The preceding is a deliberate simplification for

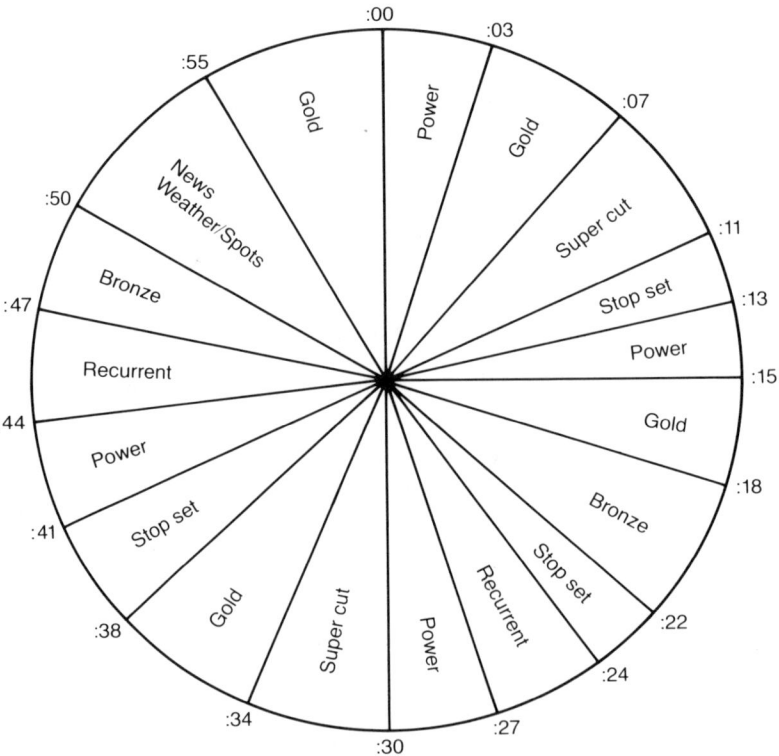

Figure 2.2 A hot clock reflecting categories discussed in the text.

```
        G                       :-)     AM     (-: :-)      PM     (-:
  r     R                    12M 1 2 3 4 5 6 7 8 9 0 1 M 1 2 3 4 5 6 7 8 9 0 1  -
  a     a     05/20/85 MON  c-: : : : :-d : : : : :-d : : : d-: : : d-: : : :
  p     d     05/21/85 TUE  d :-: : : : d-: : : : : d :-: : d : : :-d : : :-:
  h     i     05/22/85 WED  d : : : :-: d : : :-: : d : : :-d : : : d :-: : :
  i     o     05/23/85 THR  c : : :-: : d : : : : :-: d : : d-: : : d : :-: :
  c     w     05/24/85 FRI  d : :-: : : d :-: : : : : d : :-: d : : :-d : : :
  s     a     05/25/85 SAT  c-: : : : : d : : :-: : : d : : : d :-: : d : : : :
        r     05/26/85 SUN  d : :-: : : d : : : : :-: d : : : d : : :-: d : : :
  H     e     05/27/85 MON  d : : : :-: c : : : : : d-: : : d : : : d-: : : :
  i           06/28/85 TUE  d : : : : :-d : : : : : d : :-: d : : : d : :-: :
  s     1     05/29/85 WED  c : : : :-: c : : : : : d-: : : d : : :-d : : : :
  t     9     05/30/85 THR  d : : :-: : d : : : : :-d : : : d : :-: c : : : :
  o     8     06/31/85 FRI  c : :-: : : d : : :-: c : : : : d : : : d : : : :
  r     5     06/01/85 SAT  d :-: : : : d : : :-: : d : : : d-: : : d : : : :
  y           06/02/85 SUN  c-: : : : : d : :-: : : d : : :-d : :X:XcX X:X:X
```

```
: Scheduled up to :
: 06/02/85 - 6p   :     : CHANGES/                              :
:_____:     : DAVID BOWIE                           :
                        : Cart    1.    D: RECURRENT            :
  _____       : A=3 B=1 C=0 D=1 E=0 F=0 G=1           :
: P)rint        :       :                                       :
: C)ontinue     :       :                                       :
: A)bort        :       :                                       :
:_____:       :_____:
```

The song's title, artist, category and characteristic values will be displayed on the screen. Each dash indicates that the song played within that hour. The X's indicate that no history exists for the hours so marked (i.e. they have not been scheduled as yet).

After any grid has been displayed you may get a hard copy of it by keying P)rint. Keying either C)ontinue or A)bort will return you to the MAIN MENU (shown on page 1).

Figure 2.3 Computerized music library entry.

the sake of illustration. A program consultant constructs a music clock to reflect dayparts and audience demographics. At many stations computers are an integral part of the playlist and rotation process.

News

On most music stations, news is the second largest consumer of airtime, although the five-minute newscast has become a universal. In the past stations were obliged by the FCC to set aside a percentage of their broadcast day for the purpose of nonentertainment programming—namely news and public affairs features. In the early 1980s this requirement was abandoned, and broadcasters were free to approach news programming in the manner they felt most appropriate. While some stations have dropped news broadcasts from their daily schedules, most continue to present news, even when demographics are skewed to the 12–18 age group.

Youth-oriented formats, such as CHR and AOR, tend to downplay

RADIO PROGRAMMING

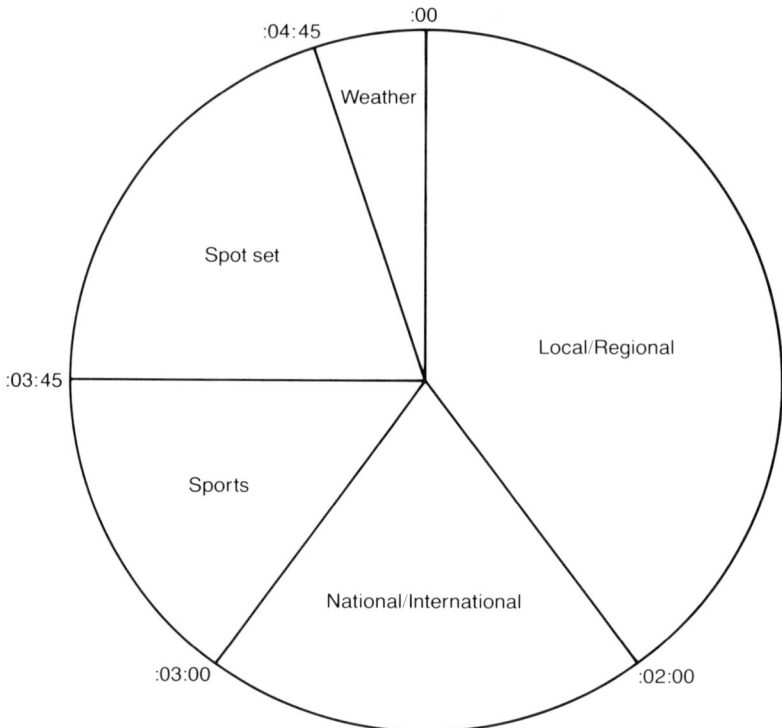

Figure 2.4 A typical five-minute news clock.

their news offerings. That is to say, news is not a highly touted programming ingredient. You seldom hear "For the hottest hits and most comprehensive news tune to W– – –." Yet news has a place on these stations.

The approach to news on a hit music station would scarcely resemble that of an old-line MOR. News is the cornerstone of most well-established, Full-Service MOR stations, and it often dominates drive periods in particular. Twenty minutes of news each hour is not uncommon. Some MOR outlets adhere exclusively to nonmusic clocks between 6:00 and 9:00 A.M. and 4:00 and 6:00 P.M. Top-of-the-hour, five-minute newscasts are most commonly scheduled in other dayparts.

Music-intense formats, such as Easy Listening, are mindful that their listeners wish to be kept informed but that they tune in for the generous amount of music offered. Thus, news is programmed sparingly, except during drive periods.

From the budget-conscious manager's perspective, news often is viewed with a wary eye, especially at stations targeting young audiences. The feeling prevails that news is an expensive tune-out factor. Stations programming to older listeners recognize the value of a solid news operation but fret over the investment.

In the 1980s the Radio and Television News Director's Association (RTNDA) voiced fears, substantiated by certain surveys, that local news is a less integral part of station broadcasts since the FCC relaxed its position on nonentertainment programming. Program consultant Jim Smith claims that the FCC's ruling has not affected his attitude or approach to news programming.

"News has always been an important radio programming element and will continue to be so," Smith says. "People want radio news. They rely on the medium. I don't detect any big move by station managers to eliminate that service. In fact, most of the stations that I advise value their news presentation. Most local stations would witness a sharp decline in their listenership if they dropped news and information features. News is an essential offering at most stations. Of course, the type and quality of news presentation make a great difference to audiences, too. As a programming consultant, it is my job to assess this area and get the station on the right road. A weak news service can inspire tune-out."

Public Affairs

As with news, the FCC saw fit to scrub its public affairs programming requirements in the 1980s. Despite the fears of many public service officials, however, public affairs programming has not vanished from the airwaves. Radio continues to be responsive to community issues and problems. Small market stations, in particular, recognize the importance and advantages of airing community-oriented features. Meanwhile, metro market hit music stations catering to teens might be somewhat less enthusiastic about scheduling public affairs features, at least in abundance.

Sunday morning traditionally has been set aside for religious and issues-oriented programs. While some stations have reclaimed the time for format material, most continue to reserve this time slot for public affairs programming.

Of course, not all stations confine public affairs features to a single designated time period. What percentage of the broadcast week should be devoted to public affairs features and where they should be scheduled is another important programming consideration. The audience sought by the station and the format employed determine this to a great extent. An AM station with a news and information format will air more public affairs features than an FM station with a music format.

The content and quality of a public affairs program or series is a key factor affecting its scheduling. For example, a program on drug abuse hosted by a major rock star would be particularly attractive to a station targeting teens. Because of the topical nature of the subject and the special appeal of the host, the feature might even be afforded special airtime. Program directors are always on the lookout for exceptional public affairs features that not only are compatible with the format but also enhance it.

Sports

Sports programming is a key factor in the ratings of many stations. WHJJ-AM in Providence, Rhode Island, is a case in point. "We carry Red Sox baseball, and in our fall book the numbers invariably reflect that fact," notes program director Ron St. Pierre. WHJJ experiences an average increase of two ratings points as the result of its baseball coverage.

Sports is far more prevalent on AM than on FM. News and Talk audiences are the largest consumers of sports features. MOR and Full-Service stations also find sports programming a profitable adjunct to music and other features.

Stations emphasizing music, especially Top 40, Easy Listening, and Urban Contemporary, rarely broadcast sporting events. Yet sports scores and stories, especially of a local nature, are included in newscasts in almost all formats. "People tune in radio to get the latest sports results," St. Pierre says. "It really doesn't matter what a station is offering as a format. Whether Classical, Country, or Album Rock listeners, they still want to know if the home team won. If they don't find out from you, they'll tune in elsewhere."

A music station might increase sports information during the morning commute and cut back to key scores at the conclusion of newscasts during the remainder of the day. While sports is not a primary programming element at most stations, it is one that few broadcasters ignore. "Sports is important," says Gary Begin, sports director at WTVL-AM in Waterville, Maine. "If you fail to give a particular score, you'll hear about it, and there will be a hundred more you won't hear from who will simply tune in another station."

Weather

Weather is a quintessential programming element. It is one of the primary reasons people listen to radio, especially in the morning, and its importance cannot be stressed enough. As with other ingredients, the amount of weather information programmed depends on a station's particular format. The nature of the climate in an area also has an impact on this decision. Usually the more unpredictable or inclement the weather, the more airplay it gets. A more-music station concerned with keeping talk to a minimum might schedule weather updates once or twice an hour. During a storm, however, it probably would consider breaking format to keep its listeners apprised of conditions.

Weather can become a news item when its effects result in life-threatening situations, property damage, and school and work closings. During the summer vacation period and on holidays, the weather is of prime importance to listeners, many of whom make plans based on forecasts.

The weather is of interest to everyone—it has a universal appeal. The absence of weather information can drive listeners to other stations. Deciding on the right proportion of weather programming is a serious matter.

Announcing

The announcer or air personality is the programming at many stations. In markets throughout the country, superjocks rule the airwaves. Radio stars such as KIIS-FM's Rick Dees and WNBC's Don Imus are given conditional carte blanche to allow their unique talent the freedom necessary to work ratings magic. There are really three deejay types. For the sake of illustration, they may be termed heavy, medium, and light. The term "heavy" applies to that type of announcer just cited. This person has the highest visibility, or presence, on and off the air. He or she is the station's product, and this fact generally is promoted through the use of billboards, newspapers, and television. The station's top announcer also is the highest paid and generally fills the crucial morning slot—the proverbial "bread and butter" shift.

Announcers in the medium category seldom achieve the level of notice accorded the superjocks. They are allowed less latitude and presence and are more a function of the format. This is not to suggest that deejays in this category are prevented from exhibiting personality. The medium category jock is expected to communicate a personality that often is more an extension of the station's general persona than his or her own.

Stations with a light announcing approach deliberately keep personality out of the picture. More-music stations that promote less talk obviously see fit to keep announcing to a minimum. Announcers at many Easy Listening stations are confined to reading liner cards and pressing automation buttons. Sometimes they are referred to as operator assists and seldom are known by the listening audience as other than the voice at the conclusion of lengthy music sweeps.

Announcing styles reflect formats. Teen-oriented stations want energy and sometimes unbridled enthusiasm from the air people. This occasionally manifests itself in what can best be described as screaming, although few stations in the 1980s are proponents of the "holler and shout" announcing technique. The more austere adult formats, particularly Easy Listening, MOR, and Adult Contemporary, are inclined toward the soft talker who has a relaxed, conversational style.

Dayparts affect both the amount and style of announcing at the majority of stations. Whereas most morning listeners expect to be informed, encouraged, and cajoled, an energetic and gregarious personality fills the bill.

The foot is eased off the accelerator during the 10:00 A.M. to 3:00 P.M. daypart because the midday audience tunes in for slightly different reasons. This audience is not as concerned with getting somewhere but rather is interested in companionship. Deejays working the "homemaker" shift must be affable and genial and are expected to work the music more than their morning counterparts.

The afternoon commute jock is nearly as active as his morning colleague at most stations. The audience needs less prodding ("Time to get up and roll out!") but wants information and empathy ("Whew, what a day, eh?"). The tone generally is more businesslike during the afternoon commute than it is during the morning, but listeners still expect a lively, upbeat delivery.

Adult stations typically become more low-key at night. Announcers often play a diminished role, whereas the percentage of music is increased. Announcers are more laid-back and less ostentatious. The idea is to match the mood and tenor of the daypart. Adult Contemporary and Easy Listening stations tailor their sound to the adult who is interested in relaxing and unwinding after a long day.

Youth-oriented stations usually maintain their high-intensity announcer approach throughout the day and night. The evening daypart is a big listening period for hit music stations catering to a more energized clientele.

Spots

Commercials are a fact of life. They pay the station's bills and generate profits. Yet they usually are the least welcome part of programming for both the program director and the listener. "Too many spots kill us in the ratings," laments the director, while the listener complains of frequent interruptions and not enough music: "All they do is play commercials!"

Programming commercial-free segments—"Another hour of spotless rock"—is especially attractive to listeners, regardless of format. Stations have drastically reduced or actually done away with commercials for a period of time in an attempt to draw a larger audience. One such example was WAPP-FM's commercial-free summer of 1983.

"We went to the top by airing a careful mix of hit AOR without commercial intrusion," says Joe Krause, former program director of the New York station. "It was a great way to introduce ourselves. We became number one in our target. When the spots returned, some of the audience began button punching, but by then we were a force to be reckoned with in the Big Apple. Obviously we could have retained our huge audience edge if we had remained totally commercial free. The station also would have gone broke."

A station determines the amount of time it will allocate to commercials by first considering the effects on format and station revenues. For instance, an Easy Listening station wishes to keep music to a maximum and talk to a minimum, but it must show a profit to satisfy ownership. While two commercials an hour might enhance the station's more-music image, they might not generate enough funds to sustain operations, not to mention generate a profit. Alternatively, twenty commercials an hour would raise more immediate income but clutter the sound, thus resulting in listener dissatisfaction, a decline in ratings, and eventually advertiser apathy.

The National Association of Broadcasters (NAB) suggests that stations hold the line at eighteen minutes of commercials an hour, while the FCC imposes no strictures. Most broadcasters abide by the NAB's recommended maximum.

Once the percentage of time reserved for commercial material is established, the hourly distribution or placement of spots is determined. Again, a station's format and approach to dayparts comes into play. For example, many Easy Listening and Adult Contemporary stations cluster commercials in spot sets at roughly twelve-minute intervals. More-music station spot sets typically contain two to three commercials, depending on the daypart. During commute periods, spot sets might contain two sixty-second commercials and one thirty-second commercial and be scheduled at more frequent intervals—every eight or ten minutes. In other dayparts, two minutes of commercial matter might constitute the maximum spot set load. Commercial clustering is a particular characteristic of automated stations that program in sweeps.

Contemporary Hit, MOR, Urban Contemporary, and Country stations usually designate spot breaks in a somewhat more random fashion. Since lengthy music sweeps are less common in these formats, spots are scheduled between songs yet away from quarter-hour points for the sake of ratings. Ratings surveys count listeners each quarter hour if they are tuned in for at least five minutes during that time. Thus, stations are inclined to sweep, or "hot track," the quarter hour to retain listeners until they have been counted. This is called quarter-hour maintenance.

Programmers must be sensitive about the quality and content of commercials, too. A poorly mixed spot can hurt the image of a quality-conscious station. Sloppy production or inferior fidelity (the consequence of tactics such as excessive dub-downs) reflects negatively on a station. "A spot that is not on par with surrounding program elements because it is muddy or badly tracked simply doesn't make it on the air here," observes Peter Fenstermacher, production director of WMJX-FM in Boston.

CONSULTANCY AND FORMATICS

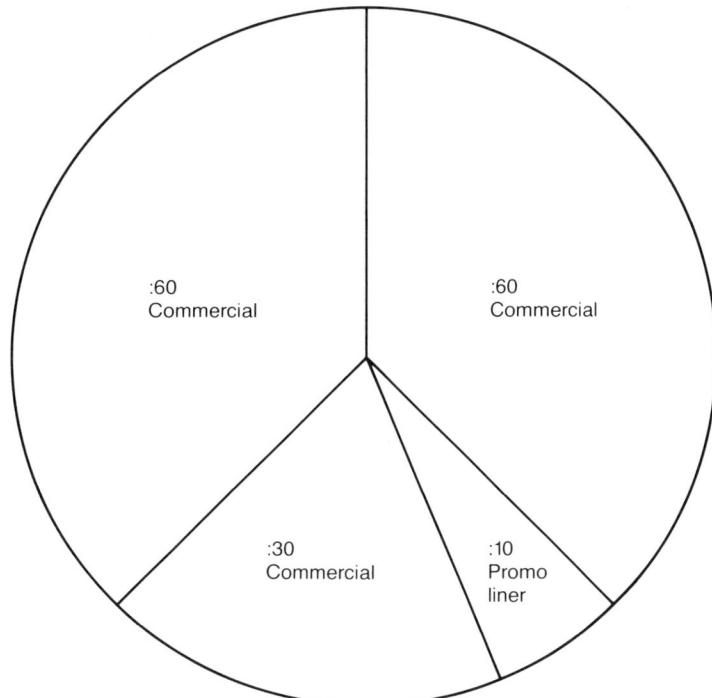

Figure 2.5 Easy Listening spot set.

Production values, such as beds (background music), sound effects, and voice tracks, can cause problems if they run counter to the overall sound of the station. For instance, a commercial with high-intensity production elements (strident bed and cacaphonous sound effects) would send the listeners of a soft adult format running for cover, while one featuring chamber music would upset the pacing and flow of a hot hit station.

Commercials must be compatible with a station's programming, or they weaken it. "Spots are as much a part of a station's sound as its music," Joe Krause notes. "A bad spot will have nearly the identical effect as a bad song. Too many bad spots can cause lasting damage."

Contests and Promotions

You do not give away water beds on a Beautiful Music station or symphony tickets on a CHR station. These prizes obviously would miss their intended demographics, since sixty-year-olds are not particularly big purchasers of water beds and teens are not noted for their affinity for classical music.

Contests must be relevant to the life-style and interests of a station's audience to accomplish their objective. Stations run contests to draw new listeners and retain existing ones. Promotions and contests are much more prevalent during ratings sweeps for obvious reasons.

An effective contest, whether long- or short-term, involves an entire audience, nonparticipants (known as passives) as well as participants (actives). A contest that is unimaginative or has a weak payoff will do little to attract attention.

Contests that violate the station's sound alienate listeners. An extreme example, but one that effectively illustrates this point, is the misguided Easy Listening station that runs a mystery sound contest featuring the hair-raising squeal of a dentist's drill. Good-bye audience. Not only would this jar format continuity, but it ultimately would damage the station's soothing adult image.

As with any other element of programming, contests and promotions must fit in with the surrounding landscape. The integrity of a station's format should not be sacrificed because of gimmickry.

Jingles

Jingles convey the mood and personality of a station. They are image orchestrations that can be of high or low intensity to suit a particular format and daypart. An Easy Listening station might use up-tempo jingles during commute periods, while a CHR station employs high-intensity jingles around the clock.

Jingle length is another consideration. Positioning usually determines the length of a jingle aired. Whereas a brief (five-second) jingle is used to break loaded spot sets, a lengthier jingle might be employed as a bridge between music cuts. The interminably long jingles common during the 1950s and 1960s have given way to the more laconic ones of the 1970s and 1980s.

To work effectively, jingles must be well produced and timely. Jingles on hit music stations must reflect the contemporary nature of the chart toppers, or they will sound out of place and dated. At the same time, jingles with weak arrangements or performances contrast negatively with the professionally produced songs they bridge. The result is inconsistency. The purpose of the jingle is to remind listeners that they are tuned to the best station, not to create a negative impression.

Noted consultant Mike Joseph has long been a proponent of jingles. His clients use jingles extensively, especially in and out of stop sets. He believes they help strengthen a station's hold on its audience. Joseph is particularly known for his use of short, two- to four-second jingles that promote calls and slogans.

Call Letters

The value of a good set of call letters is inestimable. All stations want meaningful and memorable IDs. Ratings companies use call letters and station slogans to credit listenership. It follows then that a catchy, vivid ID is desirable. WTOP is simply much easier to remember than WXUI, and in the battle for ratings prominence, this constitutes a distinct advantage. "You use whatever you have, and super calls make the job easier," programming consultant Tom Hotchkiss notes.

Stations with unmemorable calls also take to grafting logos or slogans onto their frequency (Kiss 102, Power 103, EZ 93) or create alphanumeric IDs by combining a call letter with a frequency number (X-104, Z-95, A-101) as a way of impressing survey respondents. A station's ID or slogan is its name, and the more distinctive it is, the more likely the listener will be to recall it during the crucial ratings sweeps.

Features

Features add color and texture to programming and also give salespeople something additional to sell. Like other programming ingredients, features must be designed to reflect, rather than detract from, the station's primary product, be it music or talk. Features also must be fashioned to appeal to the life-style and interests of the audience. For instance, a rock report on an AOR station, a political commentary on a Talk station, a syndicated countdown show ("American Top 40") on a CHR station, or a nightlife update on an Urban Contemporary station would appeal to their respective audiences. Traffic, weather, and sports reports have broad appeal and, therefore, are common fare in most formats. Of course, certain features are intended for broadcast during specific dayparts. Traffic reports during commuting hours are a good example.

CRITIQUING TIME: METHODS AND PROCEDURES

To examine a station's state of health, a consultant ("radio doctor") usually must make a house call. In many instances, this requires flying to the station's market. Consultants are no strangers to airports. "Sometimes I feel like I spend half my life walking through metal detectors," Donna Halper says.

While some consultants limit themselves to serving clients in specific geographic regions, say New England or the Midwest, others have clients all over the country. "We contract from coast to coast, and then some," Rick Sklar notes. "As a national consultant, our clients take us everywhere. This is not a business for a homebody."

When a consultant hits town, he or she will begin to monitor the client station. This usually takes place in a hotel where distractions and interruptions are minimal. "I sit down in a quiet place—if I'm out of town this usually means a hotel room—with a cassette recorder and notepad," Halper says. "I take notes as I listen, but I also record to check myself later on and pick up anything I may have missed. I listen for the right music mix, how comfortable and listenable the station is, how effective the announcers are, whether or not the station has a clear image—is it allegedly Top 40 yet playing lots of nonhits? Is it allegedly AC yet using Top 40 singles and screaming jocks? —and what problems are evident. I also listen for technical quality and for the things the station does well, since no critique should be all negative.

"I have a form that I fill in as I monitor, noting what time a song was played, whether there was a front or back sell, use of call letters, and so forth. Later I read it all over, listen to tapes, and then compile a comprehensive report on the station's strengths and weaknesses as I perceive them. I monitor each of the dayparts, and I try never to judge a station on only one day's listening, because anyone can have an off day. I prefer to monitor at least two days before I prepare my report."

Chicago-based programming consultant Jim Smith contends that close, in-person listening provides the basic data from which to construct a remedial plan, if necessary. "I prefer actual listening in the market itself," Smith says. "Some consultants may try to do it by mail with cassette air checks. In my opinion, this is a 'half-a-loaf' method used to fill the gap between on-location

RADIO PROGRAMMING

MONITOR SHEET

Station: WXXX

DATE: 7-6-87

Time: 2pm–3pm

COMPETITOR 1	COMPETITOR 2	WXXX
1. Station ID	Stations ID	Station ID
2. Madonna—Live to Tell	Genesis—Invisible Touch	Bob Seger—Like a Rock
3. Peter Cetera—Glory of Love	Robert Palmer—Hyperactive	Billy Joel—Modern Woman
4. Stop Set 2:10	Giuffria—I Must Be Dreaming	Stop Set
5. :30 Second Spot	Janet Jackson—Nasty	:60 Second Spot
6. :30 Second Spot	The Outfield—Your Love	:30 Second Spot
7. :60 Second Spot	Nu Shooz—I Can't Wait	Jingle
8. Weather	Andy Taylor—Take It Easy	Stones—Harlem Shuffle
9. Jingle	Force M.D.'s—Tender Love	Rod Stewart—Love Touch
10. Moody Blues—Wildest Dreams	Stop Set	Contest Promo
11. John Waite—Missing You	:30 Second Spot	Lauper—She Bop
12. Liner—LP Giveaway	News 2:00	PSA & Jingle

Figure 2.6 Consultant/programmer's monitor sheet setup for side-by-side comparisons. Here the consultant or program director will check for the following: (a) the strength of each song compared to the competition's; (b) where spot sets fall in comparison to competitors'; (c) length of spot set and unit count compared to competitors'; (d) is the station into spots when competitors are playing music?; (e) is the station into news when competition is airing music?; (f) is the LP giveaway on number one effective?; (g) is the station's contest promo more effective than competitors'?

tuning. I would rather critique the station within the context of its own competitive radio marketplace. This is the true litmus test.

"There are certain basics that always need to be covered in appropriate depth: music, air talent, production, stop sets, news, features, and promotions, and this can't be done effectively by mail. There may also be special issues involved for specific situations. One recent example for me involved stop set placement in what was becoming a front-loading battle. I use a somewhat helpful form I devised for my own particular approach. Most consultants create forms that reflect their own monitoring strategies."

CONSULTANCY AND FORMATICS

Programming consultant Mike Joseph employs the following procedure when arriving in a client's market as a prelude to any format or programming recommendations:

1. Checks into a hotel (incognito if the situation warrants).
2. Monitors the competition, devoting a full day to each meaningful facility.
3. Listens around the clock, up to twenty hours a day.
4. Logs everything heard: announcing, music (every artist), contests and promotions, information, newcasts (story by story), jock ad-libs, jingles, and so forth.
5. Conducts a record store survey to ascertain what is happening musically in a market. This involves in-person interviews with store employees and customers.
6. Examines the demographics of record purchasers and prepares ethnic breakouts.
7. Analyzes the locations of record stores.
8. Researches the market flow (where people are at different times of the day: schools, plants, offices) to determine availability of specific demographics for listening. Dayparting is determined by audience flow.
9. Analyzes market ratings and composes individual ratings breakouts for each station.

Joseph is very selective about the clients he assumes. He insists on creative control and total cooperation from station management. While his services do not come cheaply, the time he devotes to a client is extraordinary, and his success ratio is high.

Upon conclusion of the monitoring phase, a consultant meets with station management to discuss his or her findings. "We monitor the market and the client station thoroughly and review the station's goals with management," programming consultant Eliot Keller says. "Then we prepare a situation assessment. If included in the contract, we then prepare recommendations. We also work with management to assist with implementation if that is stipulated in the agreement."

Rick Sklar involves the client station in the analysis process. "We have the station management do an all-inclusive preliminary analysis of their station and the market, and then we do one," he notes. "We then listen extensively to the station and the competition and do local music testing and other research. In our work we try to measure human behavior when it comes to listeners, rather than rely on what they believe their behavior is or what they say about it."

Research Techniques

To ascertain just what the listening public wants from a station, consultants employ a number of techniques, including focus groups, call-out research, and music testing.

Focus groups provide stations with data concerning the attitudes and feelings (emotions) of listeners about elements of programming. Ideally four to six groups, each with eight participants (called informants), are queried at length by an interviewer (called a facilitator), who often is a consultant, as to

Figure 2.7

what they like or dislike about a station's music, deejays, news, contests, and so on. To acquire the necessary data, the facilitator plays representative air checks of various programming elements to the informants. The findings are used to help station management develop winning programming strategies.

Focus group research is expensive. Research on two groups with eight members each costs between $1,500 and $2,000 to conduct. That's approximately $93 to $125 an informant.

Call-out or telephone research is another method of gauging a listener's perception of a station. Call-out research is similar to focus group surveys in that questions are asked by an interviewer and responses are analyzed in an attempt to bring music in line with station programming objectives. Consultants work independently or with station staff in preparing questions, gathering call-out data, and analyzing the information. One approach used in call-out research involves playing extracts of preselected songs for a sampling (one hundred calls is typical) to rate on a scale of one to seven. The scale might appear as follows:

1. Never heard song
2. Strongly dislike song
3. Moderately dislike song
4. Indifferent to song
5. Tired of song
6. Like song
7. Favorite song

Some consultants and programmers dislike call-out research. Mike Joseph believes that call-out research can be invalidated by faulty survey techniques, which can lead to numerous programming problems, such as lopsided playlists. Nonetheless, call-out research is a widely used method of determining what and what not to air.

CONSULTANCY AND FORMATICS

```
Typical questions that can be answered using Focus Research from
BOB HARPER'S company:

Is my advertising working?

How would a listener describe my station?

Why are people spending less time with my station?

Who do they turn to first for news?  Weather?

Should I be more aware of the music on MTV?

Do they know our announcers' names?

Do the listeners think we've changed?  For better or worse?

Why do people listen to the radio?

Do the listeners think of my station in the same ways I do?

Am I playing too many commercials?

Why did people first start listening to their favorite stations?

Does the audience know my dial position?

Do listeners want personalities or more music?

Why do people listen to my station?

Am I wasting money on contests and promotions?

What features could I add to attract listeners?

Am I playing the right music?  Are some songs repeating too
often?

How much news do listeners need?

How can I get a new listener to sample my station?

When does my audience listen to the competition?

If you need answers to four or more of these questions, you need
Focus Group Research from BOB HARPER'S company.
```

PROGRAMMING, MANAGEMENT, SALES AND TECHNICAL CONSULTANTS

Figure 2.8 Focus group piece from Broadcasting Unlimited.

Music testing often is conducted in an auditorium setting with up to two hundred paid participants who are asked to evaluate several dozen songs as a means of determining their rotation on station playlists. While this research method is expensive, it is regarded by many as more accurate and reliable than call-out. Consultant George Harris of Harris Communications has conducted auditorium music testing for several years with considerable success for his station clients.

Not all consultants engage in outside audience testing. Many confine their services to the monitoring and analysis of their station's existing sound. Of course, the purpose of a consultant's critique is to point out both the strengths and weaknesses of a station's programming to help it reach and keep the audience.

memo: ALL CLIENTS   24 AUGUST 1984

FROM: JAY WILLIAMS

As you know, although Broadcasting Unlimited subscribes to the trade publications, we are increasingly distrustful as to their usefulness in programming music. The reason is twofold: first, trade publications are relegated to broad-based format descriptions, i.e., adult contemporary, CHR, etc. Real station formats, in order to serve a more concentrated core audience, must be more specific than that. No one would seriously think that an AM MOR in one market should play the same music as an adult contemporary FM station in another market -- yet there is only one chart to use for both. But secondly, and even more importantly, the real problem lies in the creation of the chart itself -- a combination of sales, radio station airplay, and the chart editor's opinion. <u>None</u> of these factors is relevant. What is relevant is how <u>listeners</u> to a particular station <u>feel</u> or accept a record that is played -- which is why Broadcasting Unlimited relies more on music testing than any other factor to determine whether or not a song is played, in what rotation, and the like. Listener acceptance, in other words, has a direct correlation to ratings; we have never seen such correlation using trade publications.

You may see songs, Julio Iglesias and Diana Ross, for example, which are selling well and are high on trade publication charts, but test poorly. In reverse, you may see records in a lower chart position that test exceptionally well -- thus they are moved up more quickly and played more frequently. You may recall that we put "Jump" by the Pointer Sisters on the chart long before it was a factor in the trades -- for that very reason. Music testing -- not our opinion or the opinion of anyone else but the listeners -- is the single largest determinant in selecting music for our lists.

/r

PROGRAMMING, MANAGEMENT, SALES AND TECHNICAL CONSULTANTS • 16 Coltsway, Wayland, Massachusetts 01778 (617) 358-4828

Figure 2.9 Memo warns of dangers of relying solely on trade music charts. Courtesy Broadcasting Unlimited.

Consulting Obstacles

Consultants, perhaps because they are a relatively new phenomenon, face problems of acceptance by some of the people they hope to serve. According to Donna Halper, the greatest challenge confronting radio consultants is overcoming the negative perception of some managers and PDs. "We are not all charlatans intent on cleaning house and selling fad formats," she says.

"We are not the bad guys in dark suits with sneaky plans to destroy the lives and tranquility of the programming staff. We don't have all the answers or any magical solutions. A consultant is only as good as the staff working with him and the level of commitment from management to improving the station."

Broadcasting Unlimited's Jay Williams expresses concern over a lack of understanding concerning consultants by radio management: "In the main, station heads are either small businessmen, entrepreneurs, or corporate people who are seeking to improve or protect their positions of power. Many of these types of managers don't know how to use a consultant properly or understand the value of one.

"To begin with, they do not know how to evaluate one potential consultant against another. Research and track records often pale beside a good pitch. But the greatest single problem facing consultants is the attitude that we are a necessary evil. This attitude is sometimes held by the people who hire us. Many stations do not fully utilize the consultant's valuable resources and talents, preferring to take from the tip of the iceberg. Getting adequate compensation for expertise and experience, especially for work done away from a station, is also a problem."

Eliot Keller concurs with Williams regarding management's sometimes limited awareness of a consultant's potential contribution to a station: "The biggest problem facing consultants, I believe, is that station staffs often do not clearly understand how to use us. A station's staff must know why the consultant is there. Management has an obligation to make this clear to its people. When a staff is suspicious and confused, it hinders the consultant's ability to function one hundred percent."

Rick Sklar considers the relationship between the consultant and station PD one that requires careful attention and nurturing. "It is no small challenge to effectively relate to program directors," he notes. "There can be resentment of the consultant's involvement. It is the role of the consultant to educate the PD concerning his function and contribution to the station."

The perception held by many broadcasters that all consultants are pretty much alike has had a negative impact on the profession, contends Jim Smith. "Despite the fact that there are countless consultants available, all offering different services using different approaches with different degrees of success, the typical station owner or manager regards us as a monolithic block," Smith says. "How should we deal with the comment that someone else passed along to me: 'I had Kent Burkhart in here the year before last, and our ratings went down. Why should we hire another consultant?' That's like saying 'I used to drive a Pinto, but the gas tank blew up. Why should I buy another car?' The appropriate action would be to buy another make of car, if you need a car. Just don't buy another Pinto. This is not a major problem to me personally, since most of my business comes from referral. But for many other consultants, this is a most serious obstacle to have to overcome."

Finally Halper observes that too few stations effectively follow a consultant's prescriptions once he or she has departed. "I can do a flawless critique, implement a new format, and train the staff, but if there is no follow-through when I leave, the station will not derive the most value from the time I spent there," she says. "Unfortunately, this happens too often. For consulting to work well, it has to be a partnership between the station and the consultant, and everyone must cooperate.

"Some owners expect a quick fix and instant ratings, and when that doesn't happen, they blame the consultant. Good consulting can identify a problem right away, but an effective solution may take some time to implement. Similarly, even if I do have a quick fix (in some cases the problem is very obvious), I must also have the trust and the patience of the staff as we go through the transition period necessary to fix a station in a way that will have enduring results.

"It's tempting for some owners to bring in a consultant one time and then figure they can take it from there themselves. That doesn't usually work because stations with problems didn't get that way overnight, and it takes a while to really make sure the station has overcome what was debilitating it. I don't think it's realistic or fair to expect me or anyone else to solve five years' worth of image problems in one visit."

INDUSTRY NOTES

Midwest consultant Jim Smith discusses his particular approach to station critiquing:

I bring certain biases to each situation, as presumably anyone would. There is a human tendency to do a comparison/contrast evaluation of any new item encountered. That is, how is this like something seen before? How is it different?

This may give a useful framework for the initial assessment but should not be taken too far, since no two competitive arrays are ever identical.

To an extent there are certain biases, of course, some of which are relatively unquestionable, on which just about everyone can agree. The disagreements come in the interpretation.

For a simple example, probably no one in the field would suggest that a station identify itself only the legal minimum of once per hour. Frequent presentation of the name of the station—whether that means the call letters, the dial position, or some identifying slogan—has obvious multiple benefits that need not be outlined here.

But that given tells us neither the optimum frequency nor the method of that identifying. Here is where the consultant draws upon experience: what has worked before, here and elsewhere.

Not all consultants agree on the approach. There are those who may dictate, say, a fixed number of jingles at specific points in the hour, as supplemented by a rigid—or at least a minimum—number of live announcements of the calls or slogan.

My approach would vary with the situation, and my approach to communicating this would vary with the reader of the critique. To continue with the simple example of station identification, "I think the station could be more frequently identified," "Is there a reason for the station to be so infrequently identified?" or something similarly non-directive might be sufficient for an initial evaluation or perhaps for a subsequent critique to an owner in a situation where it is a minor deficiency and not a huge problem.

On the other hand, a subsequent monitor for the client PD of a station that, in my judgment, is falling short in this area might take a different tone. Let's assume this seems to be a failing only in one air shift and has not been a consistent failing month after month. Perhaps my written evaluation might be telling him or her—I'll use the masculine from here on, since that is usually the case—something he hadn't noticed in his own listening.

All that may be needed is one note, as part of my item-by-item monitor of what took place, such as "Burt Curtis is regularly missing the jingle going into the weather—any reason?"

The wording might be more pointed, of course, if he were a problem-attitude jock, this were a consistent failing of his or part of a particularly lax air shift in this one critique, or this were to have extended to other air shifts also.

I only reach the extreme—which some consultants seem to hit upon the slightest provocation, or even none at all—when it can clearly be shown that there is a serious problem caused by the deficiency being spotlighted.

To manufacture an example, let us assume that the station had recently changed call letters or identifying slogan, changed format, or gained a direct competitor. Or perhaps an Arbitron diary review had shown problems of the station's not receiving proper listening credit due to sloppy identification. Or maybe station-commissioned research had shown listener confusion about the name of the station.

In short, if for any reason station identification was a major issue, then is the time for the written monitor to foreshadow the no-kid-gloves discussions that will surely follow.

For me, a nonoffensive, nondirective posture—the diagnostician—is one I most often assume in an initial critique. While it would be absurd of me to presume to know the theory behind everything on the air, it is not unreasonable to ask questions.

So my approach—both in the written evaluation and in the oral—tends to start from that framework. Whether it stays there depends very much on the situation. Some station personnel need more authoritarian direction than others; some owners and managers prefer it.

Some consultants, however, seem to operate only in that more authoritarian mode regardless of the circumstances. What is fine for them may or may not be fine universally, and it is certainly not fine for me. I'd rather be Aristotle than Hitler, more the consultant-teacher than consultant-dictator.

Whenever feasible, the monitoring session has a tape-cassette back-up. No matter how many and how thorough are the written notes, there is always the possibility of wanting to check again what actually took place on the air.

Taping while listening also allows me to be half-listening to more than two stations at once for the sake of competitive comparisons, when appropriate, while still being relatively certain of not missing anything.

Critiquing beyond the initial or preconsulting session has the additional dimension of determining whether the various aspects of the station are on course. Concentrated monitoring will pick up patterns of performance that may be missed in casual day-to-day listening.

Here also, the objectivity of the outsider brings obvious benefits. Beneficial, too, is the outsider's multiple-market familiarity and ability to see things in a broader context.

I don't think there is any magic to the form in which the various elements are written down. My proprietary form is useful to me because it is familiar and seems most simple. Someone else may find mine convoluted but may be comfortable with one that would seem complicated to me.

The purpose for using a form at all is for the information to be easily written down quickly yet be easily read and analyzed when completed. Ideally it should have a structure for every meaningful element to be noted (usually in some abbreviated manner) and perhaps space for additional comments, conclusions, and questions.

Jay Williams, president of Broadcasting Unlimited, makes the following observations concerning aspects of radio station operation.

Personalities

A lot of people want to be stars, but they have total misconceptions of what that means. Many young jocks think it means speed breaks [stop sets] and talking up records. Even older jocks believe it has something to do with having a great voice, good production skills, and being able to read liner cards. There are a number of major market disc jockeys who make more than $100,000, but many small market jocks make under $15,000. One of the major problems within the business and with people who are trying to enter it is the complete lack of understanding of the characteristics and qualities that spell the difference between the two extremes of talent as measured in actual dollars.

First, of course, most highly paid personalities do the morning shift, although there are some notable exceptions. They become, in effect, the spokespersons for the radio station. They are its warmth, its community involvement, its keen eye for observation, its wit and charm, its laugh or smile, its community image, and so forth. Most highly paid personalities know the mayor, many business and community leaders, and many club owners and concert managers. On the other hand, most disc jockeys know the names of the newest songs, the names of the people Paul McCartney has done duets with, the names of the disc jockeys at the other stations, the amount of promotion their station is or isn't doing, the name of one or two female bartenders, and the name of their landlord. In short, most jocks are into radio, and most highly paid and tremendously successful personalities are into the community and all aspects of life.

Sales

Radio is an advertising medium that gets approximately five percent of all advertising dollars. That figure has not changed in twenty years. No one with a modicum of talent would consider going into a no-growth industry in a sales position. Yet there is plenty of opportunity. Radio sales has been plagued by people who use the immediacy of the medium incorrectly, often as an excuse for not planning ahead. Neiman Marcus begins planning its Christmas direct mail catalogue in January. It buys its Christmas clothes in the spring, and it does its Christmas layouts in mid- to late summer. Radio salespeople call on them in November and ask, "What's going on for Christmas?"

Radio salespeople make the same mistake radio deejays make. They're into radio. They're into immediacy. They don't plan, and they dump stuff on the air without really thinking about it. Print people are no smarter, mind you. It's just that it takes so much longer to get anything done in print that they've had to think farther ahead. This often means they get more money because they get there before radio.

Radio salespeople have to stop selling radio, per se. They have to learn advertising. Then they have to learn marketing. Radio people need to become part of the retailer's planning process. They need to think about the retailer's problems and the advertising goals to offset those problems. By the time radio people get to the dollars, the bulk has already been allocated. Radio is eating from the scraps on the floor, while newspaper and television, and now direct mail, are getting the steaks on the table. As with programming, sales needs brighter, better-educated people who think about the future.

AM stereo

Although switching to stereo is expensive, our perceptual research indicates it's a major positive with listeners. This is confirmed in a major Coleman Research study. Keep in mind one thing about listeners' buying habits: People perceive products differently than we might think. That is, they perceive products as being about the same, getting better—new and improved—or getting worse. Our research indicates that listeners perceive that FM radio is better than AM radio. Thus, AM radio is staying the same or getting worse by comparison. AM stereo is a countermeasure to that negative perception. It shows that AM radio is progressive, too. Switching to stereo is not a matter of technology as much as it is a matter of marketing.

Management

Logic does not explain, much less direct, human behavior. "You do not change people's opinions by defeating them," writes Herbert Simon in *Science* magazine. In an essay titled "Herbert Simon's Simple Economics," the 1978 Nobel Prize winner argues that human behavior cannot be logically defined. Although he says that the concept of neat behavioral rules understandably appeals to some scientists, he believes this thinking is flawed. Simon writes that behavior is governed by two factors. The first is humanity's tendency to allow feelings to overcome logic. The other is the human tendency to take shortcuts that violate formal logic.

The reason for both, according to Simon, is that individuals can possess only so much information. "The mainstream model used by economists, mathematicians, and statisticians says that a person acts rationally if he applies a consistent set of values—economists call it a utility function—over a vast array of choices in order to pick the best possible one," explains Simon. Yet Simon believes that people and classic economic assumptions are at odds. His case in point: Simon had twenty-three executives at large firms read a ten-thousand-word history of a hypothetical company, then identify the company's most crucial problem. Sales executives contended that it was in the sales area, managers saw it as a production problem, and accountants perceived it as a problem in bookkeeping.

Our conclusions drawn from Simon's assertions are threefold. Managers do not necessarily react logically because they, too, view problems with blinders on, especially if there are too many possible solutions. Secondly, the traditional economic or management model of logical behavior may not be valid. And thirdly, innovation and productivity in individual companies can best be fostered by building in allowances for invention, surprise, and mistake—the unpredictable.

Radio as a business

Radio is a rapidly changing business because of Docket 80–90; the decline of AM; the increased competition from better-educated, more aggressive broadcasters; deregulation; new technology; and much more. On the decline are egocentric programmers (and program consultants), erratic general managers, lazy sales managers, and disc jockeys in T-shirts. Radio is becoming a a business complete with computers, sophisticated sales presentations with graphics and customized plans, direct mail promotions, and the like. The efficiencies of radio properties have increased (and the economy has grown), with the result that prices for radio properties have skyrocketed. In the future, radio people will be able to rely less on their egos and their lack of education and limited world view and will have to possess greater business, marketing, and research expertise.

Dwight Douglas, president of Burkhart/Abrams/Douglas/Elliot and Associates, responds to some questions about the role of computers in the radio station environment.

Michael Keith (M. K.): What makes computers an indispensable research tool?

Dwight Douglas (D. D.): Abacuses and human brains are very slow. Computers are fast, accurate, and creative.

M. K.: In your opinion, how important are computers as a research tool on the station level?

D. D.: As important as the telephone.

M. K.: Will station computers make in-house research comprehensive to the point of decreasing reliance on the major audience research and measurement companies.?

D. D.: No. The strength that major audience research and measurement companies have is that they have credibility and informed and intelligent manpower.

M. K.: What area(s) of broadcast research has most significantly been affected by computers and why?

D. D.: The most significant usage of computers in broadcast research is the use of the PC to down-load Arbitrend and Arbitron information. This is because Arbitron has managed to eliminate the hard-copy concept as a delivering device and will cut down some of their costs. The computer is also being used as a music device, which has as much impact as the down-loading of Arbitron information.

M. K.: What is the single greatest drawback of computers in broadcast research?

D. D.: I believe it is that many people who operate computers are more hobbyists than they are experts, and this tends to make the usage of computers blurred to upper-level management who usually know little about computer dynamics.

M. K.: What role do you foresee computers playing in the broadcast research area in the next ten years?

D. D.: Call-out research, music tests, and Arbitron down-loading will all continue to be a part of the computer's job. But most significantly, I believe the computer will act as a source of information for disc jockey content to bring more high touch into the presentation and will not have much success in the area of computerized phone calls to establish research projects.

M. K.: In what way does your company use computers?

D. D.: We use computers for billing, music tests, call-outs, word processing, games, communication, and someone to eat lunch with, but mostly to save time.

3

Adult Contemporary

Adult Contemporary is like vanilla ice cream, delicious and satisfying, but too much of a good thing when overused by listeners.
—Robert E. Henabery
Henabery Associates

Adult Contemporary is the most difficult radio format to define because the phrase has been used to market everything from hits to soft pop. AC is for rockers who have grown up but haven't outgrown a contemporary feel. Some prefer rock; some merely tolerate it. AC keeps them from changing their tastes just because they change demographic group.
—Ed Shane
Shane Media Services

Adult Contemporary (AC) has been around in one form or another for a long time. In the 1960s MOR and Chicken Rockers appealed to approximately the same audience that AC does today. The cryptically labeled Chicken Rock stations were the forerunners of the Mellow and Soft Rock stations of the 1970s. The term "Chicken Rock" was inspired by the fact that these stations only flirted with rock music by playing the least raucous tunes from the pop-rock genre. While a Chicken Rocker would air "Michelle" and "Yesterday" by the Beatles, it would avoid "Strawberry Fields Forever" and "Yellow Submarine."

Most MOR stations (see Chapter 12) of the same period stuck to contemporary nonrock tunes that attracted an impressive number of young adults who were not fans of rock 'n' roll music. There were far more mainstream MOR stations transmitting than there were Chicken Rockers. Collectively, both formats reached approximately the listening audience that AC succeeds in attracting in the 1980s, the 24- to 39-year-olds. While Chicken Rockers drew more from the young end of the demographic, MOR was effective in attracting the over-thirty crowd in the 1960s.

In the early 1970s the Chicken Rock format evolved into the more distinctive Mellow Rock sound, which attracted larger numbers of young listeners who sought an alternative to the glut of heavier rock stations that crowded the airwaves. Whereas Chicken Rock stations were a product of AM, Mellow stations took up residence on the FM band, where stereo capability expanded on the appeal of the programming approach: "Mellow Rock in Stereo on FM 98…."

As Mellow Rock grew strong in the 18- to 34-year-old listening cell, MOR stations turned to the 40-year-old crowd. Initially the Mellow format playlist included a broad range of quiet rock, from relatively obscure songs to the widely popular. As the format continued its evolution in the 1970s, its playlist was narrowed and the less familiar phased out.

By the mid-1970s Mellow stations became known as Soft Rock. The term Mellow had become an anachronism, having been a part of the psychedelic drug movement lexicon of the 1960s. With this transition came a greater conservatism. Less avant-garde gentle rock and more mainstream standards appeared on playlists. The format softened in reaction to the preponderance of Album-Oriented Rock stations, whose playlists could be all-encompassing, and the expanding popularity of Top 40 on FM.

The popular, yet short-lived, Disco format of the late 1970s, the resurgence of hit music stations, and the updating of Easy Listening playlists caused significant erosion in the Soft Rock numbers. It was out of this flux that the AC format emerged in earnest.

Today only Country stations outnumber those programming AC, and that gap was growing smaller in the latter half of the 1980s. AC listeners tune in because they want popular, upbeat music without the harshness that often accompanies rock. The typical AC listener enjoys personalities, a comprehensive mix of bright contemporary music, and a sufficient amount of news and information. Of course, some AC listeners prefer more nonmusic features, while others want to hear music to the near exclusion of all forms of talk.

FORMAT CHARACTERISTICS

Music

AC takes a couple of different programming approaches. While some stations offer softer, easier listening contemporary music and refer to themselves as Lite or Soft AC outlets (Lite 106), others broadcast a more up-tempo, hit-oriented sound, referred to as Hot Adult (Hot Adult 98 FM). Regardless of the approach, AC generally stresses music, although some stations employing this format place more emphasis on music than do others. At those stations touting music, lengthy sweeps, or segues, are common. AC stations that rely more heavily on talk or features treat music in a manner similar to standard MOR outlets, where one song at a time is aired, followed by announcer discourse or commercial matter. AC stations using the Lite approach are more apt to sweep, whereas Hot AC stations typically break between cuts of music or *brief segues*.

The AC playlist focuses on music popular within the past few years, although many stations add recent oldies (1960s and 1970s hits) to their rotations. "We are flavored quite heavily with oldies here at WGAF," reveals John Clark, program director of the Valdosta, Georgia, FM station. "Our focus is on AC sounds, but we mix in classic hits of the past couple of decades and even an occasional cut from the 1950s."

Montana AC station KCAP-AM runs oldies features. "We program an oldies show called 'Noontime Nostalgia' weekdays, from noon to 1 P.M., with deejay Scott Matthews," program director Andrea Boulos says. "The show is very well received. Most ACs with an oldies orientation are targeting a broader cell than standard ACs, which are after the twenty- to forty-year-olds. Here we compete for the nineteen- to forty-nine-year-old audience, and oldies help us."

David L. Vasser, program director of WABZ-FM in Albemarle, North Carolina, contends that oldies are becoming a more integral part of AC playlists. "We utilize a very tight playlist, supplemented with an extensive rotation of oldies," he says. "Our research indicates an upswing of interest in oldies over the past couple of years, and we have adjusted our music rotation to reflect that change. For instance, not long ago the oldest song we played would have been taken from around 1970, but currently we draw music from as far back as the dawn of the rock era. This older music is not placed in heavy rotation, but once every hour a pre-1970 tune is presented. Shortly after we made this modification, an AM station in our market switched to an Oldies format. Apparently they were getting similar research results."

New York's WLTW-FM claims its Lite music approach provides a much-needed programming alternative to listeners in the nation's top market. In 1986 the Viacom station had the highest 25–54 quarter hour in the United States. "We are appealing to an adult who is bored by Beautiful Music

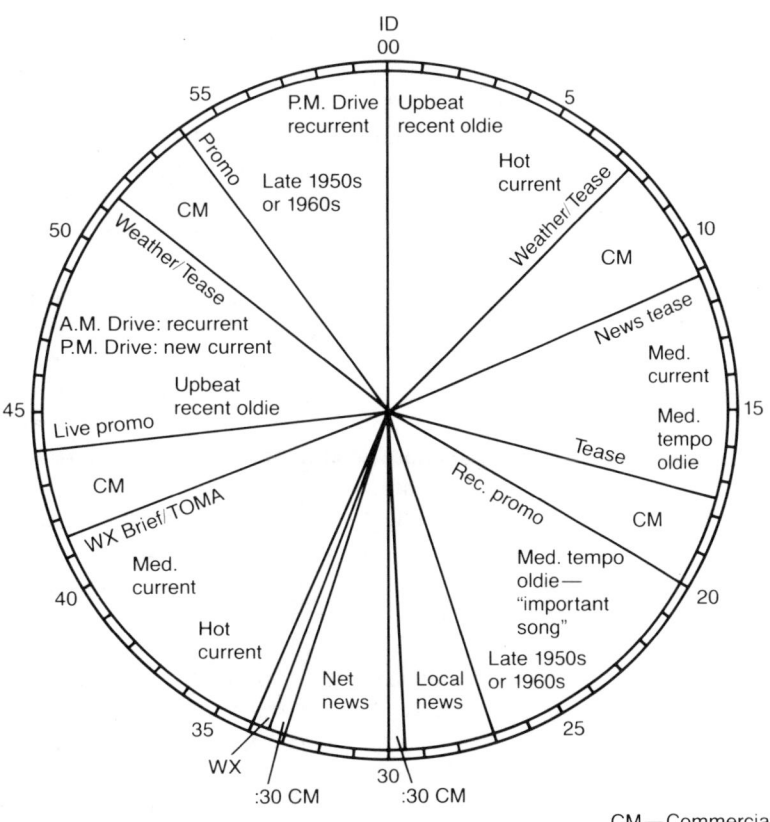

Figure 3.1 An Adult Contemporary drive-time format clock (6:00 to 9:00 A.M., 3:00 to 6:00 P.M.). Notice the emphasis on oldies. Courtesy WKGW-FM.

but who enjoys softer, melody-based music without a lot of breaks or interruptions," program director Philip L. Redo says. "We are foreground for those who wish to sing along but background for listeners who want to relax. All our music is researched to appeal to the New York market."

Keeping the music bright and adult is the objective of Hannibal, Missouri's KGRC-FM. "We have a positive, energetic sound that is especially designed to target adults," program director Chuck Yates notes.

John Carucci, program director of WUUU-FM in Rome, New York, believes that AC must convey energy and vitality: "We're basically targeting the baby-boomers, the Big Chill generation, if you will. You have to give them a sharp, with-it sound that has a nostalgic flavor, too. We try to be very listenable for long periods of time. This we accomplish by programming a wide variety of mass-appeal adult contemporary music with minimal talk."

To attract a slightly younger adult audience, many Hot AC stations draw on the Top 40 charts. "We have what could be described as a hybrid AC station," offers Ann L. Kolodziej, program director of WZOZ-FM in Oneonta, New York. "By this I mean we combine the best CHR with AC to create a very alive, now sound."

Announcing

Since AC is primarily a music-oriented format, the role played by announcers usually is not as prominent as it is elsewhere. Like most other formats, AC relies on personalities during commute dayparts, especially mornings. "Other than in morning drive, there is no talk across the quarter hours, except for the legal ID at the top of the hour. This helps us build some quarter-hour maintenance," says WABZ's Vasser.

Announcing also is kept to a minimum at WZOZ. "Like most ACs, we're music-intensive," Kolodziej notes. "Only very brief talk-ups are scheduled to create plenty of forward motion—hardly any back sells."

This also is the case at WLTW. According to Redo, "We program in sweeps designed to showcase our music. That's what Lite offers its listeners and what its listeners expect. Therefore, talk is light, also."

While music is the primary product at the majority of AC outlets, announcers do play a greater role at others, especially in smaller markets. As a rule of thumb, metro AC stations downplay talk, whereas rural stations often promote personality because of a desire to create a more active presence in the community.

"Personality is important here at KRGI-AM," says Brian Gallagher, program director of the Grand Island, Nebraska, station. "We place a lot of weight on warm, personable announcer communication. Announcers talk about what affects our community. He or she relates."

George Carpenter, program director at WKGW-FM in Oriskany, New York, concurs with Gallagher regarding the role of announcers in AC: "Many music-based stations deemphasize the involvement of announcers. To quote, 'They let the music carry the station.' At KG-104 our personalities play an important part in the overall sound of the station."

Mike Trembly, program director of WKNE-AM in Keene, New Hampshire, believes that announcers are integral to AC's personal appeal: "AC is a highly specialized form of interpersonal communication, as far as I see it. Making the listener feel a one-to-one relationship with the station is essential. A friendly voice is how I view AC. It is without a doubt the most personal format in radio, and announcers help make it so."

A station using automation generally will reduce announcer presence, so a large percentage of AC stations are automated. The majority of automated AC outlets promote music rather than gregarious personalities. "There are a lot of operator-assist operations around where the announcer reads liner cards and punches buttons," WGAF's John Clark notes. "At WGAF we are live on the air, as opposed to many of our competitors who are automated or satellite. This gives us somewhat of a competitive edge, I believe."

Most automated stations increase announcer presence during the morning commute. Even at music-intensive operations, personalities become a key element during this crucial daypart.

News

The amount of time AC outlets devote to news varies from operation to operation, although music-heavy automated stations tend to approach news more sparingly than do live operations. News does command attention during drive periods, however, and many AC stations cut back significantly on music to give news its due.

"On KCAP a popular segment is 'Radio News 90,' which is an informative ninety-minute news show aired weekday mornings between seven and eight-thirty," Andrea Boulos notes. "The program features news and topics from around the state right from our CBS network. Although we are an adult music station, news gets top billing mornings."

New York's WLTW also expands its news coverage during drive periods in an attempt to relate to its commuter listeners. "News service is expanded during drive time to include traffic reports and detailed weather information," Philip Redo says. "Most music stations, regardless of format, offer greater news and information mornings because the medium serves as the primary news source for most people at that important time of day."

In an effort to establish a strong community image, AC stations frequently devote large blocks of time during drive times to local news coverage. WABZ is a case in point. "Since we are in a small market that is just outside a major market's ADI [Area of Dominant Influence], we emphasize local news and sports," David Vasser says. "In fact, one hundred percent of our non-music programming is local in nature. We don't even use a news wire service, which is certainly atypical. Our research here indicates that what this market wants is solidly prepared and well-presented local news and sports coverage. We don't cover sports on the national level, but we do hit hard locally using our own resources. We are affiliated with CBS, but we do not carry their newscasts. Our research indicates that the majority of our target audience wants their national and world news on television or in a newspaper, unless it is of an extraordinary nature. From radio they expect localized information."

KGRC takes a strong local news slant, too, during drive periods, but it pulls back on nonmusic elements in the remaining dayparts. "Local news is important to our listeners, especially during the morning drive. However, the rest of the broadcast day is devoted fairly exclusively to music," Chuck Yates says.

Newscasts on AC stations are most typically presented in hourly five-minute blocks around the clock, although many stations drop news entirely in the evenings. Reliance on network news also is substantial. "Once we're out of drive, we present brief newscasts covering local and world events. We maintain our news profile, but music is what we market here," WKGW's George Carpenter notes.

While most AC outlets increase news during prime listening slots and then pull back to five-minute hourly reports the rest of the broadcast day, some stations maintain a high news profile around the clock. "At WLAM news is not a secondary element," program director Christopher Chapman says. "We offer full-service news and extensive information features from sign-on to sign-off. Our listeners tune us for news and information as much as they do for music."

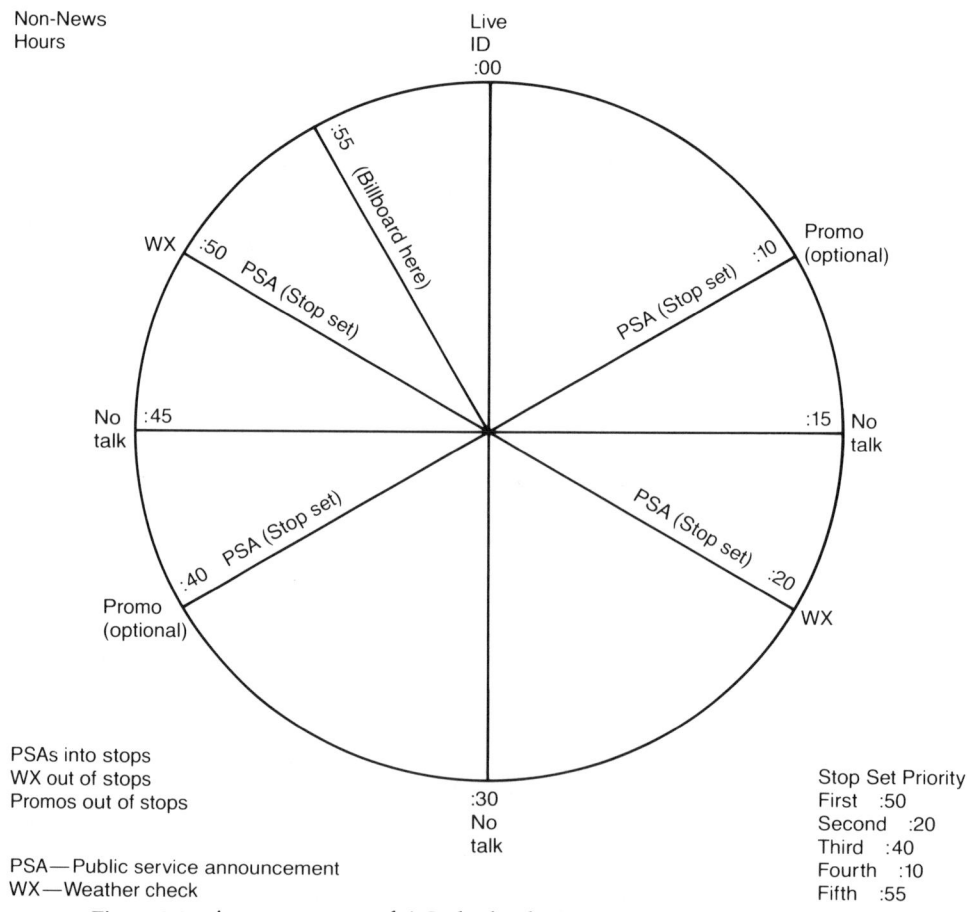

Figure 3.2 An assortment of AC clocks depicting the role of news in various dayparts. Note stop set priority. If running short of time, stop sets are eliminated in ascending order. Courtesy WABZ.

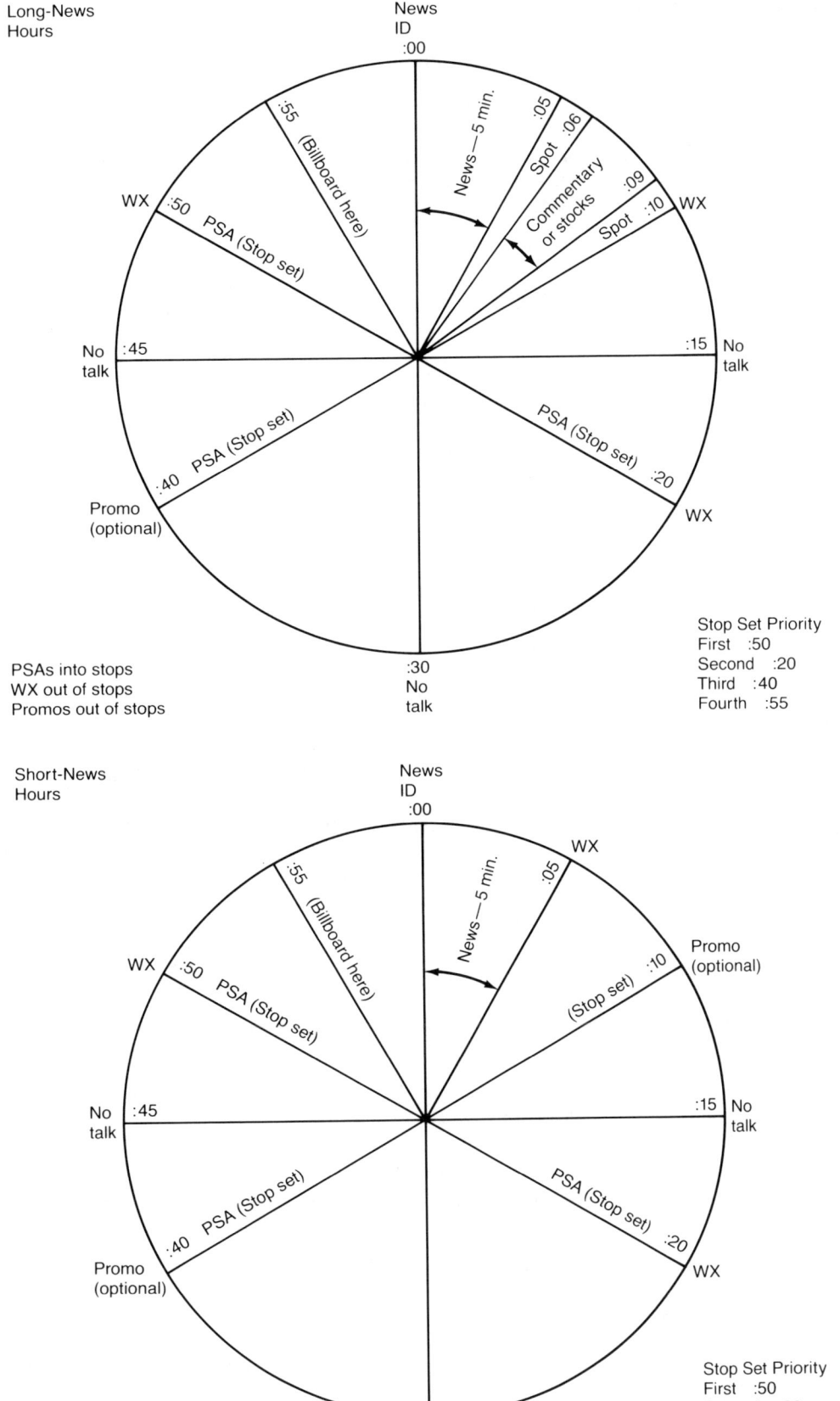

Contests and Promotions

The AC format is promotion- and contest-conscious, although not to the degree that hit stations generally are. "Promotions are an integral part of our product," WKGW's Carpenter says. "We keep them very life-style-oriented. They have to be appealing to the adult listener. A promotion should be designed to complement the format, not collide with it. The thirty-year-old isn't going to relate to a skateboard giveaway."

KGRC's Yates believes that promotions and contests on AC stations should reflect the upbeat nature of the format: "We're very promotion-minded, and we want it to be fun, too. The right promotion achieves that goal. The prizes we give away are intended to fit in with the life-style and tastes of our listeners. Of course, AC is a mature format, so balance and proportion must be kept in mind. We can't, nor should we, go as far as some formats."

The widespread application of the format—in some large metro markets as many as half a dozen stations may be airing some form of AC—has prompted some consultants to recommend that clients promote their product more extensively through the use of billboards, television, and direct mail. Outside (off-air) promotion is seen as an effective way for AC stations to distinguish themselves from the rest of the pack.

Public Affairs

Public affairs programming has been cut back slightly at many AC operations since FCC deregulation was implemented in the early 1980s, but certainly no more so than in many other formats. As with other nonmusic elements, public affairs programs are selected on the basis of their compatibility with surrounding program ingredients. The idea is to air features that target the desired cell. In truth, public affairs continues to be one of the most neglected areas of programming at many stations, regardless of format.

Commercials

AC stations commonly schedule spots in clusters at ten- to twelve-minute intervals (see Figure 3.2). This allows for the sweeping of several songs, which music-based stations desire. Spot sets usually consist of two to four commercials. Station policy will govern the actual time allotted to commercial matter. That is to say, a station can place a limit of two and a half minutes for commercials during all periods outside of drive time and raise the limit to three and a half within drive time.

Not all AC stations cluster spots. Heavy-personality stations, especially during the morning commute, might leave spot distribution to the discretion of the on-air personality, who airs spots when he or she deems most appropriate. Obviously, this must be relatively close to where they appear in the log. This method is not very common, however.

The prevailing sentiment among AC programmers is that keeping the spot load down is a worthy objective. "Commercials are necessary; they pay the bills," Ann Kolodziej notes. "At WZOZ, however, we strive to minimize the interruptions. Therefore, we impose a twelve-spot ceiling per hour."

Denise Oliver, program director at WYNY-FM in New York City, takes a similar approach to spot loading: "The AC format is a bit sensitive to heavy spotting. People tune in for quality music programming, not clusters occasionally interrupted by music."

COMPETITION

CHR and Easy Listening (EL) are the formats that compete most directly with AC. Both represent opposite ends of the AC listening demographics in terms of age. CHR taps into the twenty-year-olds, whereas EL draws some of the forty-year-olds. "CHR, which in New York has a considerable following among twenty-five-plus adults, is the most formidable format we're up against," WYNY's Oliver says.

This is true even in smaller markets. According to KGRC's Chuck Yates, "CHR appeals to a lot of young adults, and its demographic base continues to expand."

WLAM's Christopher Chapman concurs: "The all-hit station can, at least at times, be pretty universal in its appeal. Thirty- and forty-year-olds today are a lot more accepting of rock. CHR has to be monitored and added into the AC equation."

Attracting listeners from the high end of AC's listening demographics are the updated EL stations. "Easy Listening outlets, with long listening patterns, have some impact on ACs," WLTW's Philip Redo says. "Depending on their playlists, EL and AC outlets can cross over one another's targeted cells. This is especially true of some stations during the morning drive time."

Country and Oldies stations also can be a competitive factor. "The Oldies station across town lures some of our listeners," WABZ's David Vasser says. "Thus, we work many oldies into our rotation. As I said earlier, oldies are popular with AC listeners, at least that is true here."

At Nebraska station KRGI, Country is an opponent to be reckoned with. "Since they are essentially after the same target audience that we are, Country gives us a run for the numbers," Brian Gallagher says.

WKNE's Mike Trembly is more sweeping in terms of what challenges AC stations: "Anything that appeals to twenty-five-plus adults on a highly personal level constitutes a threat, as far as I'm concerned."

WKGW's George Carpenter agrees with Trembly, adding, "The overall market profile—that is, the makeup of the market, what the other guys are programming, and how well they execute—determines competition more than a particular type of format. In our market we contend with CHR and AOR more than the others."

FUTURE

The future viability of the AC format will depend on its sensitivity to the consumer. "We're constantly aware of the impression we make in our signal area, as well as our competition's, from the consumer's perspective," Carpenter says. "This we accomplish through focus groups and research by independent companies. We can then fine-tune our approach to capitalize on the perceived weaknesses of our competitors, while emphasizing our strengths."

Research will continue to play an important role, believes WLTW's Redo: "We constantly research our market to see what changes are necessary. We do focus groups, music testing, and strategic research projects so we can have the tools required to stay on target. We have finished in the top of the twenty-five- to fifty-four-year-old ratings cell for the past few years. Research should keep us in there in the future."

WLAM is another AC station that recognizes the value of research as one means of remaining strong in the years to come. "We use a consultant to keep us on course and provide us with data to enhance our position," Christopher Chapman says. "We also keep in touch with the times by reading the trades and attending seminars and conferences." WLAM also was one of the first AM stations to go stereo.

According to WYNY's Denise Oliver, constantly updating and revitalizing the playlist is a primary factor in keeping AC interesting to the listening public. "AC playlists mirror change nearly as much as all-hit playlists," she notes. "What was Neil Diamond, Barry Manilow, and Barbra Streisand evolved to Huey Lewis, the Pointer Sisters, and even Bruce Springsteen in the mid-1980s. And the evolution continues. Vitality is important in this format. The term 'contemporary' is part of our name."

WABZ's David Vasser believes that community involvement will help strengthen AC's position with listeners: "We will continue to be more visible in the community. Some ACs have a tendency to be little more than a music box. That's a particularly dangerous approach in smaller markets. AC is really America's format, and radio belongs to everyone. You can't be aloof and make friends. Our listeners are our friends because we make an effort to embrace them."

INDUSTRY NOTES

What follows are actual AC consultant station critiques. To maintain client-consultant confidentiality, names, call letters, and locations have been removed and when necessary replaced by those of a generic nature. This technique will be followed in subsequent chapters as well.

A critique from a format syndicator to a client:

> Dear Manager:
> I received the Lite 100 air check. If you included a note with the cassettes, it didn't get to me. By the way, I'm including some cassettes that I kept before and am through with now—thank you.
> Lite 100 continues to sound slick. You're dropping relate lines over the power gold intros and updating those lines regularly. Good. This makes a big difference in the sound of Lite 100. Here are some comments and suggestions to help you stay on track in AnyCity with your AC format.
> Now that Lite 100 is starting to sound less sterile and a little more lifelike, I feel you should be more involved with your listeners and their

interests. You are doing a life-style reminder, but just one an hour on this air check. I suggest you program at least two of the reminders an hour. They don't need to be more than eight to ten seconds in length and should include the station's phone number to call for more details. Giving Lite 100's number to call for information gives the impression that the station is the place to contact to find out what's going on in AnyCity that would interest your target demographic. Giving out other numbers is usually ineffective because the average listener won't remember them— and will ultimately call the station anyway.

I noticed that you're including upcoming song promos in some weathers and reminders. I also heard a dedication of sorts and a song intro done by Bill. Our experience includes a track record of many automated stations that are very successful with our syndicated format. Most of those stations avoid having a local announcer take the place of the format announcer by doing song intros and outros, promo songs, etc.

It's confusing for the listener to hear two different voices handling these announcing duties. Attempting to help the station sound live in those ways usually backfires because it only points out to the listener that the other announcer doesn't use this approach. The conclusion the listener comes to is "This is a station that tapes their programming and plays it back. That kind of a station can't possibly serve my listening needs." For this reason, I think we're our own worst enemies when it comes to programming an automated format. It really isn't necessary to "help" Lite 100 sound live in that way. In fact, it can hurt listenership.

A quick note about production. I heard a couple of commercials that had music continue after the spoken copy. It's best to fade the production music as the last word is spoken instead of trailing after the announcer finishes. Try producing your commercials this way. I think you'll find that the resulting transition is much smoother and more professional.

Finally, I didn't hear any promotions going on in this air check. If you aren't already, you should be planning some fall promotions. Have some fun and get the listeners involved. It's important to keep Lite 100's profile up in the AnyCity market. Tie in with the many fall activities in the AnyCity area. Indoor promotions are obviously more effective as the weather turns cooler: movies or theater giveaways, a "take your radio to work" day, late-night special programming for quiet times. How about something to do with keeping Lite 100 through the fall and winter months? Just some thought starters.

Keep up the good work, and keep freshening up the relate lines while exploring more ways to make Lite 100 a hit in AnyCity. I look forward to hearing another air check of KXXX.

A programming consultant's critique of a major market AC:

Monitor of WXXX: Wednesday, Thursday, Friday (16, 17, 18 September 1987)

First, lest this seem opportunistic, let me stress that my car radio has had a button set to WXXX since it first went on the air, so this is not the initial occasion that I've monitored Magic. Secondly, none of what follows is meant as criticism. WXXX does a few things very well, as I will discuss, but it also has what seems to me to be an identity crisis. By talking about this, it is my hope that we can embark upon the steps needed to bring the station the success it deserves and is capable of.

It is readily apparent to anyone who knows programming that the main difference between WXXX and, let's say, Power 106 (on one extreme) and Lite 98 (on the other end of the spectrum) is that WXXX tries to be an adult Top 40 station. It plays more recent and recurrent music than a Lite and plays more up-tempo (almost to the point of rock) music than a Lite but is not quite so young-oriented as a Power 106. Unlike most ACs, it plays larger numbers of current and recent music, yet unlike a traditional Top 40, it lacks the high energy. What then is WXXX? Is it Top 40? Is it AC? Can it truly be both? Or, rather, does it sufficiently confuse the audience to the point that it is perceived as neither?

The recent Arbitron says there is definitely an image problem, given that WXXX has perhaps the shortest average time spent listening (only thirty-five minutes) of any station in the Central City market. It's facile to say this was a bad book. Magic's numbers have been consistently eroding, and that too says to me that the listenership it seeks either does not exist or cannot be reached with the current music mix. Those people who like hard-edged rock will go for WZZZ or the various CHRs. The AC listeners have so many ACs to choose from that it becomes difficult to decide. As I recall, the original rationale behind Magic was to create an AC station that filled the void for the 25–34s who still liked CHR and didn't want heavy metal or teen music.

The trouble is, in Central City there are so many stations doing permutations of the same thing that it truly becomes difficult to distinguish between the competitors. The increased play of recent hits that at first made WXXX unique has long since been met by an adjusted music rotation on the various Top 40s, so WXXX is no longer the only place to hear the hits of the past year without having to put up with the tight playlisted CHR approach. One can hear recents on KISS 102, WBBB, Power 106, and WRRR to a lesser degree. Thus, what is left to WXXX as a way to position itself in the face of its competitors now?

Evidently it was felt that "variety" should be the key word. I noted that several jingles and a liner or two stress that Magic plays the best variety of music. Sadly, in all my years doing research, I've never found that variety was a quality that radio listeners sought. Consistency, yes. Friendliness, yes. But variety? What constitutes variety, and what does it mean to the average passive? While variety may be a good selling point for a department store or supermarket, I'm not convinced that it is a good strategy for a radio station, nor am I sure that it clearly conveys a benefit that the audience feels they lack. All too often, variety is merely a euphemistic way of saying "We aren't sure how to position ourselves." I would thus ask: What is Magic trying to offer to its listeners that is a reason to listen? Let's discuss this in more detail.

There is a certain schizophrenic feel to the station. At times it sounds almost typically AC, but then at other times it sounds very much CHR.

The announcers are competent but sound directionless. I worked with Todd Johnson back when he was "Guy Purdue" at Top 40 legend WIII in the late 1960s, and I do respect him, but he sounds somewhat lost on WXXX. He alternates between a very adult approach and a pseudo-friendly delivery reminiscent of MOR. He seems unsure just how up he should be, but when I've heard him, he sounds a lot more restrained than I'm used to hearing. His newswoman is competent and has a good voice, but again, I get no sense of a morning team. I'm not asking for funny jokes or zoo voices, but once more, I feel a lack of guidance, and that shows up on the air like radio that is done correctly yet with no excitement. Again, why listen to WXXX when I could get the same news, information, traffic reports, and much of the same music on any of numerous ACs and several of the CHRs? I just don't feel any sense of energy. Everyone is doing his or her job, yet something is missing.

The midday announcer tries hard and, like much of the station, is not bad but not memorable either. Again, he alternates between trying to be a Top 40 jock and trying to be AC, with the result that he ends up very ambiguous. I liked the two promos he played ("It's never too late to listen to Magic" and "Better variety, more music"), but they struck me as somewhat preachy and thin. More than two promos are obviously in order here, especially if we are in fact claiming to give more variety.

The jingles are well done, and while I'm not exactly certain how they contribute to the station's image, they certainly don't sound bad. On the other hand, I still have a problem with what people perceive the station's identity to be, and the jingles don't clarify the issue.

The afternoon announcer has decent pipes, but the station certainly seems a lot more Top 40 when he is on. This further confuses the issue. Each announcer seems to be going in his or her own direction, leaving me puzzled about the station's overall direction and who enforces it.

Regarding the music policy, some of what I heard struck me as far too young for a station that claims to be adult. On the other hand, sometimes I would hear as many as three down-tempo songs in a row. I also heard the same artist within forty-five minutes. This too adds to my confusion about what the station wants to be.

In general, the quality of the songs technically was superb, so when I did hear one that sounded scratchy (Journey's "Who's Crying Now"), it stood out. The station doesn't sound too processed or too thin, and the engineers obviously did a good job.

I heard a woman on the air Sunday morning who sounded more enthusiastic and warm than several of the full-timers. The entertainment reports are well done and contain useful information, especially regarding places to go and things to do locally.

I could go on, but let's look at options. One would be to remain the same, but I feel this is not working. While Big Media is obviously committed to adult radio, there are some markets where it has already been overdone. This presents a new problem—deciding to cut your losses and reevaluate, or insisting on improving what you have and sharing a very small slice of the AC pie. There are two major voids in Central City: one is for a full-time black station (a difficult move for whoever does it, given that Central City is perhaps 7 percent black and

Arbitron is famous for not collecting diaries in great amounts from our HDBAs [High Density Black Area]) and the other is for a station to do what WTTT once did—go up against WVVV and do some version of album rock. Lite seems to be trying to move back toward what WEEE-FM once did, a Soft Rock with lots of nice folksy tunes, which always went over well in a market as filled with college students as ours is. Still, WVVV's numbers say to me that they could use some form of competition, and adult Album Rock is alive and well in several markets.

I'm willing to help you determine a direction and then make it manifest to the air staff, but I'm concerned about the lack of any standouts on the staff. I'm not a believer in firing people. On the other hand, we need some good and memorable reasons to listen, or we will just vanish amidst all the other ACs and CHRs. I'd welcome the opportunity to take Magic on a new path or, if you wish, to work with you in giving the station some more energy and consistency.

4

Contemporary Hit Radio

CHR, when properly delivered, has the potential to deliver broad demographics to a station—not just teens and young adults. It is the selectivity of the single—the best cuts from pop albums and the cuts that are big enough to cause a record company to invest in a video—that forms the mainstream of American pop music. The strongest selections that we eventually hear in Adult Contemporary formats had their origins in Contemporary Hit Radio.

—Rick Sklar
Sklar Communications

The basic programming concept behind hit music stations is quite simple: Confine the playlist to those songs that are currently the fastest selling and most popular (sales being a barometer of popularity). This is the approach the Contemporary Hit Radio (CHR) stations take, and it is the same approach that CHR's forerunner, Top 40, employed.

This idea first struck programmers Todd Storz and Bill Stewart at KOWH-AM in Omaha, Nebraska, in 1955. As the story goes, both broadcasters were in their favorite watering hole and observed that patrons poured money into the jukebox to hear essentially the same songs. It struck Storz and Stewart that basing a playlist on the most popular songs of the moment would attract radio listeners. They were right. Soon KOWH-AM led in the local ratings. Not long after, the Top 40 programming approach was earning stations top ratings throughout the country.

At the onset, Top 40 playlists primarily consisted of ballads by artists such as Nat "King" Cole, Tony Bennett, Perry Como, Les Paul and Mary Ford, The Four Lads, and others. As the rock 'n' roll sound became more widely accepted, however, it received greater airplay. Artists such as Bill Haley and the Comets, Chuck Berry, and Elvis Presley were selling millions of 45 RPMs to enthusiastic teens, and Top 40 stations reflected and fostered this phenomenon. Before long, Top 40 radio was synonymous with the new sound simply because rock tunes dominated the charts.

By the late 1950s Top 40 stations were among the most successful in the country. Rock and radio formed a perfect union. The recording companies needed the medium to promote their product, and Top 40 stations depended on the recording industry for the most recent tunes.

The Top 40 audience continued to grow into the 1960s as the "doo-wop" sound underwent a metamorphosis with the arrival of the Beatles and other British groups. The "King," Elvis Presley, whose songs had dominated the pop charts for nearly a decade, found that he and his sound had been supplanted by that of the "mopheads" from Liverpool. In the mid-1960s rock music became more diffused and sophisticated, which ultimately led to the fragmentation of the rock audience and the birth of new formats to accommodate their needs.

In 1965 the Top 40 format was refined by programmer Bill Drake, who felt it had become flabby and listless. Drake's plan was to revitalize the format by getting rid of unnecessary clutter, which he perceived as counterproductive. Deejay clutter was cut back and spot loads reduced. Dead air was regarded as anathema. A jock who could not run a tight board was soon shopping for another gig. The idea was to keep the hits rolling and the gab down as a means of retaining the interest of the easily distracted teen listener.

Although the ultraslick, ultratight presentation came under attack by some critics, who regarded the format as dehumanized, stations that had been "Draked" won the approval of the audience. Top 40 remained a force to be reckoned with as the result of Drake revisionism.

During the first decade and a half of its existence, Top 40 maintained exclusive residency on the AM band. In fact, Top 40 was practically nonexistent on FM until the early 1970s. The notion of hit radio on what was perceived by many as the alternative listening medium met with resistance. FM had long held a reputation as the source for urbane programming, a fact that kept its audience relatively select. The introduction of Top 40 was inspired by the desire to increase profits, which were still small compared to AM's. The transition to FM proved to be revolutionary in many respects. By the latter part of the 1970s, the bulk of the nation's hit stations were broadcasting on FM, which now drew the majority of music listeners.

By the 1980s Top 40 had become known as Contemporary Hit Radio and was all but nonexistent on AM. The retitling of the format came about as the result of a facelift orchestrated by consulting pioneer Mike Joseph.

Joseph's CHR playlist formula included, among other things:

Tight playlist of around thirty records
Up-tempo sounds
No oldies
No declining records
Limited play of recurrents
Chart hit countdowns
Fast rotations

In CHR, the buzzword is "narrow." Today Contemporary Hit stations focus on the top 30 or 40 best-selling songs, whereas hit stations in the late 1960s and 1970s expanded to include more oldies and sometimes even new, untested songs.

Sensing a good thing, many broadcasters abandoned their Soft Rock and AOR formats, among others, in the early 1980s in favor of CHR. As a consequence, many medium to large markets had two or more CHR stations by the mid-1980s. This significantly fragmented the all-hit audience, as well as ratings shares. At this writing, however, the CHR format continues to be one of the most viable formats around.

FORMAT CHARACTERISTICS

Music

As previously stated, CHR outlets essentially base their playlists on record sales. All-hit stations derive their information from a variety of sources, including trade and industry publications such as *Radio and Records* and *Billboard*, record stores, call-out surveys, and other types of audience surveys. Keeping up with what is hot is vital.

"The music has to be right on target; it can't grow stale," says Chip Mosley, operations manager of KSYZ-FM in Grand Island, Nebraska. "It is important to us, and I suppose most CHRs, to get the hits on first, ahead of the competition. We are constantly working at adjusting playlists to keep things fresh sounding. Repetition is a factor in this format. It can work for or against you. We have no fixed music rotations, which allows us to fine-tune as we go along. I'm not an advocate of fixed rotations, which many consultants tend to be. We work our own roster in an extemporaneous way. It works for us."

G-105-FM in Raleigh, North Carolina, takes a similar approach with their music programming. "Here music is the product," program director Mike Edwards says. "Our objective is to keep the hits rolling and relative. CHR is really a recycling of the 1960s Top 40 station, and the idea then was to program from the summit of the hit charts without getting too bogged down. Keep it up and to the minute. Today's hit is quickly tomorrow's oldie. You can't turn your head for a moment, because you're liable to miss something."

WLRS-FM in Louisville, Kentucky, does the same thing. "We air the hottest songs—the biggest 'adds' and 'breakers'—and don't deviate," promotion director Pru Radcliffe notes. "Songs are established as best-sellers before they get rotation, and the hotter they are, the more air they are given. When they cool, they lose power cut status. CHR is designed to be hard-hitting and ultratrendy. If an artist is burning hot, he or she gets top billing. When a star fades, his or her rotation is reduced proportionately. We go with success to be successful."

Oldies play a role at some CHR outlets, although songs that were hits more than five years ago seldom are aired, and then only if they were number one at the time. "We rotate some golden heavies with our power hits primarily because our market is particularly receptive to popular oldies or classic hits," says Wes McShay, program director at KMON-FM in Great Falls, Montana. "Oldies do not constitute a substantial part of our playlist, but they do help us draw more listeners."

While CHR stations pay close attention to the hit charts and parallels (station add-ons in various markets) in national trade magazines, the majority also adjust their playlists to reflect the particular preferences of their market.

RADIO PROGRAMMING

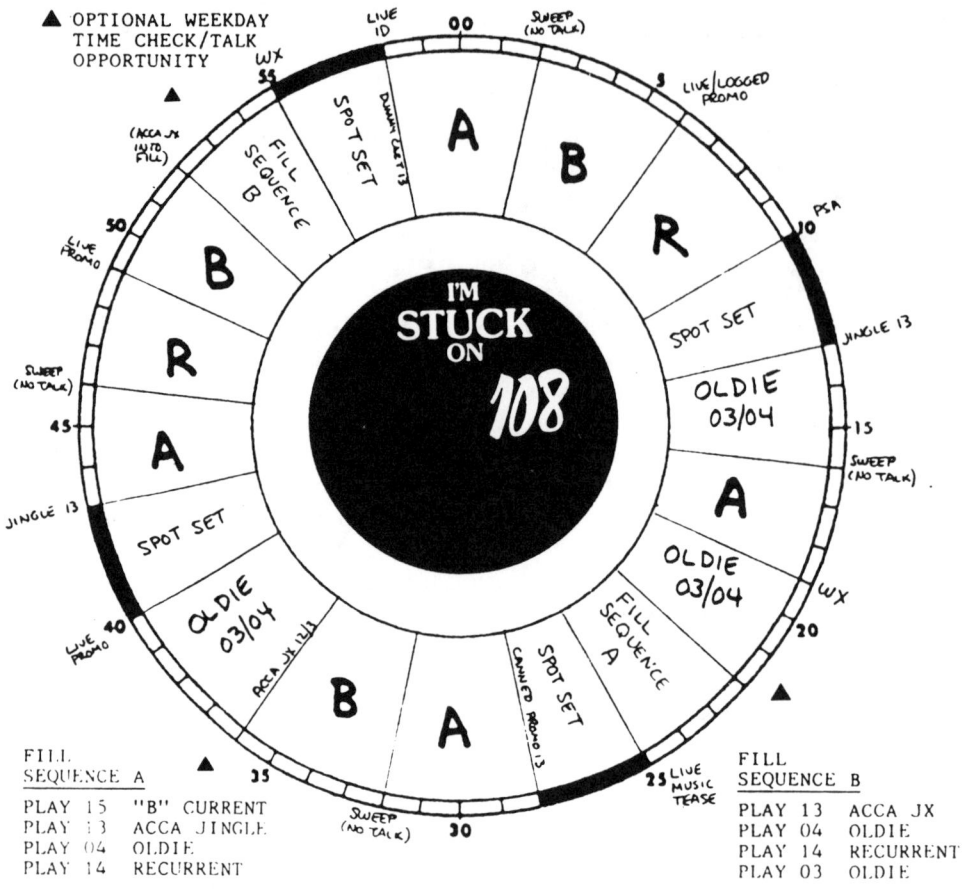

SEQUENCE	SOURCE	TIME/EVENT	SEQUENCE	SOURCE	TIME/EVENT
1850	PLAY 12	:55 LIVE WEATHER	1875	PLAY 12	:25 LIVE MUSIC TEASE
1851	NEXT C	Commercial Cluster	1876	NEXT C	Commercial Cluster
1852	PLAY 13	DUMMY CART (Live ID)	1877	PLAY 13	CANNED PROMO/GREAT 108 JINGLE
1853	-------		1878	-------	
1854	PLAY 12	CURRENT MUSIC SWEEP (A/B/R)	1879	PLAY 12	CURRENT MUSIC SWEEP (A/B/ACCA)
* 1855	-------		* 1880	-------	
1856	PLAY 12	:10 LIVE PSA	1881	NEXT B	OLDIE (PLAY 03/04)
1857	NEXT C	Commercial Cluster	* 1882	-------	
1858	PLAY 13	KSYZ JINGLE	1883	NEXT 12	:40 LIVE PROMO
1859	NEXT B	OLDIE (PLAY 03/04)	1884	NEXT C	Commercial Cluster
* 1860	-------		1885	PLAY 13	KSYZ JINGLE
1861	PLAY 14	"A" CURRENT	1886	-------	

Figure 4.1 CHR music day clock and content breakdown. Courtesy KSYZ.

CONTEMPORARY HIT RADIO

```
  1862   -------                              1887   PLAY 12   CURRENT MUSIC SWEEP (A/R/B)
  1863   NEXT B    OLDIE (PLAY 03/04)       * 1888   -------
* 1864   -------                              1889   PLAY 13   ACCA JINGLE         FILL
  1865   PLAY 15   "B" CURRENT      FILL     1890   PLAY 04   OLDIE                     B
  1866   -------                            * 1891   -------
  1867   PLAY 13   ACCA JINGLE       A       1892   PLAY 14   RECURRENT
  1868   PLAY 04   OLDIE                   * 1893   -------
  1869   -------                              1894   PLAY 03   OLDIE
  1870   PLAY 14   RECURRENT               * 1895   -------
  1871   -------                              1896   END OF BLOCK
  1872   END OF BLOCK                         1897   JUMP TO 1850
  1873   -------                              1898   -------
  1874   -------                              1899   -------
```

* These positions are available for an optional TIMER function in the automation system. To use, find the sequence number, press EVENT EDIT, enter the sequence number, press TIMER SET, enter the length of the record as a four-digit code (example: 0405) and either press AUTO/MAN to return to main screen or EVENT EDIT to enter more timer functions.

NOTE: If you use timer functions, be sure to remove them!

THE BASIC DAY CLOCK

Every hour starts with the top of the hour station ID, and jock shifts change during the spot set at :55. When a new shift begins, the oncoming jock is expected to be here prior to the start of this spot set in order to make the shift change during the commercials.

The following is a break-by-break schedule of what is expected at each point on the clock:

:55 - (following spot set) STATION ID/TIME CHECK/MUSIC TEASE & INTRO

:02 - segue - no jock talk here

:05 - LIVE/LOGGED PROMO (read over song intro)

:10 - EXTRO SONG/TIME CHECK/PSA
    Spot Set
    Jingle - no talk after jingle

   NOTE: If there are no commercials in this spot set, the PLAY 12 in the NEXT position is removed and the order is changed to

   Jingle/TIME CHECK/PSA (read over song intro)

:16 - segue - no jock talk here

:19 - TIME CHECK/BRIEF WEATHER/SONG INTRO (If time allows) (read over song intro)

:25 - EXTRO SONG/TIME CHECK/YOUR NAME/TEASE UPCOMING ARTISTS
    Spot set
    Jingle or promo - no talk after jingle or promo

:31 - segue - no jock talk here

:35 - a cappella jingle between songs - no jock talk here

:40 - EXTRO SONG/TIME CHECK/LIVE PROMO
    Spot Set
    Jingle - no talk after jingle

   NOTE: If there are no commercials in this spot set, the PLAY 12 in the NEXT position is removed and the order is changed to

   Jingle/TIME CHECK/LIVE PROMO (read over song intro)

:45 - segue - no jock talk here

:49 - TIME CHECK/LIVE PROMO/SONG INTRO (If time allows) (read over song intro)

:55 - EXTRO SONG/TIME CHECK/YOUR NAME/WEATHER FORECAST
    Spot set
    (sequence returns to the top of the page)

REMEMBER: Open and close every talk set with the station call letters (KSYZ) or the station slogan (either THE GREAT 108 or FM 108).

Follow the clock and the computer screen...they are the best director you can have!

Figure 4.1 *(Continued)*

RADIO PROGRAMMING

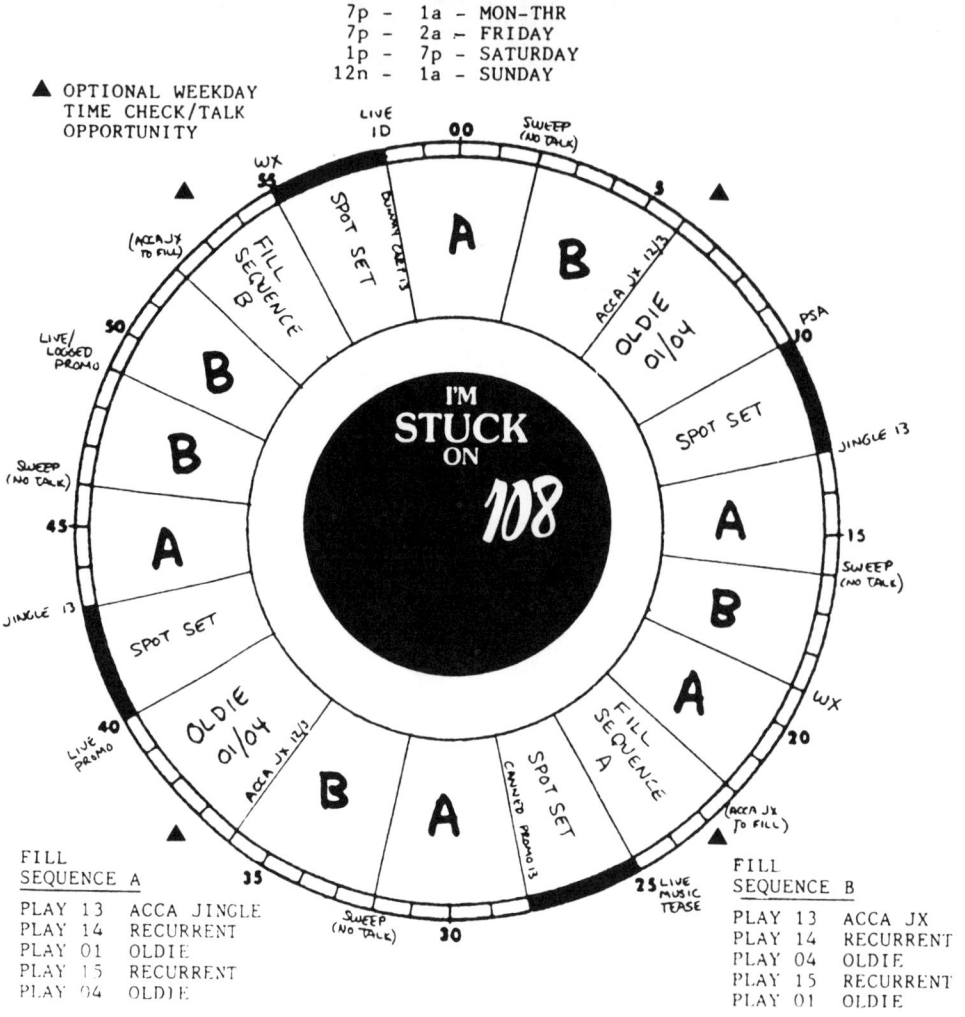

Figure 4.2 CHR music night clock and content breakdown. Courtesy KSYZ.

1914	PLAY 13	ACCA JINGLE	FILL	1939	PLAY 13	ACCA JINGLE	FILL	
1915	PLAY 14	RECURRENT	A	1940	PLAY 14	RECURRENT	B	
* 1916	-------			* 1941	-------			
1917	PLAY 01	OLDIE		1942	PLAY 04	OLDIE		
* 1918	-------			* 1943	-------			
1919	PLAY 15	RECURRENT		1944	PLAY 15	RECURRENT		
* 1920	-------			* 1945	-------			
1921	PLAY 04	OLDIE		1946	PLAY 01	OLDIE		
* 1922	-------			* 1947	-------			
1923	END OF BLOCK			1948	END OF BLOCK			
1924	-------			1949	JUMP TO 1900			

* These positions are available for an optional TIMER function in the automation system. To use, find the sequence number, press EVENT EDIT, enter the sequence number, press TIMER SET, enter the length of the record as a four-digit code (example: 0405) and either press AUTO/MAN to return to main screen or EVENT EDIT to enter more timer functions.

NOTE: If you use timer functions, be sure to remove them!

THE BASIC NIGHT CLOCK

Every hour starts with the top of the hour station ID, and jock shifts change during the spot set at :55. When a new shift begins, the oncoming jock is expected to be here prior to the start of this spot set in order to make the shift change during the commercials.

The following is a break-by-break schedule of what is expected at each point on the clock:

:55 - (following spot set) STATION ID/TIME CHECK/MUSIC TEASE & INTRO

:02 - segue - no jock talk here

:05 - a cappella jingle between songs - no jock talk here

:10 - EXTRO SONG/TIME CHECK/PSA
Spot Set
Jingle - no talk after jingle

 NOTE: If there are no commercials in this spot set, the PLAY 12 in the NEXT position is removed and the order is changed to

Jingle/TIME CHECK/PSA (read over song intro)

:16 - segue - no jock talk here

:19 - TIME CHECK/BRIEF WEATHER/SONG INTRO (If time allows) (read over song intro)

:22 - a cappella jingle between songs - no jock talk here

:25 - EXTRO SONG/TIME CHECK/YOUR NAME/TEASE UPCOMING ARTIST
Spot set
Jingle or promo - no talk after jingle or promo

:31 - segue - no jock talk here

:35 - a cappella jingle between songs - no jock talk here

:40 - EXTRO SONG/TIME CHECK/LIVE PROMO
Spot Set
Jingle - no talk after jingle

 NOTE: If there are no commercials in this spot set, the PLAY 12 in the NEXT position is removed and the order is changed to

Jingle/TIME CHECK/LIVE PROMO (read over song intro)

:45 - segue - no jock talk here

:49 - LIVE/LOGGED PROMO (read over song intro)

:52 - a cappella jingle between songs - no jock talk here

:55 - EXTRO SONG/TIME CHECK/YOUR NAME/WEATHER FORECAST
Spot set
(sequence returns to the top of the page)

REMEMBER: Open and close every talk set with the station call letters (KSYZ) or the station slogan (either THE GREAT 108 or FM 108).

Follow the clock and the computer screen...they are the best director you can have!

Figure 4.2 *(Continued)*

"The term 'CHR' is a general description of radio stations throughout the country that play hit music," WBLI program director Bill Terry notes. "However, hit music can vary from region to region. WBLI's version of CHR is particularly suited for Long Island. The hits are chosen for airplay because they are hits here first. Our music has got to touch the listener immediately. We're in the music presentation business. Basically we are a wall-to-wall music operation twenty-four hours a day, seven days a week, so it had better be tailored to satisfy our local listenership."

Announcing

The role of the deejay in CHR has gone through a cycle of change since the hit-oriented format made its debut in the mid-1950s. The hip and hyped sound was most prevalent during the early days of the format. Top 40 deejays shouted, cajoled, and held court with their audiences. The heavy-voiced, frenetic, and zany jock was the stock announcer persona of the day.

Bill Drake's move to refocus and revise the Top 40 sound in the mid-1960s resulted in the reduction of deejay presence by cutting back on chatter and emphasizing music. Deejays were told to shut up and spin the hits.

In the 1970s, as Top 40 grappled with identity problems, deejays were less strident and aggressive on the air than were their predecessors. Announcers in practically every format were going through a mellowing out phase, which was in vogue in the early part of the decade.

With the reformation of Top 40 to CHR in the 1980s, the energetic, if not frenetic, big-voiced personality style reasserted itself, and while playlists were narrowed and music stressed, deejays often did more than read liner cards.

"Hit radio KSYZ is a radio station with a personality, as opposed to a personality radio station," Chip Mosley says. "Our announcers are a secondary element—music being first—but their contributions to presentation really help set us apart from our automated and card-reading competitors. We encourage our jocks to be a little off-the-wall, to develop bits that fit into the music flow rather than stop it."

According to programmer Mike Edwards, G-105-FM expects its announcers to exude energy and enthusiasm: "In this format, on-air people must reflect the vitality and vigor of the music. We hire people who really have fun on the air and who convey that fact."

WBLI's Bill Terry concurs, adding, "Warm, bright, upbeat deejays who possess a keen wit and a sense of economy keep the sound tight, alive, and entertaining."

Morning teams enjoyed even greater popularity in the 1980s, especially at CHR stations taking the so-called "zoo" approach, wherein the overall objective is to convey a bizarre, almost circuslike atmosphere. This usually involves a menagerie of colorful, often irreverent, air personalities who keep the morning show moving at a vaudevillian pace. Several major market stations topped ratings surveys with "zoo teams."

In the latter part of the 1980s, however, this programming approach lost some of its audience appeal, and many stations reverted to more lean and traditional forms of presentation. Stations using high-profile morning teams usually abandon the team approach in other dayparts because of simple economics. Air teams are very costly, and while AM drive-time rates usually justify greater expenditure, other time periods seldom do.

News

Many CHR programmers regard excessive talk, such as news, even in five-minute hourly increments, as a tune-out factor. Thus, while CHR stations usually increase the level of information they convey during drive periods, particularly mornings, the amount of news programmed is relatively low.

Since the FCC eliminated its news and public affairs requirement, many CHR stations have cut back on nonmusic elements in an effort to retain listeners and reduce station-hopping, something CHR audiences are prone to do when two or more hit stations reside in the same town.

Not all CHR outlets have reduced their news coverage. Many continue to air newscasts hourly, but as of this writing, news is becoming somewhat less evident outside of drive times. Midday and evening, especially the latter, are music-intensive periods at CHR stations.

Features

Syndicated features that reflect the all-hit nature of the format, such as "American Top 40," help attract listeners, but nonmusic features, such as sporting events, rarely are programmed. "Our features are designed to showcase our music," WBLI's Bill Terry notes. "Countdown shows, artist specials, anything that really ties in with the top chart hits helps us strengthen our image. A feature should always enhance, and never detract from, the sound. Ours is CHR, and a feature that falls effectively into that category and hits our cell may be picked up."

Features have become an increasingly popular adjunct to CHR programming in the 1980s, and the number of syndicated features and specials available to programmers has nearly doubled since the 1970s.

Contests and Promotions

CHR is among the more promotion- and contest-oriented formats. Contests and promotions are an integral element of programming at most hit stations. Stations used to fire up the promotion machine only during ratings sweeps, but now they keep it running throughout the year, observes G-105's Mike Edwards: "We're out there all the time with captivating and involving promotions that are elaborately produced, rather than flung together to suit the moment. In the highly competitive radio marketplace, a cleverly conceived and well-produced promotion can give you the edge on the other guys."

Keeping promotions on target and interesting to the audience is the goal of WLRS programmer Pru Radcliffe. "Cold, hard cash and big prizes work better than anything else, so we give away more money and bigger prizes than anyone else in town. Major contests should be powerful and entertaining in CHR."

WBLI's Bill Terry agrees that contests must engage the audience on many levels and adds that this can be achieved without hitting the listener over the head. "Unobtrusive contests, I mean those that don't rival a Cecil B.

deMille production, can involve big cash giveaways, movie premieres, ongoing movie ticket giveaways, bumper sticker contests, and so on. Listeners love to get T-shirts, too. CHR contests should incorporate elements of current popular culture trends for added relevance. They should be as wide in their appeal and as contemporary as the hits programmed."

Since hit radio's inception, contests and promotions have played a major role. In an attempt to lure the listener, some stations have gone to strange extremes, and the results have been mixed. CHR audiences are perhaps more receptive than any other to imaginative and entertaining promotions, however, and program directors are aware that many stations have rocketed to ratings glory when they have hit the mark. At the very least, a well-prepared promotion strengthens listener retention.

Public Affairs

Public affairs programming has experienced a slight decline on the CHR airwaves in the 1980s, especially in metro markets where competition for the hit music audience is intense. CHR programmers in markets with two or more direct competitors are reluctant to break away from the music that draws the audience.

Sunday morning was the traditional time set aside for public affairs and religious programs because of the lower listenership during that time. Programmers reasoned that no one was up at 7:00 A.M. on Sundays anyway, least of all teenagers. As CHR competition increased and the FCC eliminated its nonentertainment requirements in the 1980s, however, Sunday mornings were set aside for countdown shows. This is not to say that public affairs programming is in peril of losing airtime on all CHR stations. The majority, especially in smaller markets, continue to air issues features, albeit in what are considered soft listening periods.

Commercials

Intent on communicating a "more hits, more often" image, many CHR outlets have resorted to clustering commercials in spot sets after music sweeps—"Now four hits in a row on Hot 104." Seldom are fewer than two songs aired following a spot set. As G-105's Mike Edwards stated earlier, the objective is to "keep the hits rolling." Breaking after each song with a commercial was a common practice during the pre-Drake era in Top 40, but in the 1970s and 1980s this practice fell out of favor at many hit stations, except during drive periods when spot loads and deejay involvement usually are heavier. Even during drive dayparts, however, the majority of CHR stations try to maintain the spot set technique, breaking every ten minutes or so, although the actual time allocated to commercial matter might be increased to match the demand. To maintain audience interest, stations typically break spots with a promo or teaser—"Coming up, three hits in a row on Hot 104."

The commercials on CHR stations are designed to sound as slick, entertaining, and trendy as the music they interrupt. CHR is one of the most production-intensive formats.

Jingles

As long as there have been hit stations, there have been jingles. Comedian George Carlin did a memorable parody of Top 40 radio in the 1960s. In the skit, he spoofs the format's excessive use of jingles by breaking into his jargon-riddled hit-deejay patter with the chant "Wonderful W-I-N-O..."

Jingles can detract from, as well as enhance, a station's sound. "At their best they can succeed in conveying and strengthening image while reminding the listener just who is bringing them all the great programming," consultant Donna Halper says. "At their worst they can make a station sound pretty silly. Jingles defeat their purpose if they are predictable and worn-out. To work well they must sound as hip as the hit songs they promote."

COMPETITION

Other contemporary formats pose the greatest competition to CHR stations, notes WBLI's Bill Terry: "Adult Contemporary can skew a bit of our older demos, and AOR radio can do the same for the younger. Urban can bite a piece of the pie that we do not service directly."

KSYZ's Chip Mosley concurs: "AC, AOR, and UC pinch us, if we let them. The key is to be doing our job so well that the pinch is nearly imperceptible."

AC attracts women, whereas AOR draws on CHR's male listeners, observes G-105's Mike Edwards. "AC and AOR present demo balance problems. AC is strong in 25-plus women. They always have been tough in that cell. AOR's biggest pull is in males twelve to thirty-five. They can pose a distraction, but we're pretty strong across the board."

According to WLRS's Pru Radcliffe, other CHR stations pose the most substantial threat: "The format has really proliferated in the 1980s, resulting in considerable fragmentation. Invariably, regardless of market size, there's another all-hit [station] on the block. So there's more head-to-head [competition] within the format than from without."

FUTURE

The future of all-hit radio should be as illustrious as its past, since there is no reason to believe that radio listeners will be any less interested in the hot new songs and artists of the day. To stay viable in the ratings, CHR outlets will have to remain plugged into musical trends. According to WBLI's Bill Terry, "CHRs have to change with the changes and keep up with the times. As tastes in music and listening evolve, we have to evolve with them. That is the nature of the format. We play what is hot now. In the past we decreased oldies and increased our disco slant. That was in the 1970s. In the 1980s, as Top 40 matured, we decreased the disco and increased the AC sound. In 1983, when Top 40 became CHR and was in again, we became more hit focused. This is anything but a static format. Chances are that we'll have to modify again."

Adjusting the playlist to reflect what is currently popular is a fact of life in CHR. According to G-105's Mike Edwards, updating is what keeps hit stations viable. "We play the hits ahead of everyone. That is our marketing strategy. Keeping current and making adjustments as the rankings and parallels change is what attracts our customers. If you play last year's hits, you're not a CHR station, so you can't expect to lure the all-hit fans. Staying on top keeps us on top in CHR."

INDUSTRY NOTES

This is an abridged CHR programming critique from an Iowa consultancy firm. Prior to this, the company would have done a market analysis to get a feel for the competition and the positioning of this station and others in the market.

Personalities

Morning drive: Relates well to the music. Needs to tie in better to local/regional identities. What about using more emphasis on upcoming activities in the area? Where are requests coming from? What about some live, brief phone involvement?

Midday: Needs to be more up. Needs a radio school smile—listeners can hear a smile. The smile needs to be there. Local identity is also low.

Afternoon: Needs to keep in mind target audience. Needs to be more than a rehash of *Rolling Stone*. Music information needs to be relevant. The audience, especially of your station, probably doesn't want a bio of each and every bass guitarist heard on the station.

Evening: Good talent. Good balance of talk and music. Sounds like good preparation goes into the program. It comes across well.

Overnight: Suggest intensive training or convert to a semiautomated format. Perhaps this person should be working on limited flip cards. We really don't want to hear that this person is all alone at the station. We want to be entertained . . . informed.

Production

Attached are some suggestions for improving the sales message in the commercials. More emphasis on commercial production will improve the overall sound of the station.

News

The news needs to be better targeted toward the interests of the target audience. Social Security is of little interest to folks in their teens and twenties. Drugs, sex, and rock 'n' roll, not necessarily in that order, are what your audience wants to hear about. Like it or not.

See attached suggestions for news story topics. See attached suggestions for types of stories to avoid.

Break the mold. Dare to be different. The ghost of Ed Murrow won't get you if you entertain your audience in a newscast. He might even smile, if the stories impact on the listeners.

Geographic proximity needs to be given more weight in the order of the stories. A story within a few miles is more important than most Middle East stories.

Just 'cause the wire runs it as the first story in a split, doesn't mean it's important to your audience.

News of entertainment—music, media, cinema, celebrities—is significant.

Music

In general, it appears you need to get on the hits faster and not play them as long.

We'll need to do some more detailed analysis of how long certain records are staying in the current rotation. The burnout factor can be significant.

Our music specialist will be discussing this in greater detail in an upcoming phone call.

Also, certain cuts are too far away from being hits to be appropriate for this format. These should be dropped immediately in this competitive situation.

Image

Current on-air image is solid. This needs to be supported with more tie-ins to promotions.

What other promotions are planned for the next four months? Let us know, and we'll look at some additional on-air and merchandising possibilities.

The following is an article titled "Watching a Radio Consultant Consult" that appeared in the July 1985 issue of ADWEEK. Written by Karrie Jacobs, it focuses on consultant Rick Sklar's work while at client-station WMKR-FM. It is reprinted with permission from ADWEEK.

TOWSON, MD.—"We gotta go after yuppies and we gotta go after baby boomers and we can't lose one teen in the process," declares Rick Sklar. It is Tuesday morning here, and the principal owners of Hot Hits K106, Steve Seymour and Stuart Frankel, along with program director Ralph Wimmer, are seated around a long table in the station's nondescript conference room. They jot occasional notes as radio consultant Rick Sklar coaches them in their quest for bigger numbers in the ratings book.

Sklar, who is based in New York, had come down on the train to Baltimore the previous day with Seymour, counseling him on the advantages and disadvantages of other radio stations in which Seymour and Frankel wish to invest. That evening, Sklar had dinner with Wimmer as they finalized plans to hire a new morning drive-time disc jockey from a Miami station—a move they felt would boost the all-important a.m. rush-hour ratings for K106 (WMKR-FM), but also would necessitate bumping the current morning jock to the less prestigious 10 a.m. slot.

Breaking the news to the soon-to-be dislocated deejay now was on the agenda for lunch. But first, Sklar—fresh from his five-mile sunrise run—had a pep talk to deliver.

A compact man in his 50s who alternates between fist-pounding and a reflective, almost icy deadpan when explaining his methodology to station management, Sklar is one of the handful of radio consultants

Figure 4.3 Consultant Rick Sklar.

with national reputations. His own broadcasting career—extending over more than 30 years—parallels the development and ascendance of rock 'n' roll and rock radio.

Much of what a consultant sells to a client is his own success story, and Sklar's is particularly heady. He programmed New York's WABC-AM in the '60s and '70s when that station, fueled by and building on Beatlemania, claimed gigantic 20- to 25-percent shares of the metropolitan area's listening audience. Sklar's winning format combined a short, cyclically repetitive playlist of hit songs; fast-talking, aggressively verbose deejays; and a constant stream of jingles that drilled the station's call letter, slogans and deejays' names ("Cou-sin *Bruuu*-ceee") until they were etched in the memory of even the most casual listener.

The top-40 format lost favor in the mid-'70s as more sophisticated "progressive" and album-oriented-rock FM stations moved to the forefront. Now, however, hit radio is back—this time on the FM band—with all the promotional hoopla and shtick, and even shorter playlists. Earlier this year, Sklar left his position as vice president of ABC Radio, and he now is selling his skills to a variety of radio companies. Among his clients are a talk outlet in Oklahoma City, an easy-listening station in Greenwich, Conn., and Hot Hits K106.

"The name of the game," Sklar tells the three men at the table, "is to create a kind of radio over the air that is audience-friendly." He explains that what seems like good management and sound programming to the professionals who run the station—those who consider the station's overall format in a 24-hour period—may be the opposite of what attracts the listener who tunes in for 20 minutes at a time. He points out that even a 15 share of the market (nowadays a 5 or 6 share is considered strong in most cities) means that 85 out of every 100 people never listen to the station. "We are trying literally to get 5 more people out of 100 because, if that could happen, we'd be the market leader."

Part of what Sklar has done in the month he has been working with K106 has been a winnowing of the record library, tossing out songs that don't have the clout the station is seeking in its rotation. He has instituted a system of surveying local record stores (just as he did 20 years ago at WABC) to determine the top sellers in the area. Those songs can be given maximum exposure on the air. The theory is that the more a record sells, the more popular it is, and the record that sells the most will attract and hold the most listeners. "We've identified 250 songs or so that are popular all over the country," says Sklar. "At this point in time, we're pretty damn sure of most of those records." He emphasizes that they should be added to the cartridge library (the cartridge deck has replaced the turntable at most commercial radio stations) immediately, even if that means buying them rather than waiting for the record labels to supply the discs.

Every trick in Sklar's repertoire is intended to hook listeners. More important, he aims to implant the station's call letters in the minds of the handful of Baltimore-area residents who are selected to keep Arbitron diaries, the arguably dubious but indisputably official basis for ratings that help determine ad rates. Sklar pushes for the institution of a sophisticated program of jingles: "They can do a great many jobs for a station." He advocates putting them on cartridges, in some cases tagged to the beginning of a song with a second jingle or a station ID at the end of the song, to form "multiple-element cartridges." "Look at the station the way a movie director looks at a film, with each cartridge representing a scene," Sklar suggests.

Steve Seymour looks up from a note he's just received from Stu Frankel. "I lost the concept," Seymour confesses. "Go back."

Sklar drops the movie metaphor and tries to clarify the point. The combination of elements on one cartridge scheduled into the day's programming by computer would "force the sound in spite of the deejay." His aim is to "create repeating sound patterns," which he calls, "a secret weapon."

"Everything is done," Sklar insists, "not for convenience at this end but for the convenience of those filling out the diary. This damn thing [the Arbitron diary] is an exam book. [The diary keepers] don't like it. It reminds them of school. We have to give them the answers to the exam."

As the morning progresses, Frankel asks Sklar how he feels about the station using syndicated programming from a comedy network. Sklar advises him to "pick and choose," to use the network selectively. They touch on the problem of finding a morning newscaster and debate the merits of using occasional live commercials.

Sklar summarizes what they must do by saying they have to "isolate the hit factor—from hit songs to hit personalities to a hit way of presenting news."

As noon approaches, Seymour, Frankel and Wimmer disperse to attend to last-minute details connected with their first run-through of a new promotion: playing "The Star Spangled Banner" every day at noon until the TWA hostages have been freed by the Shiites. Wimmer has located a copy of the national anthem and had it transferred to a cartridge. Seymour has called the newspapers and television stations and has been told that two different TV-news crews will film the airing of the anthem. Somebody has hung a banner with the station's logo—"Hot Hits K106" in orange and magenta graffiti-like letters on a bright-yellow background—on the wall in the sound studio and made sure that the deejay, Davey Crockett, is sporting a logo T-shirt.

Sklar assures the staff that even though stations in other cities are doing hostage promos, "as long as we're the first in the market, we're the winner." The station's managers and Sklar take turns enthusing about the promotion, citing its publicity value and its patriotic merit, in that order.

By noon, only one cameraman from one station has arrived. The anthem is aired, and afterward the deejay offers a grave explanation of its significance to the listeners. A station ID is played, followed by the upbeat strains of Katrina and the Waves' "Walking on Sunshine." Seymour, Frankel and Sklar follow the cameraman out to the parking lot and watch a replay of the video on the television-station van's color TV. All are pleased with the visibility of the station's logo in the picture.

By 12:30 they're ready to take the old drive-time deejay to lunch and let him know he doesn't have to get up at 5 in the morning anymore.

Sometime after 2, Sklar, Wimmer, Frankel and Seymour reconvene in the conference room and are joined by the morning deejay, who seems unfazed by his sudden demotion. They have cushioned the blow with promises of publicity and fanfare for his move to the 10 a.m. slot, including a staged alarm-clock smashing and contests for late risers.

Scheduled for this afternoon is a brainstorming session on promotions, particularly ones that will attract adult listeners. The managers need to devise publicity stunts and ongoing giveaways for the fall, but first they have to move on a couple of immediate matters, current events they can capitalize on. Ticket sales have just been announced for the Live Aid extravaganza, a rock festival scheduled to take place simultaneously in Philadelphia and England to benefit African-relief organizations. The station has put out feelers in all directions to come up with 10 pairs of tickets to give away on the air. Sklar says the giveaway has to be done in a big way, using lots of superlatives. "First the Beatles, then Woodstock and now the biggest concert event of your lifetime" is the pitch he suggests.

Also discussed are ways to wed the airing of the national anthem to a yellow-ribbon giveaway. The deejay notes that yellow ribbons would match their logo. Sklar proposes distributing thousands of ribbons stamped discreetly with the K106 emblem.

"Who's the woman who handles this building?" Seymour asks Frankel. "We should call her and see if we can tie a ribbon around it. . . . Find out how thick you can get ribbon."

So goes a typical day in the field for radio consultant Rick Sklar.

It was a day that could have included conferences with deejays, a brainstorming session on jingles ("K106 *music blitz, blitz, blitz*) and a music-selection meeting.

A typical day at Sklar's own office might see him sitting back, surrounded by framed black-and-white photos (old ones of Sklar with fresh-faced Beatles and newer ones with Boy George or Juice Newton) and listening to tapes of his stations, making sure his instructions are translated into on-the-air action, taking notes.

There are four times as many radio stations operating in the U.S. today as there were when Sklar's WABC was at its peak. Simple mathematics implies that rating shares must be smaller than they were in the '60s. But Sklar thrills station owners and managers with the message that double-digit shares still are possible. "I was talking to a guy yesterday," relates Sklar, "who was happy 'cause he went from a 2.5 to a 2.8. What happens is people get used to these things. They get comfortable with these kinds of shares. You have to try to open their horizons. They could even be bigger if they just believe that they can be and work at it."

5

Easy Listening

The popularity of music formats is cyclical. In many markets, Beautiful Music formats, highly rated but a few years ago, have been dropped by stations seeking different age demos and more commercial flexibility. However, Beautiful Music remains viable and with the proliferation of new licenses, should definitely be considered to fill the void in numerous markets. Programmers could well profit by new approaches to formatting the Beautiful Music/Easy Listening sound.

—Keith W. Horton
Kozacko-Horton Company

Even with fragmentation of radio listening, the Easy Listening (Beautiful Music) format remains high in ratings performance ... with a loyal following in all demographic segments from thirty-five years on up. I forecast a continued healthy life for this kind of station, as there will always be an audience for the soothing, relaxing benefits provided by instrumentally based music programming.

—Marlin R. Taylor
Bonneville Broadcasting System

The Radio Information Center in New York estimates that five hundred stations classified themselves as Easy Listening (EL) in the mid-1980s. Programming innovator Gordon McLendon introduced the forerunner of EL, also known as Beautiful Music (BM), at San Francisco's KABL-AM ("Cable") in 1959. Prior to the creation of a format devoted to what has been variously called soft, good, or easy music, several stations around the country flirted with the concept by airing segments of relaxing (another applicable term) tunes, generally at night. MOR stations, in particular, were inclined to program "bedtime ballads," and announcers with soothing, nocturnal voices worked at creating the proper atmosphere. "Settle back in your favorite chair for the restful sounds of 'Evening Orchestrations' on W– – –."

McLendon's format sparked interest in other markets, and by the early 1960s dozens of stations had made the conversion to Beautiful Music. In its early years the format was primarily found on the AM band. This would change, however, as the FCC forced AM/FM combo operations in markets exceeding one hundred thousand population to break simulcast. Many of the stations affected chose to go the automation route to keep staffing expenses down. Because of its emphasis on music rather than chatter, BM was perfectly adaptable to automation.

Interestingly, combo stations, which had always earned their big profits on the AM side, discovered that FM Beautiful Music attracted listeners. To fans of the format, FM's ability to broadcast in static-free stereo was a plus.

Within a few years, many stations that had accrued solid ratings by programming BM on AM found themselves losing substantial ground to their own FM outlets. This prompted many combo BMs to abandon the format entirely on AM. By the late 1960s, BM was one of the strongest formats in the nation, and it, along with Progressive Rock, was helping to raise listener awareness of FM.

With the proliferation of other adult-oriented formats in the 1970s, BM began to experience some erosion in its numbers. Adult Contemporary, MOR, Oldies, Nostalgia, and Country stations all competed for certain cells sought by BM. Consultants and station programmers decided BM had grown stale and was in need of revitalization. The audience for old-line BM had "died-off," to use the term bandied about to describe the situation.

Playlists were updated, as was the format's moniker. Beautiful Music became Easy Listening as more recent songs and artists were added to rotations. Rather than a steady diet of lush instrumentals and low-key vocals by artists such as Mantovani, Percy Faith, Jerry Vale, 101 Strings, and Robert Goulet, listeners were treated to popular artists of the present and recent past. Dan Fogelberg, the Beatles, Ann Murray, Bread, and Barry Manilow shared the airwaves with the more traditional EL performers. EL outlets were out to reverse the geriatric image they had acquired under the BM banner.

According to surveys in the 1980s, this goal was achieved. EL audiences are now somewhat younger than they were in the previous decade and are more on an age par with those who tuned in the format at its inception. Listeners over fifty years old, however, still represent the format's most prominent cell.

Today EL is essentially an FM offering, although some AM stations do well with the format. More than 90 percent of the nation's EL stations broadcast on the FM band, and the majority are automated, at least to some degree.

EL listeners are among the most loyal, and station-hopping is virtually nonexistent, something advertisers find very appealing. Although the format has been called a background service, audience reaction to programming, as well as promotions and commercials, is perceptible. EL listeners primarily tune in for the relaxing, laid-back programming that stresses music and deemphasizes talk.

FORMAT CHARACTERISTICS

Music

As stated previously, above all else, EL is a music format. In the past, EL stations concentrated on airing instrumentals. An average quarter hour often consisted of two to three instrumentals combined with one or perhaps two vocals. More often than not, vocals were performed by groups rather than by individuals, and male singers were far more prevalent than female. Today vocals are more common, as are female performers, although some EL outlets retain their penchant for instrumentals. "Instrumentals run about seventy-five percent to twenty-five percent for vocals," says Jim Furr, general manager of WHER-FM in Hattiesburg, Mississippi.

EASY LISTENING

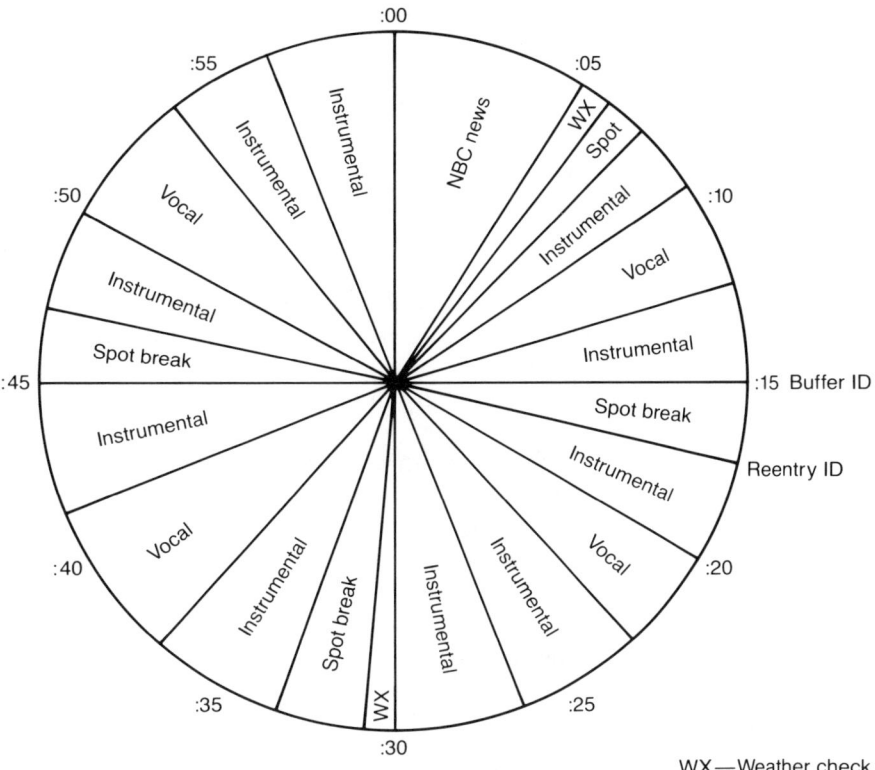

Figure 5.1 Hourly Easy Listening clock. Courtesy WHER-FM.

WX—Weather check

EL is the preeminent sweep format. The uninterrupted music approach was introduced by BM at its inception and has since served as the foundation on which the format is based. "EL is the reigning monarch of continuous music. No other format offers as much music," says Homer Odom, program director at KRUZ-FM in Santa Barbara, California.

Maintaining music flow is a crucial programming consideration, contends Al Jennings, vice president of WJCL-FM in Savannah, Georgia. "It is not enough to keep the music coming, but developing a proper balance—a harmoniously proportioned mix of songs and artists—maintains listenability. In other words, working the tempo and texture scale so that the audience is offered a pleasing ride is our primary programming objective."

Preventing music from becoming stale has been a challenge for EL programmers over the years, reflects Peter Irmiter, program director of WDOK-FM in Cleveland. "One of the reasons BM experienced a softening of its numbers in the 1970s was that the music had grown tired. The updating and renourishing of the playlists injected much-needed life into the aging sound. Today most ELs, WDOK included, work at keeping the sound fresh and vital. This is accomplished by incorporating into the programming a contemporary edge, one that doesn't lacerate the forty-five-plus demographics. This has to be approached gingerly."

WJCL's Jennings agrees: "It is important to keep life in the music, but you have to remember at all times that EL is aimed at mature adults. Like oil and water, audiences seldom mix. Usually older tastes are not compatible with younger."

Chuck O'Neil, program director of WSMN-AM in Nashua, New Hampshire, uses the AC charts as a source for updating his playlists. "We draw from the soft side of the AC Top 40 lists. You have to be very selective, but the AC chart is a real mixed bag of crossover music, so it can be useful. It tends to mirror other formats."

Syndicated music services, many of which use satellites to distribute programming, are widely used by EL stations. "We use a syndicator out of Southfield, Michigan," WHER's Jim Furr says, "What we get is a very upbeat, foreground-type contemporary EL sound that has been very effective in our market."

Syndicators have played an important role in this format since the early 1970s, and this remains the case today. More than one-third of EL stations receive some form of canned programming. The majority of syndicator formats are especially tailored to suit the client's signal area. Syndicators also offer consultancy services to subscribers.

Announcing

This is the original big-voice format. In the past, and to a certain extent today, EL stations possessed a strong affinity for the deep, resonant male voice. Until recently this was not a format prone to hire female announcers. "The big, rich voice with plenty of texture and depth is still widely sought by ELs," programming consultant Dick Ellis notes. "However, this bias has lessened to some degree, and many stations look for effective communicators first and voices second. The stiff-collared stilts no longer claim a monopoly on announcing jobs in this format."

While golden pipes are no longer the primary criterion for announcers at many EL stations, the mature delivery is, claims WJCL's Al Jennings. "This is a fairly conservative format, so announcers can't be too glib or silly, nor can they talk down to the audience. Announcer delivery in the majority of other formats just wouldn't work here. Our audience consists of adults, and this is what we expect our announcers to be on the air."

Announcer presence is relatively low in EL. The majority of stations employing the format promote music, not personalities. At many highly automated EL outlets, live announcing is secondary. Many syndicated services include premixed promos and time checks, so the on-duty announcer is more an equipment operator than anything else. Announcers at many EL stations are called operator assists. Their duties often include breaking spot sets with current temperatures and brief promos, which they read from liner cards (ad-libbing is virtually taboo), and maintaining the automation system. Announcers at many EL operations are not permitted to identify themselves. The idea is to keep the listener's attention focused on the music and the distractions to a minimum.

Announcers do play a greater role at the majority of EL stations during drive-time dayparts. During these segments, announcers often achieve a kind of semipersonality status, wherein their names are mentioned and information-oriented talk is allowed.

WDOK believes that personalities have a place in EL. "Personalities add the human touch in a format that can sound metallic at times," Peter Irmiter explains. "At WDOK the announcer is more than a disembodied voice; he or she is a living, breathing person who complements the sound."

News

While it is the goal of EL stations to establish a reputation for quality continuous music, program directors realize that news and information are important to listeners, particularly in certain dayparts. News coverage is commonly expanded during drive times.

"Of course, music is our entrée, our main selling point, but we also run extended newscasts at seven A.M., eight A.M., noon, five P.M., and six P.M.," WHER's Furr says. "We have made a rather substantial commitment to news over the past couple of years. Our news director has thirty years in broadcast journalism."

Numerous EL outlets all but suspend music programming during morning hours, substituting lengthy news blocks instead, which contain traffic reports, sports updates, and extensive weather information, among other elements.

Although certain EL stations maintain a high news profile around the clock, most cut back to brief hourly newscasts in non-drive-time dayparts and reduce news coverage even further at night. Network news is widely aired in this format.

Features

EL stations tend to be purists, adhering closely to format essentials. For this reason, features are rare and very few EL outlets air talk or sports programs. "'Flow' is the buzzword," consultant Dick Ellis says. "What breaks the music, breaks the format in EL."

Compatible music features are the exception. For instance, programs such as "Sunday with Sinatra" or "Evening with the Pops" would not alienate fans. For the most part, however, the approach to programming in EL remains basic—music, music, music.

Contests and Promotions

While EL stations are promotion-conscious, they are not ostentatious about it. High-profile on-air promotions are rare. Life-style giveaways, such as an evening for two at a local dinner theater or a vacation aboard a cruise ship, are fairly typical. Promotions are conceived to match the flow of surrounding program elements.

"Too elaborately produced on-air promotions or contests would stick out rather than match programming," Ellis notes. "They would attract attention in a way that would be inappropriate and injurious to the format. Promotions should never become an end unto themselves or an irritation factor."

RADIO PROGRAMMING

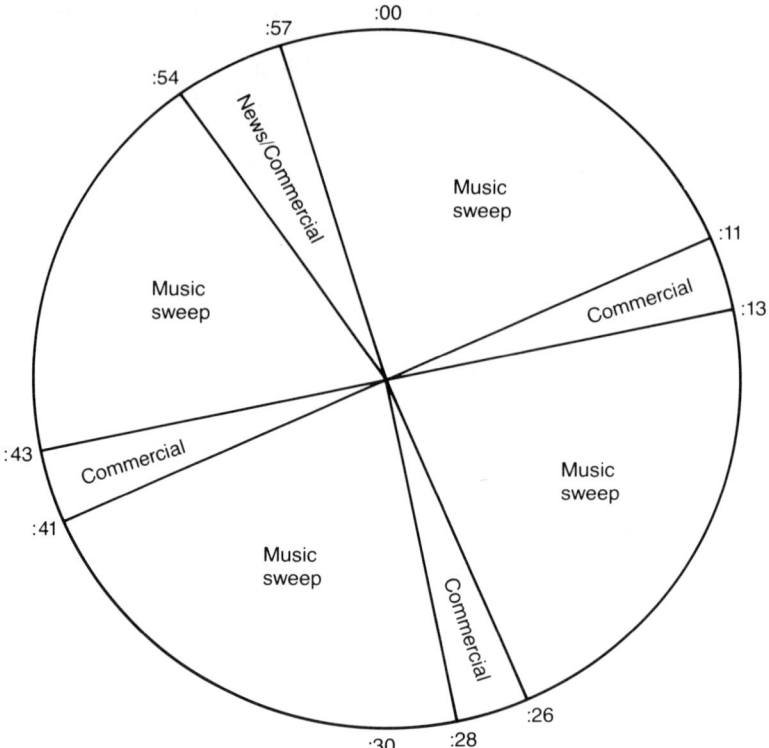

Figure 5.2 A music-intensive EL clock. Courtesy KRUZ-FM.

Public Affairs

Public affairs programs are in as much evidence in EL as in any other music-heavy format. In fact, many EL stations schedule more public affairs programs than might be expected of a music-intensive format. EL listeners are receptive to well-produced, intelligent, and highly relevant issues-oriented programs. This is not to imply that nonmusic features play a major role in the format, which has sometimes been referred to as "segue city," but public affairs features remain a solid ingredient of EL programming.

Commercials

Just as EL can claim to be the original music sweep format, it also can boast introducing the cluster or spot set method of presenting commercials. Of course, the idea behind clustering spots is to create the impression that greater amounts of music are being programmed. Spot clustering also eliminates interruptions and helps maintain flow, which is instrumental in setting mood.

Generally speaking, spot loads are kept low in EL. Lengthy spot sets are regarded as encumbrances to flow. Therefore, a station might impose an eight-minute spot ceiling per hour or a two-minute spot maximum per cluster when the hour is broken at four points. Spot loads usually are increased

EASY LISTENING

during commute periods to take advantage of the premium rates these dayparts can command.

EL stations are sensitive concerning the production value of the commercials they air. A spot with a loud, contemporary sound could offend the sensibilities of the EL listener, contends Enzo DeDominicis, vice president of WRCH/WRCQ in Hartford, Connecticut. "If we judge a spot to be too raucous for our programming, we reject it," he says. "It doesn't make sense to work all day at maintaining a certain sound and to allow a sixty-second spot to ruin everything. We have an established set of standards for commercial material, and if they are not met, the client is informed."

WHER
FM STEREO 103

Where It's Easy To Listen... 24 Hours A Day

STATION INFORMATION

```
WHER
2414 W  SEVENTH ST
HATTIESBURG MS   39401
(601) 544-3232
GENERAL MANGER: JIM FURR
```

FACILITIES

100,000 WATTS / ANTENNA 1,000' ABOVE AVERAGE TERRAIN, LOCATED BETWEEN HATTIESBURG & LAUREL.

COVERAGE, ACCORDING TO ACTUAL LISTENER REPORTS, REACHES FROM THE COAST TO WELL NORTH OF MERIDIAN, TO NORTH OF JACKSON, TO McCOMB, BROOKHAVEN AND WELL PAST PICAYUNE TOWARDS NEW ORLEANS.

PROGRAMMING

TARGET DEMOGRAPHIC: ADULTS, 25 - 65

MUSIC: CONTEMPORARY EASY LISTENING...INCLUDES BRIGHT, FRESH INTRUMENTALS (75%) AND VOCALS (25%) BY ORIGINAL ARTISTS. STATION HAS USED THIS BASIC FORMAT SINCE GOING ON AIR IN JULY 1966.

NEWS: NBC NETWORK NEWS EVERY HOUR (24 HOURS) FOLLOWED BY LOCAL RADAR WEATHER & FORECAST. STATION AIRS EXTENDED NEWS, SPORTS & WEATHER FROM 7:05-15A, 8:05-15A, 12:05-15P, 5:05-15P, 6:05-15P, 10:05-15P. STATION'S LOCAL NEWS IS DIRECTED BY 28-YEAR VETERAN JOUNALIST HANK DOWNEY. DOWNEY ANCHORS THE EARLY MORNING NEWS AND REPORTS THROUGHOUT THE DAY. A STAFF OF SEVERAL OTHER NEWS REPORTERS ASSIST WITH DAILY COVERAGE.

SPORTS: LOCAL SPORTS IS UNDER THE DIRECTION OF VETERAN SPORTSCASTER AND ASSISTANT SPORTS INFORMATION DIRECTOR AT U.S.M., JOHN COX. COX ANCHORS THE EARLY MORNING SPORTSCASTS AND REPORTS THROUGHOUT THE DAY.
WHER ALSO AIRS ALL U.S.M. FOOTBALL & BASKETBALL GAMES. STATION'S LOCAL STAFF ORIGINATES A "LIVE" GOLDEN EAGLE TAILGATE PARTY BEFORE & AFTER EACH U.S.M. HOME GAME (FEATURES INTERVIEWS WITH COACHES, PLAYERS & FANS).

2414 W. 7th STREET • HATTIESBURG, MS 39401 • (601) 544-3232

Figure 5.3 An Easy Listening profile sheet (a) and coverage map (b). Courtesy WHER-FM.

RADIO PROGRAMMING

Figure 5.3 (Continued)

COMPETITION

Lite AC stations present the most competition to EL outlets. "The Soft, or so-called Lite, ACs are everywhere, and they can bite into EL listening," WSHN's Chuck O'Neil says. "The softer they are, the greater the threat."

WDOK's Peter Irmiter agrees, adding, "Lite AC tugs at the younger end of the EL demo, while the syndicated Music of Your Life (MOYL) and Nostalgia formats play in about the same cell that we're going for."

In the South, Country stations pose the most significant threat to EL outlets, contends WHER's Jim Furr. "Country is strong in approximately the same age demo as is EL. This is particularly true in our region of the country."

KRUZ's Homer Odom perceives News and Talk stations as major competition: "Although they are not doing what we're doing, when the EL audience wanders, it is usually to nonmusic formats like News or Talk."

Odom also echoes O'Neil's and Irmiter's opinions about the competition created by AC stations. "If we're head-to-head with any other format besides EL itself, it is probably with Lite AC. I suspect that this is the case around the country in the 1980s."

FUTURE

Consultants and EL program directors believe that the way to keep the format healthy and viable in the future is to refresh playlists continually. "Retuning as the situation warrants is what has kept us on top of the market," WJCL's Al Jennings says. "You can't remain static and expect to attract listeners. They change, too. The fifty-year-old today was the thirty-year-old in the 1960s. Tastes in music change with the times. This is what many adult more-music stations failed to realize in the 1970s. The only thing that will set EL on its ear is if it allows itself to grow old again."

KRUZ's Odom is in complete agreement: "EL will remain a ratings contender as long as it doesn't lapse into complacency. Like any other format, EL must update its music and continually analyze its rotation patterns."

Like many smaller market stations, WHER believes that a strong emphasis on topics of local interest is the key to remaining salable. "We feel strongly that nonurban radio stations, ELs included, must provide local programming that means something, that is important to the listener," Jim Furr says. "You cannot get by as strictly a vendor of music. Community involvement is important, even in more-music."

INDUSTRY NOTES

What follows is an EL station programming monitor (air check critique) from a consultant:

> To: Fred Curtis
> Fr: Jean Marlowe
> Re: Monitor of WDDD-AM and WDDD-FM

To reiterate what we discussed at breakfast, let me first consider the FM. Unlike its counterpart in Hopeville, WBBB-FM, WDDD-FM still strikes me as more of a traditional Beautiful than an Easy Listening station. There seem to be fewer vocals and fewer light pop selections than on WBBB-FM. Given that Bob has the same music on both stations, I would be interested to discover why WDDD-FM has such a background-music sound, while WBBB-FM has made the transition to a somewhat more foreground sound.

Some of the problem may be engineering—WBBB-FM has much more presence, and the music tempos are much more textured. WDDD-FM seems to play more of the violin/orchestral/Mantovani type of Beautiful Music, and while its signal is loud enough, it does not seem as clean to me as WBBB-FM. Perhaps this contributes to the perception of being more like Muzak and less like Easy Listening.

Although WDDD-FM uses that liner about "sparkling sounds," for me the music did not sparkle at all. It just lay there, not offensive but nothing that anyone under fifty would find enjoyable. I realize that the very nature of Beautiful (or, if you prefer, Easy) makes it difficult to attract those younger demos who grew up with AC and Top 40 and are not accustomed to the style or the background quality of most BMs, but still many Beautifuls are being dragged forcibly into the 1980s—WBBB-

FM among them. It is still possible to be Beautiful/Easy yet not sound like a throwback to 1960.

WDDD-FM seems to be slowly evolving into a more foreground type of station, but it isn't there yet. The announcers seem convinced that they must put on a "Beautiful Music voice" when they record their drop-ins, and it's almost amusing to hear the jock who was on the AM doing very up AC/Top 40 a few moments earlier suddenly transformed into a person who speaks very slowly and carefully enunciates each word with a suitably serious tone of voice. Even those jocks who have been told to lighten up still seem a bit confused about the image they should maintain on FM.

As we discussed about WBBB-FM, and as you are certainly aware, part of the transition in today's BM/ELs is toward announcers who sound more human and friendly. While the FM jocks don't sound as dead or as funereal as others I have heard, they still seem stuck in the belief that FM is supposed to sound serious. Another problem is the length of the FM shifts. For example, I heard Van's voice, off and on, doing news or whatever else, from afternoon drive up to about 10:00 P.M. The perception there is that the poor guy never goes home.

Another major problem is one that we corrected on WBBB-FM: dead air. To my knowledge, it is not necessary to have a full five-second pause between certain songs or between a song and an announcer drop-in. It may have been part of old-line BMs not to sound too tight, but we are at the other extreme. At times we sound totally asleep or, worse, unprofessional. Listeners don't know the great reasons for dead air. They just know it's there, and they wonder if their radio is broken.

There are also minor stylistic points, such as the jingle (which I'm not even sure I like), which is used much more at night than during the day. Also, I'm not certain saying FM twice in the ID is good. It sounds a bit redundant to say FM 94 WDDD-FM, but that's a small matter. In addition to dead air, we also have traffic reports that are of horrible quality. The newspeople impressed me a lot with their general professionalism, but we'll talk more about that when discussing the AM. Also, what are the rules about vocals to instrumentals, newer music to recent to very old, etc., and how many in a row without calls do we play at night? I would like to have other voices besides Van's on the air, and more involvement from the announcers wouldn't be a bad idea.

As it stands right now, there are times when the station really does sound automated and lifeless. I also am not thrilled that Bob has no system for ever telling the nice people the name of any song they heard. It strikes me as a service to our audience. Most adults are very passive, and while they may not buy a lot of records, they like to know what they have been listening to. I don't say we have to announce every song, but it's too bad that right now we can't even do it at all. In summation, I feel the FM has come a long way, but it is still moving toward a positioning that will make it slightly more modern.

EL consultant's announcer critique:

Brian:
I meant what I said when I told you I'm pleased with your progress. The

effort you are making is definitely noticed and appreciated by us all. I critiqued two of your tapes. I am only returning one because the other broke, but the comments are similar for both shows. First, the good stuff. You have excellent rapport with the audience, and your one-on-one skills are usually very fine. You are obviously trying to be more concise and to relate better to the 34–44 end of the demo, rather than just talking to the forty-five-plus end the way you once did. By the way, you sound very good on the FM. Now let's look at some areas that are still in need of some improvement:

1. Be careful when you do your changeover with the newsperson at the beginning of your shift. Being friendly is fine, but it still sounds unprepared at times, so have some idea of what you and Suzanne are going to say and how to get out of the rap. you get in just fine but seem awkward when you have to get back into playing the next record.

2. You still have a problem doing the transition from one element of the format to another, such as from a back sell into a PSA. You seem to pause or hesitate or say something that tries too hard to be clever. Sometimes the best thing you can do is just move directly from the back sell into the PSA and don't even try to say something transitional. It just sounds forced.

3. Do you preread your PSAs? Several times you sounded surprised that the event you were reading was going on the next day, and you didn't read it "tomorrow," rather you said "Wednesday" just like it said on the card. Common sense would dictate that if you are reading something on a Tuesday and the event is taking place the next day, you would change the wording to "tomorrow." Catch my meaning? Be prepared!

4. Avoid inane remarks that are meant to sound friendly but just sound inane. After one PSA about a free concert, you said "Ah, the works of the Great Masters. I know them all. There's Johann Sebastian Bach, just to name a few." Huh? You didn't name a few. You just named one, and why name any? Just read your PSA and move on. Not everything needs to be added to or embellished. Some things are better left short and simple.

5. Beware of new and improved verbal crutches. Your latest is "Coming up." You said it twelve times in one hour. Also, beware of billboarding too much. Once in a while it's nice to say what artists are about to be played, but doing it six or seven times an hour is way too often. Adults don't know most of the artists anyway, so why overdo it?

Keep working hard. I'll be in touch.

6

Album-Oriented Rock

AOR is one of the few formats that is evolutionary in that it grows with the audience, versus CHR, which tends to have static demographic appeal. AOR also is geared to be programmed by the balance of science and emotion, where ideas are generated emotionally (creatively) and the function of research is to confirm emotions.

—Lee Abrams
Burkhart/Abrams/Douglas/Elliot
and Associates, Inc.

The Album-Oriented Rock (AOR) format was conceived out of a basic disdain for the highly formulaic, mainstream pop sound of Top 40 and other conventional forms of radio programming. In 1966 New York station WOR-FM introduced the precursor of AOR, known as Progressive or Free Form. Within a year, the format made its debut on the West Coast at KMPX-FM in San Francisco. The format focused on nonchart album cuts and featured laid-back, conversational deejays versus the usual shouters on pop stations and the heavy voicers common on adult stations. Progressive stations were motivated by a desire to bring album cuts customarily ignored by or excluded from conventional playlists to the listening public.

Initially many Progressives rejected the notion of structure and consistency, preferring to mix divergent musical forms and styles within a given sweep or hour. Others chose to block their programming day in a manner similar to this:

6:00–8:00 A.M.	Jazz
8:00–10:00 A.M.	Classical
10:00 A.M.–2:00 P.M.	Album Rock
2:00–6:00 P.M.	Folk/Ballads
6:00–9:00 P.M.	Jazz
9:00 P.M.–Midnight	Classical

By the late 1960s the majority of Progressive stations had converted exclusively to album rock and were variously referred to as Underground, Acid, or Psychedelic because of the social or cultural attitude they seemed to echo. For example, Underground rockers projected a pseudocounterculture posture to relate to listeners caught up in the social ferment of the period. In 1968–1969 the antiwar movement was in full swing, major cities across the country were experiencing racial upheaval, and the public was still reeling from a series of political assassinations. Underground stations appealed to the iconoclastic mindset—"Burn baby, burn!" and "Hell no, we won't go!"—possessed by an impressive segment of the under-thirty, primarily male demographic.

The use of mind-altering drugs also rose sharply in the 1960s, peaking as the decade wound down. Rock music containing lyrics with either overt or implied references to drugs was popular on many album rockers, which consequently became known as Psychedelic or Acid Rock stations. The latter was characterized by a decibel-devouring sound best typified by guitarist Jimi Hendrix, who died of a drug overdose in 1970 at the age of twenty-seven.

The format assumed a mellower tone amidst the relative cultural calm of the 1970s, although heavy rock remained a staple of album rockers. In fact, as other formats, namely Top 40, invaded the FM band, AOR stations became more formulaic in reaction to the influx of competition. Album-Oriented Rock stations, as they had come to be known by the mid-1970s, tightened playlists in an attempt to strengthen their competitive position. Soft and Pop Rock stations were siphoning off listeners, and by the end of the decade, Urban Contemporary and a refurbished Top 40 were penetrating deep inside AOR's demographic territory and winning listeners.

In the early 1980s many traditional AOR groups and artists, such as Bruce Springsteen, Talking Heads, and David Bowie, went mainstream with hits at the top of the pop charts, and CHR stations gleefully welcomed them. AOR stations slipped in the ratings in many markets, while an equal number converted to CHR because of tired and worn-out playlists. "How many times can you play 'Stairway to Heaven' and still be perceived as fresh and vital?" observed media critics.

The extreme replication of the highly formulaic CHR sound has renewed audience interest in AOR, which sharpened and honed its playlists in the 1980s. The refining of the format has included, among other things, playlist tightening, more segues (even in drive slots), a more mainstream product, a reduction of heavy metal, more classic rock, a higher profile personality during drive times, and wider use of compact discs.

Males eighteen to thirty-nine continue to be the biggest supporters of AOR, with twenty-four-year-olds the most ardent fans. Dwight Douglas, president of Burkhart/Abrams/Douglas/Elliot and Associates, suggests that a more appropriate title for the format, since it has become more contemporary and continues to be strong among males in the second half of the 1980s, is Male Adult Contemporary (MAC).

Today AOR remains nearly exclusively an FM format, and although the number of stations employing the format is down considerably (from 580 in 1979 to 285 in 1986), it remains viable and profitable in many markets. AOR listeners tune in for music they cannot hear elsewhere. They consider themselves hip, trendy, and music aficionados. To AOR fans, radio is an integral part of their life-style and daily activities.

FORMAT CHARACTERISTICS

Music

Perhaps no other format places as much importance on music mix as does AOR. "Music compatibility is our primary objective in sweeps," notes Paul Browning, program director of KPNY-FM in Alliance, Nebraska. "Unlike CHRs that'll go from a ballad to a high rocker because of their relative chart positions, we try to establish a sort of sound motif. Blends and transitions have always been important in album rock. We draw from the CHR single charts to augment our playlists and to keep things fresh and current, but we maintain continuity. We don't just drop in a hit because the clock says it's time. It has to mesh with the sweep, or it waits."

AOR stations are sweepers and have always been known as more-music alternatives that are not afraid to air lengthy cuts or the long versions of popular songs. "We promote the fact that we play more rock than anyone else on the block," Browning says. "Now another commercial-free quarter hour of great rock on KPNY."

AOR playlists can be extensive in that they often include records from as far back as the 1960s, says John Marshall, program director of KFMG-FM in Albuquerque, New Mexico. "The depth of tracks aired here is greater than anywhere else. For instance, we play more than hit singles, and we draw from an expansive library of older material, such as the Beatles, Led Zeppelin, and Creedence Clearwater Revival."

Bruce McGregor, program director of KEZO-FM in Omaha, Nebraska, takes a similar approach to music: "In addition to hit rock singles, we are able to go deeper on albums, both past and present. This depth keeps our repetition low and time spent listening higher than AC and CHR. We span twenty-five years of music in our library, so we don't rely only on current releases. Our mix is about sixty-five to seventy percent new and thirty to thirty-five percent old."

While most AORs have become more hit chart sensitive in the 1980s, many continue to punctuate their rotations by playing new music, notes KFMG's Marshall. "We also play new music sooner than other contemporary formats, often taking chances on new and untested bands. Of course, AOR used to be much more daring in this respect."

Marshall's point is well taken. AOR programmers became more conservative and less experimental in the late 1970s and 1980s, although a greater willingness to air untried or uncharted material reemerged at some album rockers in the mid-1980s as a reaction to the pervasiveness of CHR.

Announcing

Early AOR, or Progressive, announcer styles were in stark contrast to those in other formats, especially Top 40. Inspired by a desire to break with convention, album station announcers were conversational and low-key. The super-

RADIO PROGRAMMING

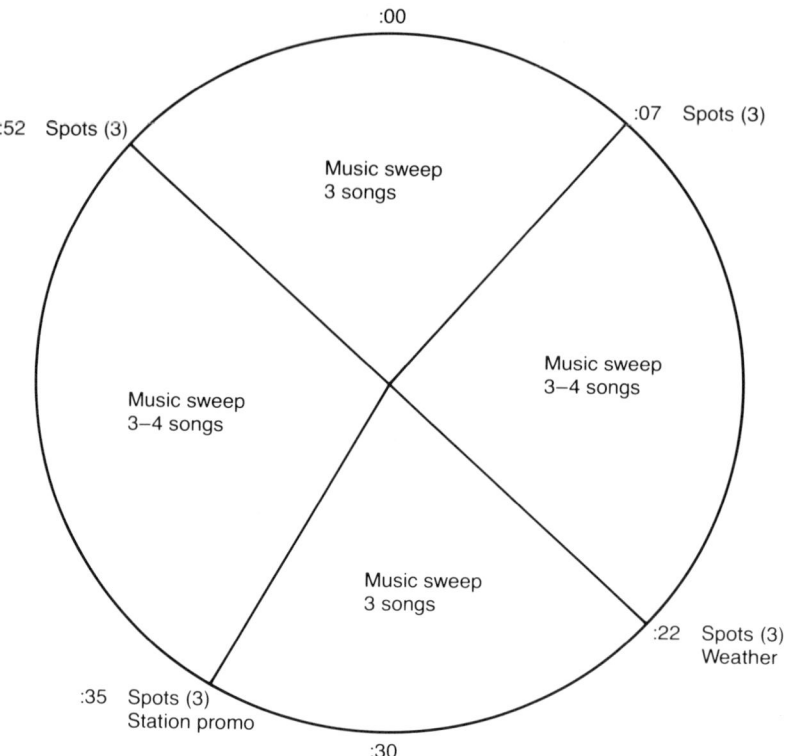

Figure 6.1 A basic "meat and potatoes" AOR clock spanning all dayparts. Courtesy KEZO-FM.

charged, high-intensity deejay delivery prevalent on Pop Rock stations fueled the move to the mellower, laid-back style. In fact, album rock jocks went out of their way to avoid the deejay stereotype of the day.

Over the years, AOR announcing has become more energetic, perhaps in response to the general softening of styles in other formats. AOR's greater adherence to formula in the 1970s and 1980s, however, has resulted in a more conventional or mainstream approach to deejaying. Album rock jocks during the early years of the format often conveyed an air of rebellion and sounded heavily anesthetized (high) while doing so. Today vitality, charm, wit, and awareness are important, contends KEZO's McGregor. "Our announcers are great communicators. They are in-touch personalities who entertain and inform their listeners in an honest, concise, and intelligent manner."

News

News generally plays a secondary role at most AOR stations. This is particularly true during non-drive-time dayparts, and many album rockers air only a limited amount of news even during drive times. At some album rockers, however, news does assume a greater role in commute periods. "We have a news commitment in the morning drive," McGregor says. "AOR listeners, especially those about to greet the day, are no different than anyone else when

ALBUM-ORIENTED ROCK

Figure 6.2 Midday AOR clock. Notice the lengthy sweep between :24 and :48 stop sets. The same station uses an alternate clock with breaks at :12 and :36 and employs ten playlist categories: three current, two recurrent, and five other special categories. Courtesy KFMG-FM.

it comes to wanting information on what is happening in the world, so we intensify information mornings."

Many AOR stations broadcast brief newscasts hourly throughout the day, while an equal number drop news altogether or air only headlines at the top or bottom of the hour. Album rockers that downplay news commonly have deejays assume newscasting duties during their shifts. Although news might be kept to a minimum, some metro album rockers consider it appropriate to have a newsperson on duty throughout the day. At night these same stations also might discontinue news service.

Features

AOR has a penchant for features, more so than other contemporary music formats. Features at album rockers range from the brief vignette to the full weekend special, notes KEZO's McGregor. "We make extensive use of drop-in type material, comedy bits, rock capsules, and so on. We also incorporate 1960s and 1970s news actualities that relate to the years of our 'goldens.' The Beatles' arrival in New York before playing a 1964 Beatles song or a blurb from Woodstock before airing an artist from that era serve as for instances. We air special shows, too, especially on weekends. A Sunday morning fusion jazz feature called 'Jazz Brunch' and a three-hour classic rock show known as 'Back Tracks' are programmed."

Consultants at Burkhart/Abrams/Douglas/Elliot, the leading AOR consultancy group in the country, have encouraged the programming of features as a method of keeping a station hot. In 1986 its feature suggestions to client station WKLS-FM in Atlanta included "Psychedelic Psupper," psychedelic hits aired during the supper hour; "One at One," a classic oldie followed by the present number one at 1:00 P.M.; "Smash or Trash," audience ratings of new songs; and "Perfect Album Side," the audience-selected six favorite hits of all time.

Live rock concerts, rock news updates, and other life-style events, especially keyed to music, are staple programming elements at many AOR stations, says KPNY's Browning. "We look for and air quite a bit of special programming, the kind of stuff that our listeners can get excited about. Involvement features, the kind that really connect with the AOR buff, are very important in this format."

Commercials

Since AOR outlets frequently work off a sweep or music-intensive clock, spots generally are clustered. "At least five songs are aired between spot sets," KFMG's John Marshall says. "To slot spots after every cut or two would frustrate our listener. After all, Album-Oriented stations have established a reputation for long, uninterrupted music segments. That is an approach that sells the format."

Of course, AOR is no different from other formats in that it often relaxes this rule during drive dayparts, particularly the morning, when listeners are more receptive to talk.

AOR spot production can be elaborate, although at the format's inception, commercials were designed to be inauspicious or innocuous in an effort to keep a station from sounding too commercial. Today the live, a cappella spot, sans sound effects and beds, is less prevalent than the premixed commercial containing a host of production ingredients.

Jingles, Contests, and Promotions

AOR has never used produced jingles to the extent other contemporary formats have. Early AOR was primarily concerned with defrilling its sound and cranking out the music. In the 1970s contests became more prevalent, and by the 1980s many AOR stations were as promotion-heavy as chart hit stations.

"Promotions are a major programming ingredient at today's album rocker," Bruce McGregor says. "You hear almost everyone in the business say it, and I'll say it again: The idea is to construct promotions that are fun and reflect the life-style—1980s radio's super buzz term—of those tuned. I think AOR promotions must be more sophisticated than those on CHRs. We earn our audience here at KEZO; we don't try to buy it with money or merchandise."

While contests and promotions have become a solid part of AOR programming, the use of jingles has not. "The idea in AOR is to play the music rather than sing about playing the music," KFMG's Marshall notes.

COMPETITION

Other contemporary rock formats present the most competition to AOR, especially CHR. "The hot hit stations have given album rock the most difficulty in the 1980s," Marshall says. "They are stronger in young women, a cell this format has always been light in. CHR also can cut into the eighteen- to twenty-nine-year-old males, depending on their playlists or what artists occupy the top chart slots. For example, when Dire Straits or Pete Townsend are power cuts on hit stations, we experience some station-hopping, something that was uncommon in the earlier days of the format."

KPNY's Paul Browning also perceives CHR as his biggest foe: "Contemporary Hit has been a problem for AOR since the early 1980s, although we've rebounded in the latter part of the decade. The CHR/AOR hybrid creates the biggest headache for the pure album rocker."

KEZO's Bruce McGregor considers AOR to be without any specific competitor: "I feel that no other format directly impinges upon us. When programmed properly, there is no other format like AOR. We are a male-centered, eighteen to thirty-four/eighteen to forty-nine/ twenty-five to fifty-four-year-old format. Most other formats just don't offer the energy that these people grew up with. Just because you reach thirty-five doesn't mean you're ready for Adult Contemporary. People stay with the music they grew up with. That's why AOR will be a great growth format if it's done in an entertaining, no b.s. fashion."

In some markets Oldies and Urban Contemporary stations have nibbled at AOR numbers, especially when AOR outlets focus on 1960s rock or on new rock.

FUTURE

KPNY's Browning believes that the depth of the AOR playlist ensures the format's hold on listeners in the future. "As long as we dig beneath the hit charts and probe popular and new albums, we'll remain a fresh and attractive alternative. If we become superficial or redundant, then we're in trouble."

Bruce McGregor concurs: "In the early 1980s, AOR was thought to be fossilized, on its deathbed, but it has adapted, adjusted, and evolved. We've updated our playlists, but we have not changed the practice of presenting depth. In the 1970s AOR was geared to hard rock and heavy metal. Only eighteen- to twenty-four-year-old males were excited about that. Older males, who came through the 1960s, were disenfranchised until AOR began to open up their older music libraries and began focusing on quality bands and their music. Many of the progressive bands, like Yes, Genesis, etc., enjoyed renewed success in the 1980s. The consumer has become very much 'show me' when it comes to new bands. An album now must have substance and depth. AOR fills the depth, whereas other Contemporary Hit rockers tend to remain bubble-gummers."

Consultant Lee Abrams notes that "AOR radio is based on the principle of changing the familiarity factor of music from title to artist. On a CHR station the titles are familiar, whereas with AOR the familiarity is based on the artist, allowing depth in the selections from the given artist, thus the album identity." Abrams believes that this formula will keep album rockers appealing to a whole new generation of radio listeners.

KFMG's John Marshall contends that as long as AOR remains quality-conscious and in touch with its followers, it will enjoy continued prosperity. "By keeping our promotions active, interesting, timely, and life-style relevant and by spending a great deal of time selecting the best music of the rock era, past and present, we'll stay ratings contenders."

INDUSTRY NOTES

Consultant's AOR station critique:

I believe the image of WZZZ-FM is very solid. With the market so crowded with mainstream ACs, we're in an excellent position to tug on their 24–39 demos. Our TV spot says it all in a very succinct manner to raise cume [unduplicated listeners], and hopefully that will transfer to more AQH [average quarter hour listeners]. But I believe more can be done on the air to increase the time spent listening.

For the most part I think WZZZ lives up to its claim of "less talk, more rock," but I think we should take advantage of the cume and try to increase the quarter hour by doing more effective recycling. The liners are somewhat stiff and don't sell the station effectively.

First, I would break out the Arbitron for the strongest and weakest dayparts, set up a rank order system on what dayparts need the most promotion, and begin to promote them in a specific order to ensure that the entire audience hears the promo. It probably takes about four to five promos per day for one week for the entire cume to hear one announcement.

Secondly, I would rewrite all the promos so they sell the jocks, programs, weekend, or daypart we want them to tune. I think our liners are too basic and don't sound like the way our audience talks. Liners should be written with more sell, excitement, and in the audience's language, not radio's.

Thirdly, I would have most promos and liners produced. Much like our current listener's promo. The produced promos always sound much more exciting and refreshing than does the talent reading the liner. I would do more producing of the promos with more cuts, edits, and some specific music identifier that could become synonymous with WZZZ. Use some quick music that stands out, and always include it in the carted [taped] promos and IDs. I would use the same music in any new television spots to create consistency both on the air and for cume building off the air.

Finally, I think the live liners need to be made more fresh, exciting, and motivating. Give the listeners a strong reason to stay tuned. I would be more specific and take advantage of the live liners to again recycle the audience in specific times. For instance, our Gale Lawry liner says "Wake up with a Gale of rock." That really isn't incentive enough for people to do it, despite the connotation. I would have that liner carted by Gale, with other pertinent info. "Wake up with some rock on and me, Gale Lawry, mornings seven to ten. I'll have our morning feature artist and a special giveaway." Give the audience the when, where, and why, and he might tune. The open-ended, data-less liner wastes time and creates confusion. Sell your dayparts with a targeted pitch.

On another subject, I believe the air staff could be strengthened in some dayparts. Overall, however, it is sufficient. I would work on the presentation and delivery of some of the air staff. At times WZZZ sounds a bit stiff and canned. We by no means have to feign happiness. There is nothing worse than a pretentious or affected jock in my estimation. While we should live up to our "less-talk" promise, a friendlier, less-liner-card announcer sound should be our goal. The air staff could be critiqued more often by the program director. Have him set up some type of air check session with the staff. This should be a positive, reinforcing session rather than a critical one. A two-way discourse gets the best results in the long run. Create team spirit through greater interaction and team-devised strategy.

On yet another front, I would establish more explicit criteria for music on WZZZ. As the market has become more competitive, the need to play on-target material is obvious. Listeners have so many choices. Fortunately we're the only album rocker in town. The ACs have provided us with a clear path. I have never seen a market so redundant, but that's fine. WOOO runs the hits. However, like so many CHRs, it runs them into the ground, and their audience with them, too. Careful of "popping" out. Last week I heard three Top 10 tracks in succession. For a moment I thought I was tuned to WOOO. What followed was fine, but inconsistencies like that will hurt in the long run. Playlist and rotation modifications seem warranted, and I will be up as planned on the nineteenth to work with your PD. Balance problems exist.

Per our phone conversation regarding WZZZ promotion, I think we can become more aggressive and strengthen the link with the community at the same time. We need promotions that generate call letter awareness within our target—promotions that inspire talk about WZZZ, as well as newspaper and television coverage. I have a proposal that I'll bring on the nineteenth. I'd also suggest more remotes and deejay appearances. Get the Z-Van on the road again with giveaways. Has it been restored to running condition yet?

Enough for now. See you the nineteenth.

7

News and Talk

News and Talk radio may be the savior formats for AM radio in America. Without them AM would have little purpose in the 1990s.
—Dwight Douglas
Burkhart/Abrams/Douglas/Elliot and Associates, Inc.

There are All-News, News/Talk, News Plus, and All-Talk radio stations. Each offers a fairly distinctive blend of programming, although all focus on broadcasting information.

In the 1950s, when telephone reception underwent significant upgrading, many adult music stations aired two-way conversation programs, especially during soft periods, as a way to boost listening. It was not until 1960, however, that a station, KABC in Los Angeles, went All-Talk.

All-News radio followed shortly after. Format innovator Gordon McLendon introduced the News format on Mexican station XETRA ("X-TRA") in the early 1960s. XETRA's signal handily reached several southern California cities, including Los Angeles, where the station did surprisingly well in the ratings.

In 1964 McLendon brought his News format stateside to WNWS ("News") in Chicago. Impressed with the success of the format, several major market stations, including WINS-AM in New York, converted to All-News a year later.

At about the time that All-News was making its mark, KGO in San Francisco unveiled the News/Talk format, in which conversation is scheduled between lengthy news blocks. In the 1970s this hybrid approach became more popular than its nonmusic forerunners, and it remains so today.

News Plus is another hybrid that often incorporates elements of both News and Talk as well as music formats. The majority of News Plus stations program adult music, such as Nostalgia, Easy Listening, or Adult Contemporary, around the news and talk features that represent their primary product.

In the mid-1980s the Radio Information Center counted 50 All-News operations nationally compared to 150 News/Talk outlets. Only a handful of News Plus stations were beaming signals, although some Full-Service MOR stations with heavy schedules of information features came close to falling into this hybrid category.

All-News began as a major market format and, with few exceptions, continues to be so a quarter century later. Economics is the reason for this: All-News is twice as expensive to program as music formats. News/Talk stations are more common than All-News in medium markets, and both are rare in smaller markets.

News stations have a fairly broad demographic, and they draw a slightly younger listenership than All-Talk. Both appeal primarily to the thirty-plus audience and became a mainstay for AM as FM became the preferred music band.

The desire to stay informed motivates the News or Talk listener. Fans of nonmusic formats run the gamut from the serious-minded, who are seeking up-to-the-minute information and hard-hitting features, to those primarily tuned in for companionship.

NEWS CHARACTERISTICS

Reflecting the approach that more-music outlets take in the presentation of their primary programming element, All-News stations typically air news in extended sweeps. Twenty-minute news blocks are fairly standard. Within this time frame, local, regional, and world news is presented. Traffic reports, sports scores, and weather also are parts of the block. Heading the segment is the top story of the moment, usually of a local nature, but occasionally a national or international news item will take precedence.

A major news operation might involve up to a dozen people during key dayparts. As many as half a dozen individuals might participate on-air. A station offering three news blocks an hour alternates newscasters in an effort to keep the sound crisp and fresh. Here is a rotation scheme at a large metropolitan All-News operation during morning drive time:

	6:00–7:00 A.M.	7:00–8:00 A.M.
:00–:20	Emond Lopez	Whalen Emond
:20–:40	Whalen McKenna	Merrigan McKenna
:40–:60	Merrigan Crosley	Crosley Lopez
	8:00–9:00 A.M.	9:00–10:00 A.M.
:00–:20	Merrigan Whalen	Crosley Whalen
:20–:40	Emond Crosley	Lopez Merrigan
:40–:60	Lopez McKenna	McKenna Emond

NEWS AND TALK

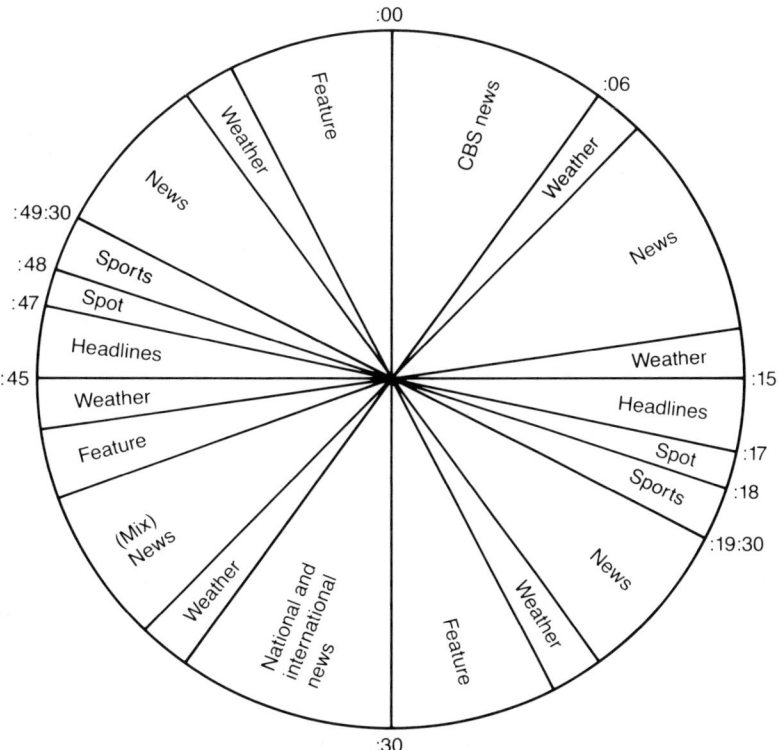

Figure 7.1 An all-day clock at an All-News station. Notice the affiliation with a network. Many All-News stations broadcast network feeds at designated times, usually at the top or bottom of the hour. Courtesy WTOP-AM.

In addition to newscasters, metro All-News stations employ newswriters, producers, sportscasters, street reporters (stringers), meteorologists, and others. When not on the air, newscasters update the stories contained in their forthcoming segments.

Holland Cooke, operations manager at WTOP-AM in Washington, D.C., views the All-News operation as a team effort. "Everyone must pull together to make the thing work effectively. A newsroom can become a scene of chaos if things are not meshing. Here at WTOP, our objective is to get news out instantly. 'You push the button, you get the news.' The Washington audience knows where to tune for the latest information—WTOP. That's quite a responsibility—one we take very seriously."

KOH's news director, Dan Vaneno, shares Cooke's sense of responsibility. "We're not 'spinning the hits' here in Reno. We leave that to other stations, of which there are plenty. Our function as an All-News station is to be the best source of news and information in the city. News is a foreground format. People pay attention and listen closely; therefore, the investment is significant on both sides. Of course, to our advertisers this means we deliver a conscious, astute, if not captive, audience."

Features

Features are an integral programming element on News stations, notes Cooke. "We schedule six traffic and weather reports hourly throughout drive time and go heavy on play-by-play sports around the clock. For example, to give you some idea, we carry Capitols hockey, Bullets basketball, and Orioles baseball."

Topical features dealing with a variety of subjects appealing to the News format fan are programmed either as part of a news block or independently, depending on their nature and length. Features on money, politics, sex, and health invariably are among the most popular on News stations, as are issues-oriented national and local commentaries.

Programmers are partial to information features because they spice up the sound and prevent it from becoming too predictable. Dozens of nationally syndicated and network features are available, and a number of public service organizations provide excellent programs free of charge.

Commercials

Commercial matter is presented in spot sets or scattered, depending on individual station policy, although news blocks usually contain designated break points. For example, spots might be slotted at transitional points between local and national stories, sports, weather, and so forth. Since News stations target an adult audience, spots containing rock beds or strident sound effects are avoided, but spots with low-key musical beds are common.

It is standard practice at the majority of stations, All-News or otherwise, that newscasters not announce commercials. Programmers contend that this hurts credibility, claiming that a person cannot report on nuclear disarmament talks one moment and sell cars the next without losing credibility. "News is serious business, and if the audience doesn't trust and believe in the newsperson, you may as well pull the plug," consultant Rick Sklar says.

TALK CHARACTERISTICS

Two-way (telephone) talk shows comprise the major part of the program schedule at All-Talk stations. Interview programs, wherein a host grills a guest, and advice shows dealing with popular and timely subjects also are prominent.

Most Talk outlets concentrate on local issues. "Our talkmasters focus on what is on the minds of people here in New York," says Jeanne H. Straus, vice president of operations at WMCA-AM.

Mike Edwards, program director at KSTP-AM in Maplewood, Minnesota, agrees with Straus that addressing local issues is a key to success for Talk stations. "More than any other station, the one presenting Talk is the voice of the community," he says. "Talk stations are involved."

The Talk listener is an important ingredient in programming. Without callers, two-way talk shows would not exist, and Talk stations would be severely limited. For this reason, talk must be evocative, contends Craig Ladd, program director of WKDR-AM in Burlington, Vermont. "While the other stations are playing 'the hits,' 'the greatest hits of all time,' 'the hottest hits prior to Moses,' and 'the hits that hit the hit list the hottest,' we are not playing the hits at all. We will talk about the hits and report the news about the artists who make the hits, but while people turn on music stations for background, our listeners turn to us to listen and participate. To get the

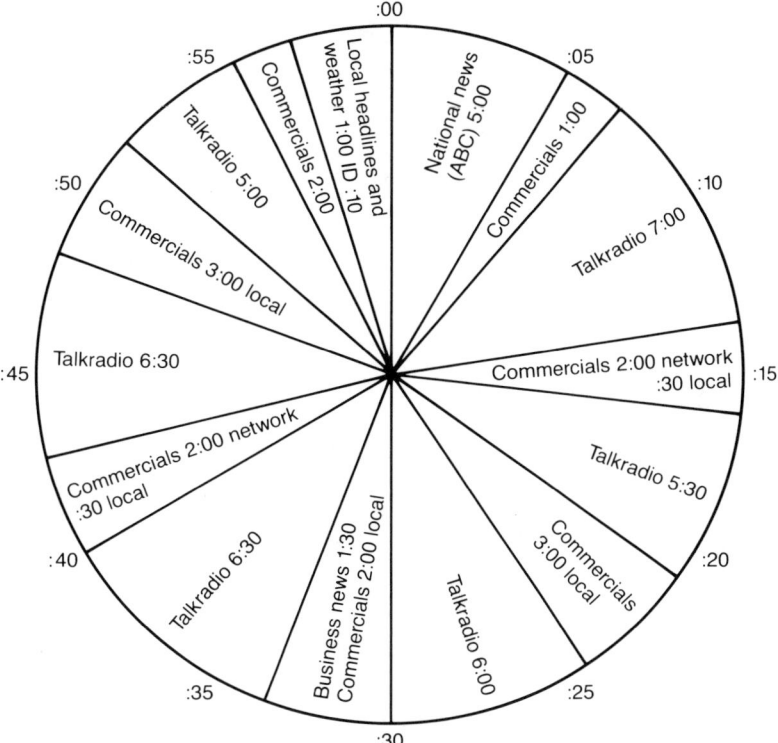

Figure 7.2 A non-drive-time Talk station clock. During drive periods this Talk station, as do most, presents lengthy blocks of news. Courtesy WKDR-AM.

audience to pick up the phone and dial Talkradio 1070, we've got to be working emotions, and to do that we have to be aware of who and what is out there in the community for starters."

Announcing

There has been a plethora of talkmaster styles since the inception of the format. In the 1960s talk show host Joe Pyne achieved national notoriety by lashing out at guests with his scalpellike tongue and volatile temper. By the end of the decade, however, the audience had tired of such caustic sensationalists.

In the 1970s a mixed bag of announcer styles, ranging from the acerbic to the genial, were familiar to talk audiences, and this is also true of the 1980s. No single style is dominant, although the Joe Pynes have lost out to the less abrasive and more tolerant, yet no less incisive, Larry Kings.

Effective talk show hosts must possess a wide range of talents and skills, notes Ron St. Pierre, program director of WHJJ-AM in Providence, Rhode Island. "To do Talk well you must be intelligent, knowledgeable, witty, sensitive, entertaining, and combative to a degree. You also have to be part psychologist."

RADIO PROGRAMMING

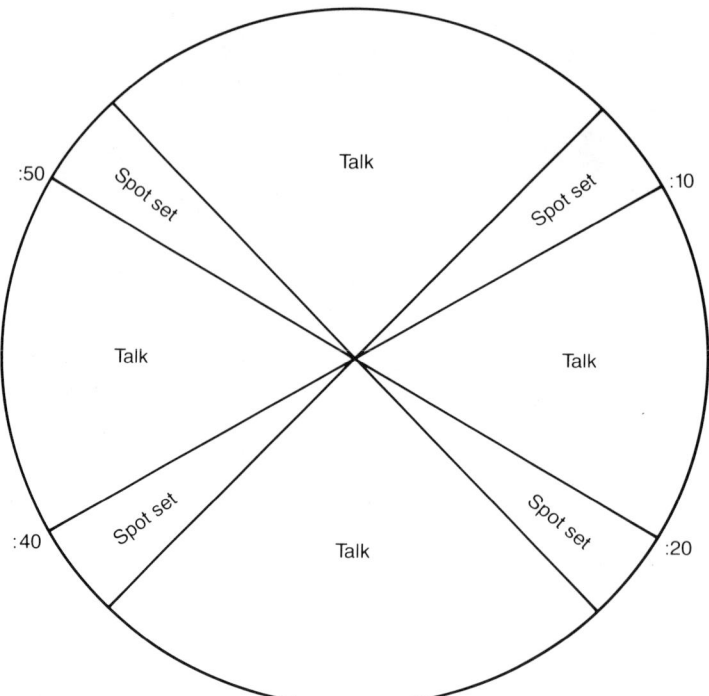

Figure 7.3 Metro market, non-drive Talk clock. Courtesy WMCA-AM.

News

As might be expected, Talk stations offer an abundance of news. As we have seen time and again, the morning drive, and to a lesser extent the afternoon drive, are news-oriented dayparts, even in most music formats. A significant percentage of Talk outlets revert to solid news during these periods, and the remainder often expand coverage. Despite the emphasis on news in particular dayparts, the primary programming element is Talk, just as it would be music in Adult Contemporary or Easy Listening that increase news coverage during the morning drive. Again, most Talk stations approach programming the way music stations do, but instead of music sweeps, there is talk.

Features

As a general rule, Talk stations are feature-intensive, even more so than All-News. The Talk audience is particularly receptive to topical and timely programs relative to its life-style. Since Talk stations are more frequently tuned in by lower- to middle-income listeners and retirees, features dealing with subjects such as the economy, politics, and health attract much interest. Many Talk stations fill up to a quarter of their program schedules with syndicated, network, and locally produced features.

Contests and Promotions

Usually Talk stations are not as contest- and promotion-oriented as are music stations. This has to do mostly with the nature and tenor of talk programming and the demographics targeted. Some Talk stations run contests year-round with considerable success and therefore regard them as integral elements of programming. At the same time, an equal number of Talk stations perceive contests as incompatible and inappropriate. Like any other station interested in attracting and maintaining an audience, Talk stations promote as much as their budgets allow.

Commercials

Of course, the presentation of commercials in this format, as in others, depends on the way the hour is structured. Talk outlets either sweep conversation and cluster spots, or they insert spots at opportune times throughout the hour. The spot set approach is most prevalent.

Talk stations usually are receptive to all levels of production in commercials. Spots with rock beds or jarring sound effects are avoided, since they might offend the predominantly over-forty audience.

While policy generally prohibits newscasters from voicing commercials, it is not uncommon for talk hosts to do so. At the majority of Talk stations, staff announcers are assigned the task of spot voice tracking.

Jingles

Jingles are as common on Talk stations as they are on music outlets. Many talkmasters have specially tailored jingles for their particular shows. Compared to jingles on many contemporary music stations, however, Talk jingles are low-key, if not austere. Many Talk program directors believe that well-produced jingles add spice to the station's sound, while others take the opposite stance and keep jingles to a minimum or off the air entirely.

NEWS/TALK AND NEWS PLUS CHARACTERISTICS

The News/Talk hybrid approach is at once All-News during key dayparts, usually drive times, and All-Talk the balance of the broadcast day. Not all News/Talk stations separate these programming genres so distinctly, but many find this arrangement most effective in attracting an audience.

News Plus mixes a variety of format genres—news, talk, music, and so forth—but typically reserves drive periods for extended news coverage. For example, after designating 6:30 to 9:00 A.M. as all news and information, WXXX airs a two-way talk feature until 11:00 A.M., after which it schedules a mix of Adult Contemporary music through the lunch hour. At 2:00 P.M., WXXX returns to talk until 3:30 P.M., when it goes all news through 7:00 P.M. Nostalgia music is broadcast until 9:00 P.M., at which time talk takes over until the next morning. From midnight through 5:00 A.M., WXXX carries network talk programming. The station is also affiliated with major league baseball and basketball teams, whose games are a key offering of this News Plus station.

WBCM-AM in Bay City, Michigan, is representative of the News Plus approach. "We offer an abundance of news and information that is pertinent to our service area, as well as agriculture updates, elaborate weather reports—AG, marine, inland—entertaining and in-depth talk shows, and music geared to our thirty-plus audience," program director Conrad

RADIO PROGRAMMING

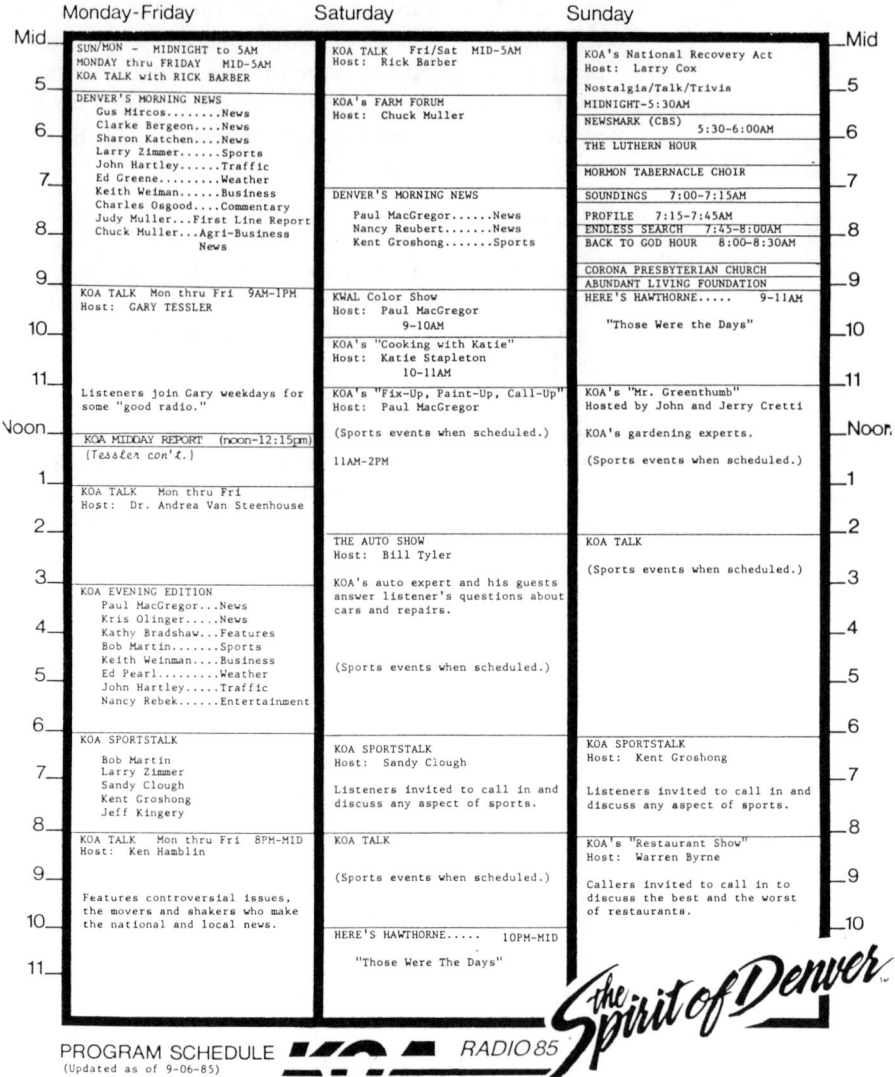

Figure 7.4 A News/Talk program schedule. Courtesy KOA-AM.

Michaels notes. "Special programming and live sports coverage of local and pro teams highlights our programming."

During talk dayparts, news still plays an active role. Some News Plus outlets offer up to fifteen minutes of news and information features hourly, around the clock.

Since this is a format more germane to larger rather than smaller markets (News Plus is available in smaller markets more than All-News), on-air talent usually is longer on experience. News Plus stations hire the widest range of announcers, since they have slots for newscasters, talk show hosts, and deejays. The mixed programming bag that typifies this format sometimes resembles Full-Service MOR stations, but News Plus is unique unto itself.

"We're a News Plus facility, or as we call ourselves 'News MORE,'" says Byron K. Johnson, program director of KHMO-AM in Hannibal, Missouri. "We are a heavy news information station with strong news blocks in several dayparts. However, we also block music that is skewed toward an older, more affluent crowd, who come to us primarily for our award-winning news."

COMPETITION

News, Talk, News/Talk, and News Plus stations generally perceive one another as primary competition, but there is seldom more than one All-News or one All-Talk station in a medium-size market. Major markets are the exception. Of course, News stations do regard Talkers as rivals and vice versa. "All-News stations definitely draw on a similar listening cell," WMCA's Jeanne Straus says.

John Hoffman, program director at WSLI-AM in Jackson, Mississippi, agrees with Straus: "So far we're the only News station in the market, which makes things a lot simpler. The emergence of another News or Talk station would give us pause if it were as well executed as WSLI."

KOH's Dan Vaneno concurs with both Straus and Hoffman: "We're the only News/Talk game here in Reno. That distinguishes us from everyone else. Another entry into this format would definitely heat things up."

Full-Service MOR, Easy Listening, Adult Contemporary, and Nostalgia are among the most competitive music formats, contends KSTP's Mike Edwards. "Any format that draws on the over-thirty audience is a potential competitor, especially those music formats that heavy-up on news and go talk, as many MORs and ACs do, at night."

Country stations, especially in the South and Midwest, pull News and Talk numbers, claims Byron Johnson. "Since we decided that our demo should be skewed toward the thirty-five-plus listener, our chief problem is the Adult Country stations that surround us."

Gene Holly, program director of WKCT-AM in Bowling Green, Kentucky, combats Country as well. "Country music appeals to a particularly wide demographic, including the adults to whom we program. No other music format in this part of the country is as adversarial."

WTOP's Holland Cooke says that News stations are a pretty distinctive breed. "We share with several other formats but compete directly with none." But WKDR's Craig Ladd contends that other media pose as much competition as do other radio formats.

"In one sense, no other format directly competes with News and Talk," Ladd says. "On the other hand, all other radio stations surrounding you are after the coveted radio listener. Newspapers and television and cable stations that offer news and information munch on the same wedge of pie, too. An All-News video service like CNN is bound to siphon off a few listeners. The marketplace is complex and becoming more and more competitive for all of us. That's why program consultants are in such demand."

FUTURE

News and Talk will likely remain strong in the future, and AM no doubt will continue to be the home base for nonmusic formats, although information and conversation formats probably will become more prevalent on FM. "In the past decade or so, music radio has become nearly the exclusive territory of FM stations," WKDR's Ladd says. "Until AM stereo becomes a wider reality, rather than a limited experiment, this condition will persist. Right now in the 1980s AM radio is the news and information center."

To maintain its hold on the listening market, News and Talk stations must continue to investigate audience interests, tastes, and preferences, believes WTOP's Holland Cooke. "As we can interpret research that reveals to us what kinds of information people want, we can target and fine-tune our programming to stay vital and fresh. You can't cloister yourself and remain relevant and popular."

WMCA's Jeanne Straus concurs: "We are constantly doing research on topics and issues about which people want to know more."

Maintaining a strong local image keeps News and Talk stations prosperous. "We are emphasizing a greater amount of information with a decidedly local bias," KSTP's Mike Edwards notes. "The audience can get plenty of world news and information, but a hometown Talker can and should be the hotline to what is going on in the neighborhoods the signal covers."

KOH's Dan Vaneno sees future technology playing a greater role in nonmusic formats. "National talk shows originating hundreds, perhaps thousands, of miles away will become more localized through the use of satellites and computers. Of course, these innovations are already here, but they will transform radio by the turn of the century. Also, I think that News and Talk can stay healthy by taking advantage of the currentness and spontaneity that so characterize the medium and are what the medium is all about."

In the future, more specialized features will become common on News and Talk stations, predicts KHMO's Byron Johnson. "As the competition heats up, I think stations will offer highly targeted life-style feature blocks or segments. This will be particularly true in the nonmusic and hybrid formats. In fact, there already is ample evidence to suggest that popular life-style programs will be the audience grabbers."

WSLI's John Hoffman shares this opinion: "The personal advice programs are extremely popular already. They are more candid and topical than they were a few years ago. Dr. Ruth Westheimer's 'Good Sex' is an example. Features that pack a clout are in demand now, and the demand will grow."

Johnson and Hoffman suggest that audience participation advice shows and life-style features help keep News and Talk stations strong as they enter the 1990s.

INDUSTRY NOTES

Consultant's memo to client station program directors.

The news director of our Centerville client station has some suggestions on how to develop a traffic image for your station. I think you will find these suggestions helpful. Even though this is a thumbnail sketch of the techniques used, it has proven to be very effective.

1. Get a grip on the overall travel picture in your market.
   a. What is the average commute time? By looking at the Arbitron, you should be able to determine the average commute time in your market.
   b. Where are most of the people going at a given time? This could include major companies in your area, schools, shopping centers, and from time to time, major events taking place on a certain day.
2. Find out the local hot spots in traffic. If there is a traffic tie-up, even a small one, where are the spots it is likely to occur? Those are the places to keep tabs on. Most cities, regardless of size, have a few places that stack up at certain predictable times on a given day.
3. Relate the traffic information to your audience. Nobody knows where the forty-five-mile marker is on a highway or takes the time to translate mentally a statement such as "We have a two-car accident about a mile south of the Jones Street/Hyatt Avenue intersection." It is much more accessible to say "There's a two-car accident on Mechanic Street. It's just before you get to the Dunkin' Donuts shop."

There are all sorts of relatables available to you. Some examples: major companies in your area, shopping centers, popular restaurants or night spots, sports arenas, large schools, parks, natural landmarks that most people know, even an unusual or clever billboard that people have probably noticed.

These give you a chance to name-drop. There is probably no more effective way of planting the thought with listeners that you are on top of their lives than by talking about the places they work, shop, play, etc.

4. Be positive.
   a. For years hospitals made the mistake of treating childbirth as an illness. It is not. Broadcasters often make the same perceptual judgment when it comes to information. We only think it is worthy if it is bad. What's wrong with saying that traffic is moving well through the Jones and Hyatt intersection? This is especially true if that is a likely spot for a problem.
   b. The other thing that name-dropping does for you is to give you the perfect excuse or lead-in to talk about things going on that your listeners may be wondering about. For example: What are all the construction workers doing at a certain spot? Are they building a new shopping mall or fixing a sewer drain that's been a problem in the past? Is a new business opening up or a new road being built that might make a listener's life a little easier?

It takes time to keep tabs on these things and check them out, but in the long run it is more than worth it.

Century 21 Programming offers the following advice on building strong newscasts six ways. Reprinted with permission of Century 21 Programming.

1. *Tailor the news to your audience.* Emphasize news of local interest.

Use your regular newsbeats—police and fire department dispatchers, city hall sources, the school board, the newspapers, etc.

Also seek other sources off the beaten path. For example, many of the local civic groups are sending you notices of their activities. Instead of just running a PSA for them, why not follow up with a news story?

Be highly selective in airing national news. Unless the topic is unusually important, headlines or briefings are sufficient. Wherever possible, look for local angles. Example: Instead of just reading wire copy about the famine in Africa, find out who in your town is coordinating relief activities.

Avoid stories that are strictly political in nature and have minimal actual impact on the lives of your listeners. Keep police blotter and ambulance-chaser stories to a minimum, as well. Avoid obituaries entirely, unless the deceased is a public figure or otherwise well known.

Season your newscasts with life-style information appropriate to your audience. *The Christian Science Monitor, The Wall Street Journal,* and *USA Today* are excellent sources of news your listeners can use.

2. *Use actualities to involve the listener.* Actualities take the listener where the news is. Creatively handled, they can bring a newscast to life. Don't confuse actualities with "beepers." Beepers are recorded telephone interviews. We recommend minimal use of beepers simply because of their poor audio quality.

Actualities should be made with good-quality cassette recorders and outboard microphones to achieve the actual sound of being there. Pocket cassette recorders with built-in mikes are handy in some situations but tend to produce recordings with too much hiss and distortion.

We've heard many instances of a newsperson taking longer to introduce the actuality than it would have taken just to tell the story. An actuality should carry the story, not the other way.

3. *Know what you're talking about.* Great news content can be negated by a weak delivery. Listen to your news readers. How many sound like they know what they're talking about? How many sound like they're sight-reading unfamiliar material for the first time? Make sure your newscasters have enough time to rehearse, to eliminate stumble and uncertainties.

Nothing destroys that sense of credibility faster than obvious mispronunciations. How many of your announcers would get "Coeur d'Alene" right the first time? A pronunciation guide should accompany every news story containing names or words likely to be mispronounced. Be sure your newspeople have a list of frequently mispronounced local names as well.

The days of the lecture-style newscast are long over. Do your newscasters sound relaxed and friendly? Do they talk to the listener one-on-one?

4. *Make the best use of your network.* We hope your local news staff is strong enough that you can avoid network newscasts during prime listening times. While network news programming has improved immensely within recent years, research shows it's not all winning the hearts of the mass audience. And none of it is locally oriented. We recommend using the network as a source of life-style stories or actualities or to relate the top national story.

If you are forced to use network newscasts, try to get some customized opens recorded by their reporters. Your regional rep or the affiliate relations department can usually arrange this. Another technique is to have your own newsman record a local news promo to run just ahead of the network news.

5. *Keep your news schedule flexible.* Unless you're running a network operation, newscasts don't have to start and stop precisely at a certain time, nor do they need to last a fixed amount of time each and every hour.

Such timing restrictions can turn news into a tune-out. Hitting a specific start time in an automated operation means either fill music or dumping songs. DJs must watch the clock like a hawk, fill with patter of PSA, rush their delivery, or dump songs. When a newscast becomes repeatedly associated with these irritants, the whole association becomes a negative.

Instead, air the newscast as the next event after a certain time. Eliminate padding and dumping. In live operations you should also set a time beyond which you don't want the news to run.

Work with your PD and/or news director to establish a minimum and maximum allowable amount of news time for different dayparts. The length of your newscasts should relate to their meaningful content. They should not run any longer than necessary to tell the news worth reporting. That amount will vary from hour to hour and day to day.

6. *Monitor the competition.* Your news director should listen to the other guy's news operation for stories he doesn't have. Make some careful comparisons between your news and the competition's.

8

Classical

There is something the classical music listener knows that the nonclassical listener rarely even suspects: that this music and the people who know and love it are not snobbish or exclusive. This music is still around and speaking meaningfully to anyone who will really listen, because it is as powerful and enriching today as the day it was written, and it will always speak to those wise enough to really attempt to listen to its message.

—Norman Pellegrini
WFMT, Chicago

Broadcasts of classical music date back to the medium's experimental period. For example, Enrico Caruso's 1910 performance from New York's Metropolitan Opera House made its way into the electromagnetic spectrum, as did many other operas and symphonies during the first and second decade of the twentieth century. By the 1920s fine music broadcasts were common fare.

The networks offered classical programming throughout the 1930s. Some popular features included "Cities Service Concerts," "Bell Telephone Hour," and "Voice of Firestone." The "NBC Symphony Orchestra" under conductor Arturo Toscanini and live opera from the Met also attracted considerable audiences.

In the late 1930s New York's WQXR-AM began broadcasting an extended schedule of classical music, making it one of the first stations to do so. Years later it would expand its classical music programming to its FM outlet. Today WQXR-AM and FM remain among the more successful fine arts stations in the country.

Classical music was a staple of FM stations at the medium's inception in the late 1940s and 1950s. In fact, many people regarded FM and classical music as synonymous until the 1960s, when other formats made the conversion to the newer band. The static-free nature of FM and the relative absence of classical music on AM created the proper atmosphere for the limited appeal format, whose followers desired cleaner audio reception. Thus, classical music found a home and moderate success on the alternative dial.

Throughout the 1960s classical audiences grew but remained minute compared to those of other formats. The advent of stereo broadcasting in the early part of the decade gave FM broadcasters a significant boost, particularly those programming classical music. In fact, the newest innovation in sound fidelity attracted some hitherto mainstream music buffs, who were enamored of the superior reception they received on their stereo component systems. The allure of stereo classical music was mitigated somewhat by the appearance of Beautiful Music, which began to make inroads into the FM band. Many of the experimental mainstream outlets found the soft standards programmed by the self-proclaimed "good music" stations very appealing. Nonetheless, stereo remained a key factor in drawing listeners to the Classical format.

By the early 1970s FM was no longer perceived as the fine arts band. Pop music stations were more prevalent than either Classical or Beautiful Music. Stereophonic reception had become as important to the majority of radio's contemporary music listeners as it had to those who preferred the more demure.

Today only a few dozen commercial stations devote themselves exclusively to classical music programming, and those that do attract about 2 percent of the total listening audience. Since the 1970s noncommercial Public radio stations have created problems for some commercial stations employing the Classical format. The primary cause for the defection of listeners from commercial to noncommercial Classical broadcasts is fewer interruptions. Noncommercial stations programming classical music are able to present lengthier selections because they are not confronted with the need to air commercials. In many markets this is a competitive advantage, especially during the morning, when advertisers wish to reach commuters. Commercial stations must generate revenues, and this often requires programming shorter pieces of music in order to broadcast spots.

Boston is one example of a market in which a Public radio station has outdrawn the local commercial Classical station in the ratings. WGBH's "Morning Pro Musica" attracts the largest chunk of the 25–49, upper-income, college-educated fine music audience. Public radio outlets around the country have found that programming classical music is an effective way to establish a substantial following.

The Classical format is most prevalent in metro markets and exclusive, upscale communities. Although commercial Classical stations seldom boast large ratings shares, they often are very profitable. WGMS, Baltimore; KFAC, Los Angeles; WQXR, New York; and WCRB, Boston, are some of the more successful commercial Classical stations. Nearly two-thirds of the members of the Classical Music Broadcasters Association are noncommercial, while the majority of the commercial Classical stations belong to the National Association of Broadcasters.

FORMAT CHARACTERISTICS

Music

Classical stations concentrate on airing pieces of music rather than cuts. Unlike a contemporary music station that might program four cuts of music

CLASSICAL

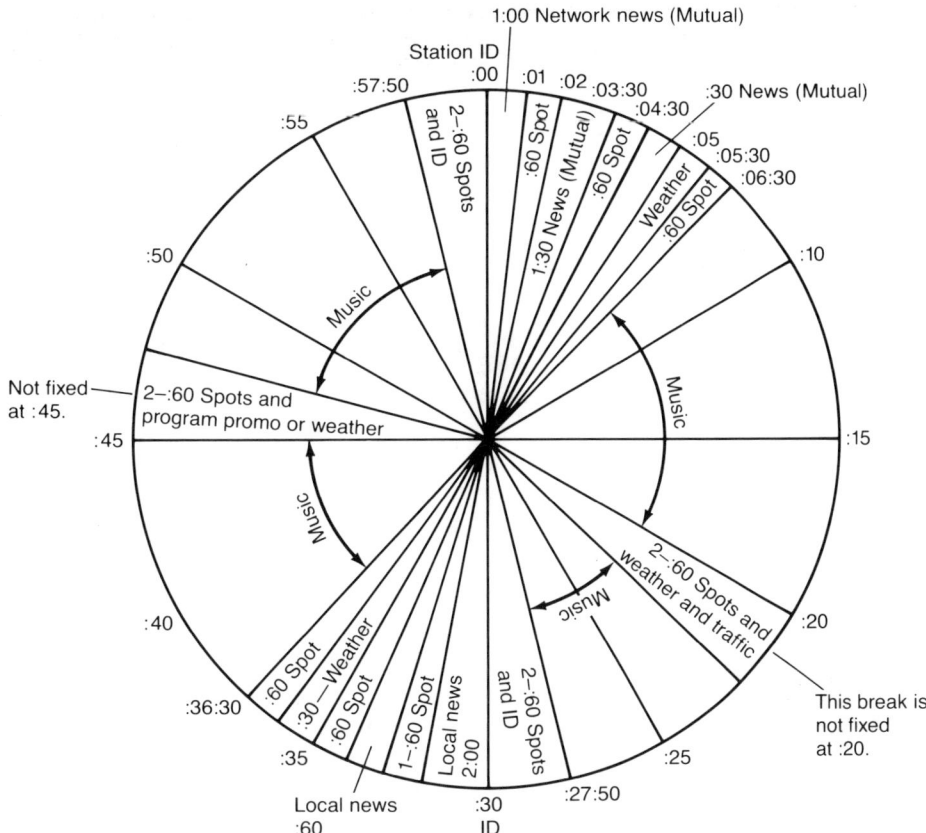

Figure 8.1   Morning drive commercial Classical clock. Courtesy WGMS-FM.

in a single twelve- to fifteen-minute sweep, the Classical outlet must deal with individual selections (symphonies, concertos, operas, and so forth) that often run the length of a standard sweep. As noted previously, due to spot load strictures, commercial Classical stations are forced to schedule shorter pieces of music, especially during prime dayparts. Airing a lengthy selection would be out of the question on most commercial Classical stations during the morning drive (see Figure 8.1). Both noncommercial and commercial Classical stations strive for the full presentation of selections regardless of length, pausing at appropriate or opportune places between selections to air information or commercial matter.

Many Classical stations employ program clocks and approach the hour much as their contemporary music brethren do, using the sweep and spot set method. Of course, many also find the system untenable. "Our programming is so varied and diverse that an hourly clock would serve no useful function," says Mike Langner, program director of KHFM-FM in Albuquerque, New Mexico. "Take a look at our program guide and you'll understand."

Generally speaking, Classical stations are not concerned about tempo. That is, there is seldom a conscious effort to avoid too many slow or up-tempo pieces, although certain Classical stations attempt to keep exces-

RADIO PROGRAMMING

Figure 8.2 Classical station program guide. Courtesy KHFM-FM.

sive amounts of down-tempo music out of drive periods. Like any other format, Classical is interested in providing its audience variety, which is not a problem since playlists span hundreds of years and dozens of countries. There is a formidable pool of musical art in the period between Bach and Copland.

Announcing

Classical stations do not hire deejays but rather employ program hosts, who are expected to communicate intelligence, knowledge, and sophistication, notes Robert Sherman, program director of WQXR AM/FM in New York. "A cultured and educated presence is very important considering the demos we target," he says.

Sherman, along with Classical station programmers Carlo Princi (KFAC-FM, Los Angeles) and David Tucker (WCRB-FM, Boston) prefer a somewhat conservative, yet conversational, announcer style. All indicate that their announcers must be adept at foreign pronunciation. "Language skills are especially important in this format," Princi says. "An announcer who mispronounces an artist's name creates credibility problems."

Until recently, in the late 1970s and 1980s, most classical programming deemphasized announcer presence. Classical announcers told listeners the names of the artists and titles of the works broadcast and very little else. In the past few years some Classical stations have found that personalities can mesh successfully with the music.

"What distinguishes us from other Classical stations is that we combine the elements of personality radio with the basic product—classical music," says Paul Teare, program director of WGMS-FM in Rockville, Maryland. "This approach has done wonders for our ratings and has brought an expanded audience to the station. Our focus, particularly in morning and afternoon drive, is this so-called peripheral audience, who say that they can take or leave classical music. The music we offer at those times is classical, but the wit and charm of the program hosts serve as a bridge between these listeners and the music. At the same time, we try to balance things so as not to lose the hard-core classical music lover."

Years ago, some Classical stations hired announcers with British accents to help promote an image of sophistication. Today most Classical stations try to avoid sounding haughty or pretentious. "Our personalities don't come across as overly sophisticated, musical elitist snobs because they air classical music," KHFM's Mike Langner says. "Some Classical stations ooze culture, but most prefer an unaffected announcer style, one that incorporates warmth with astuteness."

News

News is an important programming element at many Classical stations, particularly those in metro markets, but large news departments are rare in this format. Although the Classical listening cell is news-oriented and does desire to be informed, music is the prime reason audiences tune in to Classical stations.

An inspection of the WGMS morning drive clock (see Figure 8.1) bears out the fact that news assumes prominence in this particular daypart. In fact, many commercial Classical outlets resemble full-service operations in the key listening times. "We provide the commuter total information coverage because we have found that it is what he wants," WGMS's Paul Teare notes. "Network and comprehensive local news, along with traffic reports, sports results, and weather provided by a professional meteorological service, constitute a significant part of our morning programming."

In contrast, some Classical stations broadcast what amounts to little more than news updates or headlines. Stations adopting this approach usually assign program hosts the chore of presenting news, if and when it is scheduled. Even Classical stations that deemphasize news often employ at least one full-time news person, especially in larger markets.

As with most news-intensive formats, Classical stations frequently cut back or drop news entirely during evening hours. Perhaps the most common approach to news outside key dayparts is a recap once every hour or two, depending on what is scheduled to be broadcast.

RADIO PROGRAMMING

Features

Features are a popular ingredient of Classical programming (see Figure 8.3). Live music programs originating from distant symphony halls, as well as from station studios, round out the air schedules at most Classical outlets. "WGMS offers live in-studio chamber music and a variety of live operas from the Met and elsewhere," Teare says. "I'd have to say that this format is the most live-music-oriented of all."

Many Classical stations program periods of jazz and folk music. This is the case of WGMS, says Teare. "We broadcast three hours of jazz on Saturday nights. There is a demand for it, and it complements and blends well with our primary product."

Concert and theater reviews, along with financial features, also are on the feature roster at both WGMS and KHFM, as well as at the majority of other Classical stations. "We have a prodigious schedule of special feature programming," KHFM's Langner notes. "Classical is far from a docile or static format. It is probably one of the most active and vibrant in radio today."

Figure 8.3 A listing of features on Classical station KHFM. Courtesy KHFM-FM.

FEATURE PRESENTATIONS

A GREAT AWAKENING: A great way to start the day! Your favorite music and Gordon Spencer Weekdays at 5:30 am

ADVENTURES IN GOOD MUSIC: Karl Haas explains, explores and entertains as host of this one-hour program of music and witticism   Monday through Friday at 9:00 am

CLASSICS & CO.: KHFM's answer to the afternoon drive dilemma — classics from around the world   with Phil Dougharty   Monday through Friday at 4:00 pm

DINNER CONCERTS: Music to accompany your dining   Daily from 6:00 to 7:00 pm

ARTS AND PUBLIC AFFAIRS: Interviews of local interest with Mike Langner   Sundays at 10:30 am

SOHIO/CLEVELAND ORCHESTRA RADIO BROADCAST: Christoph von Dohnanyi and guest conductors put this great orchestra through the paces   Sundays at 12 Noon

LINCOLN/MUSIC IN AMERICA: A weekly overview of music in America   Sundays at 5:00 pm

EXXON/NEW YORK PHILHARMONIC RADIO BROADCASTS: Hear this great orchestra with various conductors   Mondays at 8:00 pm

FIRST EDITION: Your chance to be the critic of the best in classical releases. Keep up to date with Don Hoyt Tuesdays at 7:00 pm

PLAYBACK: Clears up the mysteries of sound reproduction. Get the facts   Sundays at 3:00 pm and Wednesdays at 7:00 pm

AT&T PRESENTS CARNEGIE HALL TONIGHT: Hear a wide range of music taped live at Carnegie Hall Wednesdays at 8:00 pm

CIGNA/PHILADELPHIA ORCHESTRA RADIO BROADCAST: Riccardo Muti and other guest conductors lead one of the nation's greatest orchestras   Wednesdays at 9:00 pm

GUITAR SPECIAL: A special program highlighting music for the guitar   Thursdays at 7:00 pm

RADIO SMITHSONIAN: An exploration of the infinite variety of the world around us   Saturdays at 8:00 am

THE OPERA OF THE WEEK: Listen to recorded operatic performances from KHFM's library   Saturdays at 12 Noon through October 12

CANADIAN OPERA COMPANY RADIO BROADCAST: Live recordings of this unusual opera company Saturdays at 12 Noon 10/19 - 11/23

AMOCO/CHICAGO SYMPHONY ORCHESTRA RADIO BROADCASTS: KHFM presents another great orchestra, conducted by Solti and others   Saturdays at 7:00 pm

JAZZ PERSPECTIVES: Albuquerque's longest running jazz show hosted by Gordon Spencer   Saturdays at 10:00 pm

BUSINESSDAY SOUTHWEST: Hear the latest in business news from New Mexico and the nation   Monday through Friday at 7:15 am and 5:15 pm

THE KHFM COMPUTER MINUTE: News and information you can use from the fast-paced and fascinating world of personal computers.   Monday through Friday at 7:45 am and at 5:30 pm

UNITED PRESS INTERNATIONAL NEWS and **CULTURAL CALENDAR:** Monday through Friday at 6:30 am, 7:30 am, 8:50 am, 11:50 am, 1:50 pm, 5:50 pm, 9:50 pm, and 11:57 pm. Saturdays and Sundays at variable times

WILLIAM WEINROD	General Manager
MICHAEL LANGNER	Station Manager
CHARLES MALDONADO	Program Director
ROXANNE ALLEN	Sales Manager
LINDA EWING	Advertising Sales
KAREN FERGUSON	Advertising Sales
CYNTHIA ADAMS	Production Director
SHIRLEY POWELL	Administrative Assistant
FRAN BALDERRAMA	Accounting

KHFM ANNOUNCERS

SUSAN BERNADETTE	DAVE DAWN
PHIL DOUGHARTY	LAURA HANNAN
DON HOYT	PEGGY PIERCE
PHIL PRATT	CHERI ROHN
ALESSANDRO SALIMBENI	GORDON SPENCER
MARSHA STARR	RON TEARE

ALL PROGRAMMING SUBJECT TO CHANGE

From a programming perspective, I am interested in fine-arts-related features that meet a determined need and that entertain."

Contests and Promotions

Ostentatious contests and promotions seldom are a part of Classical programming. Concert tickets, trips, and dinners at fine restaurants are among the more common giveaway items. In the 1980s a West Coast Classical station awarded a BMW to a contest winner; on the East Coast another station gave away a thirty-two-foot cabin cruiser. While the prizes presented by Classical stations sometimes are extravagant, the manner in which they are awarded generally is in keeping with their more demure image—no "Right now, drop what you're doing and dial C-L-A-S-S-I-C to become eligible to win an outrageously exotic and super-fun-filled weekend for two in passion's playground, the fabulous Poconos! More details following this by Dvorak."

Public Affairs

Public affairs programming generally is plentiful in the Classical format. Issues-oriented programs, especially those focusing on the economy, politics, and health, find a receptive audience. "Public Affairs is part of our daily programming," WGMS's Paul Teare says. "We strive for topics that mean something to our listeners. While pearl diving in the Indian Ocean may be a fascinating subject in and of itself, it really doesn't hit home with listeners in Maryland. Nonmusic programming must appeal to the same people who tune in for music. It must be germane to the audience."

Commercials

It was mentioned earlier in this chapter that many Classical stations air commercials in spot sets. Spot loads vary from daypart to daypart and are affected by the time of year. "Our morning drive clock [see Figure 8.1] reveals that we allot fourteen minutes for commercials," Teare notes. "Granted, that is a lot for a fine music station, but the seven to eight A.M. hour is our bread and butter, as it is for most commercial broadcasters, Classical and otherwise. Of course, this clock also reflects the time of year, which happens to be November, as opposed to a less busy time, say the summer months, when we reduce our spot load. Each hour is somewhat different, too."

Minimizing talk during music-intensive segments is a goal of most Classical stations, and keeping the spot count down helps accomplish this. A four- to six-minute spot maximum per hour is the rule (outside of drive parts) rather than the exception at numerous Classical stations.

COMPETITION

There is rarely more than one Classical station in a market, except in the top metro markets (such as New York, Los Angeles, and Chicago), where there may be a couple. Thus, direct format competition is usually not an issue. In markets with strong Public broadcasting operations, however, the effects of noncommercial Classical stations can be significant.

The commercial formats regarded as most problematical for Classical

RADIO PROGRAMMING

are News, Talk, and Easy Listening. "The nonmusic formats hit our cell and provide Classical listeners extensive amounts of information and news, which is a primary reason why they tune the medium to begin with. This fact has inspired us to heavy-up on news," WGMS's Teare says.

KHFM's Mike Langner cites Easy Listening outlets as competition. "ELs can and do cut into Classical numbers. In some markets, Easy Listening can really deflate the figures, while in others they are less offensive. ELs that are instrumental-intensive, those that are known in the trades as the 'all the Mantovani you can stand' stations, warrant observation and attention."

FUTURE

According to Langner, it is doubtful that the Classical format will undergo any significant change in the future. "The musical Beethoven is unchanging," he says. "Classical probably is the most stable of any format out there. Of course, that doesn't mean we can rest on our laurels. Fine-tuning and updating our presentational methods will keep us from sounding stale. Classical music will always have an audience, but the style in which it is presented will make the difference."

Since its inception, the Classical format has been particularly sensitive to the quality and fidelity of its sound, and this, according to WGMS's Teare, will continue. "Upgrading the audio has been and will remain a foremost concern in Classical. Like many Classical stations, we're in the process of converting our music library from long-playing vinyl discs to the new digital compact discs. At this stage of the game, we have around five thousand CDs, as compared to sixty to seventy thousand LPs. This conversion is enormously important to future generations. If the compact discs live up to expectations, they will represent the first time that a permanent record library can be built without fear of fidelity and quality deterioration due to repeated playing. For our immediate purposes, the discs provide a clean on-air sound with non-distorting range capability beyond anything the standard LP can offer."

INDUSTRY NOTES

A consultant's weekly monitor notes for a Classical station:

Levels: Spots very hot at times, as were announcers.

Spot beds/jingles too contemporary (Philip's House Restaurant . . .) in contrast to classical music. Coming out of a Brahms symphony, the Crown Camera donut was both loud and discordant.

Delivery on Bender's Dairy spot too hyped for station.

Too many breaks 7:30 to 8:30 A.M. Pair spot load. Handing over audience to NPR Classical. Recall our conversation about reducing A.M. logjam? Needs to be done.

Too much Gershwin. "Rhapsody" Monday, 7:15 A.M.; "Porgy" Monday, 8:41 P.M.; and "Rhapsody" again Tuesday 11:16. Perhaps just a rotation coincidence?

Dirt/scratch on Mozart Piano Concerto 21, Mozarteum Orchestra of

Salzburg. Same on Dvorak's "New World" Symphony, Bruno Walter conducting Columbia Symphony Orchestra.

Dolby audio processing sound superior. However, worn LPs detract.

Sound is best with CDs. What is timetable on conversion?

Haydn Guitar Quartet in E Major, Op. 2 No. 2 faded prematurely on Finale to meet spot set. Ouch! Worst possible practice! Classical devotees will assemble a lynch mob. Quentin Simons shift.

Simons too "tight-board" conscious, again. Pacing needs work. Pronounced pause between all elements, including spots, necessary. He is a bit erratic in delivery department, too. Sounds almost AC at times and too subdued (contrivedly so) at others. Needs some coaching. Air check?

Newscasts too nationally oriented. More local slant needed. Newspeople are excellent. Only weakness I detected other than national skew was a propensity on the part of Gene Lippett (10−3) to overdue "voicyness." He has a good voice without artificially lowering it. Would sound better if less self-conscious.

Saturday opera matinee sponsorship (Mendley's Furniture) spots should be updated and remixed. Same two spots have run as long as I can remember. Maybe a year? So old and lackluster, they actually are a distraction.

Bob Lyman's "Opera Talk" following matinee, while informative to hard-core opera audience, strikes me as too long. Forty-five minutes this particular monitor week. Suggest shortening to maximum of fifteen minutes and back to music. Think I commented on this some months ago?

Time-check liners, such as "WXXX Music Maestro Time," archaic. Drop liners. Try time with calls grafted, rather than logo. It is cleaner and less pretentious.

What happened to the stock market reports during P.M. drive? Heard only one at 5:15 on Monday and Wednesday. None elsewhere. Closing stocks are of interest to your drive home clientele.

Brian Sanders continues to have pronunciation difficulties, although I'm no expert in the pronunciation of classical composers and compositions. Sanders seems very tentative and stumbles more than he should. On a positive note, he has improved some since last monitor.

Recorded intro to "Midday Symphony" muddy. Should be recut.

Mike clicking problem cited in last monitor has been eliminated.

Twenty seconds dead air before spot set Thursdays at 8:18 A.M. Too much time for commuters to punch over to WZZZ.

Let's discuss another time slot for "Composer's Corner." WZZZ is into music at same time. Think 11:00 P.M. a better time than the current 8:30 slot.

"Evening at the Philharmonic" promotion has outlived its appeal. Suggest retiring it, at least for a while. Last year's CD giveaway worked well. Time for a new promotion vehicle.

Note: A more detailed report focusing on some of the preceding points will follow within a couple days. Next monitor sometime early December, per your request.

9

Country

When programming country music, remember that what's "country" is what the listeners think *is country.*
—Joel Rabb, Consultant

Stations have been airing country tunes since the medium's infancy. In the 1920s Nashville station WSM began broadcasting live from the Grand Ol' Opry. Other large market stations (WLS, Chicago; WSB, Atlanta; WBAP, Fort Worth) programmed live country shows as well, and more stations followed suit in the 1930s and 1940s.

The meteoric rise of rock 'n' roll in the 1950s slowed the growth of Country radio because many of the major artists of the day (Elvis Presley, Jerry Lee Lewis, Conway Twitty) brought their country flavor to the pop charts, resulting in a minor migration of Country fans to Top 40 and the diffusion of Country's listenership.

Today Country is the most widely programmed format in the nation. According to the Radio Information Center, 2,346 stations broadcast Country in the mid-1980s. As recently as the 1960s, however, Country (Country and Western) was relatively obscure, especially in the North, although country music has always been a mainstay at southern stations. What changed things for Country radio was the musical crossover explosion in the latter half of the 1960s. At that time numerous Country artists began making the transition to the pop charts. Singers such as Glen Campbell, Bobby Goldsboro, and Johnny Cash, to name a few, who had enjoyed popularity on the Country charts, had tremendously successful crossover Top 40 tunes. This raised the general public's awareness of country music, while inspiring interest in the Country format. The 1970s "rebel rock" sound popularized by the Allman Brothers, Lynrd Skynrd, Marshall Tucker, and numerous others also expanded the base of Country's appeal.

In the 1970s many Country stations shed their rural image by implementing a more sophisticated, formulaic sound that meant narrower, more contemporary playlists and a tighter, slicker presentation. The conversion of New York station WHN-AM to Country in 1973 was an auspicious sign that the format had, indeed, finally arrived in the big city. Today Country radio has nearly rid itself of the hillbilly, hayseed image that had inhibited its growth.

Advertisers no longer perceive the format as an exclusively lower-income, blue-collar draw. According to the Organization of Country Radio Broadcasters, the Country format is much more upscale in the 1980s, and no format can boast a better distribution of the 25- to 54-year-old male and female listener or a more loyal following.

Country remains primarily an AM format, although its presence on FM is growing rapidly. Both full-service and more-music programming approaches are found in Country, which has spawned several subgenre format categories.

FORMAT CHARACTERISTICS

Music

Traditional Country Most Country stations fit into one of the following groupings: Traditional, MOR, and Modern/Contemporary. Stations assuming the Traditional approach concentrate on old-line country classics of twenty or more years ago. At WRRZ in Clinton, North Carolina, program director C. David Denton allows his listeners a voice in what is aired. "Double R Country doesn't just play the traditional top country songs according to any music chart," he says. "If a listener wants to hear something that was popular forty years ago, we play it. One never knows what to expect next when listening to WRRZ. That's why we're a solid number one in our market. In a small radio market, there is no one particular way to produce a sound that your people want to hear, so you let them tell you. Here Traditional is our product."

Many Traditional Country outlets assume a full-service posture, contends John Austin, program director of WITL-FM in Lansing, Michigan. "We are a little more traditional sounding than other FM Country stations. We also regard ourselves as a good radio station that just happens to play country music. This means our focus isn't on being Country in terms of wearing boots and hats and having names like Coyote and other things often associated with country music. We feel you don't have to drive pickup trucks to like country music, so we approach programming in a more full-service way, with lots of news, weather, sports, and information for an adult audience. Apparently it's working. We are far and away number one with adults over thirty-five and do very well twenty-five to fifty-four in a northern market that is both a state capital and a college town."

MOR Country Middle-of-the-road (MOR) Country stations work with broader playlists. Following a contemporary song with an old-line standard is common, notes Gregory Raab, program director at WCXI-AM/FM in Detroit. "We recognize the origin of country music and understand that the genre needs to evolve as time passes. Consequently we play traditional artists like Hank Williams, Patsy Cline, Roy Acuff, Porter Wagoner, and Eddy Arnold, as well as modern country acts like Exile, The Judds, Ricky Skaggs, and Restless Heart."

WTCM-AM/FM in Traverse City, Michigan, programs similarly. "Ten years ago I would have said that fiddles, steel guitar, and down-home honesty in the lyrics best characterized this format, but country music is going through so many changes that it is rather hard to depict," program director Ryan Dobry says. "Many songs are so pop that you can't tell if you're listening to CHR, AC, or Country. Our station, in particular, tries very hard to get a good mix of traditional country and the newer stuff."

MOR Country outlets are likely to be full-service stations. "We provide our listeners with a variety of news, information, and entertainment features, in addition to music that runs the gamut from big band country and western songs to pop-chart MOR tunes. We could be called 'Variety' Country," observes Bruce W. Allen, program director of WDLC in Port Travis, New York.

Contemporary Country Contemporary Country programming was born out of the crossover explosion of the 1960s and 1970s. Contemporary Country stations, also referred to as Countrypolitan, Urban Country, Modern Country, and Hit Country, focus on current artists and songs and reflect the style and tenor of CHRs. "We utilize a contemporary approach to country music, borrowing from CHR some of the elements that make it exciting," says Skip Walters of KEIN-AM in Great Falls, Montana.

Brad H. Peterson, operations manager at WATN-AM in Watertown, New York, fashions his Country station after CHR. "We highlight what is currently taking place on the charts in country music, and we keep pace and tempo lean and clean."

This also is true at KAFY-AM in Bakersfield, California. "Our sound is 'Uptown Country,'" programming consultant Jack Hayes says. "It is upbeat, modern, and hot. KAFY is a tight, Contemporary Country station. Contemporary Country serves the broadest audience."

KSDY-FM in Sidney, Montana, takes the Contemporary Country approach but attempts to avoid the repetition found in CHR. "Because we are a rural area with fewer choices on the dial [a six-station market], we cannot play songs with the frequency of the larger market stations," program director Edward McIntosh says. "We base our playlist on the current hit charts, but the airplay is about half as often as the national average. Because of the trend in modern country music toward more of a pop sound, we have updated our library. Surveys in our area indicate that country is the most acceptable type of music, and the Modern Country sound allows us to attract the light or soft rock listeners, too."

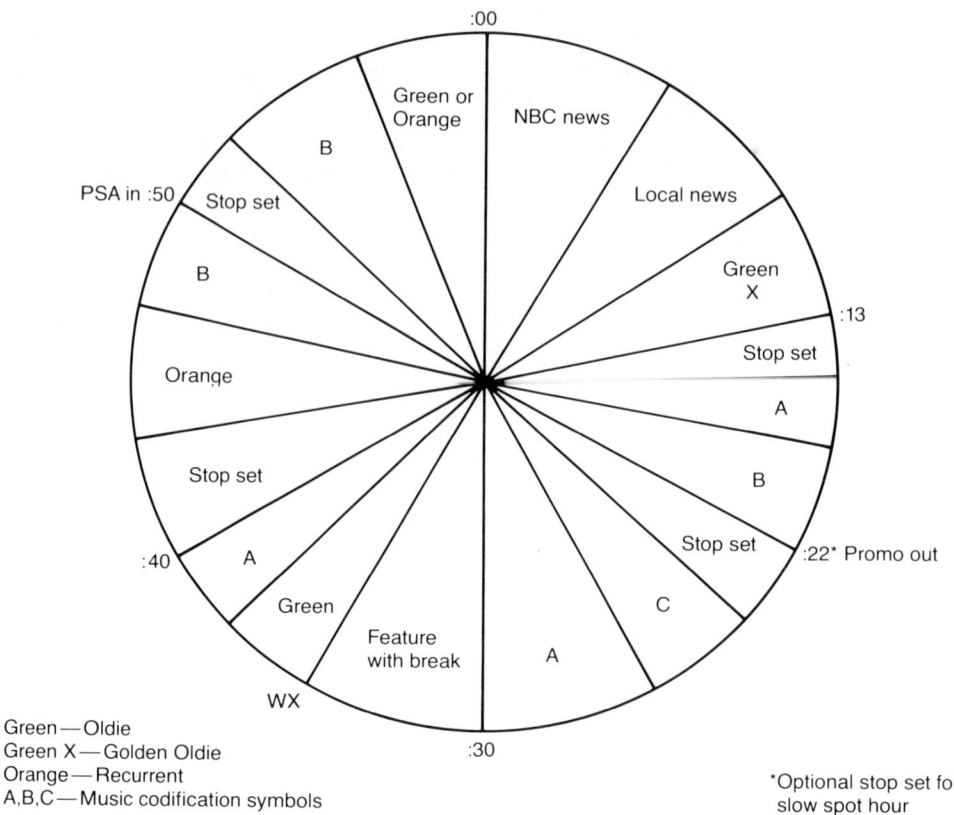

Green—Oldie
Green X—Golden Oldie
Orange—Recurrent
A,B,C—Music codification symbols

*Optional stop set for slow spot hour

A

F   Break Hour

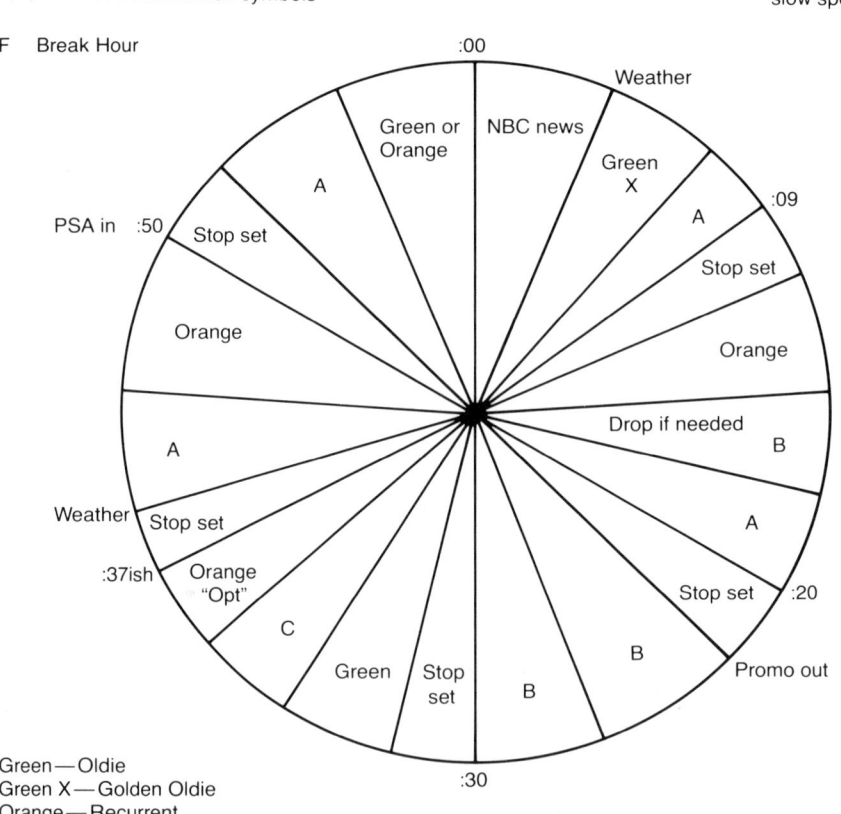

Green—Oldie
Green X—Golden Oldie
Orange—Recurrent
A,B,C—Music codification symbols

B

126

COUNTRY

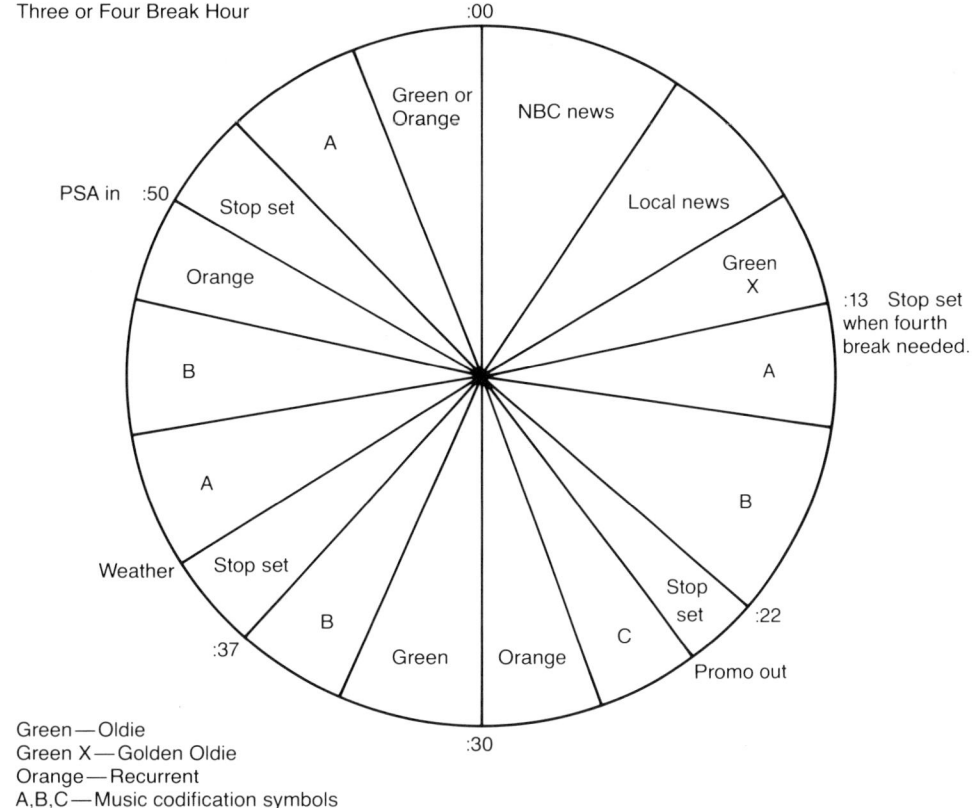

Green — Oldie
Green X — Golden Oldie
Orange — Recurrent
A,B,C — Music codification symbols

Figure 9.1 Country clocks for several dayparts. Clock A is used between 6:00 and 9:00 A.M. Clock B applies to the hours between 5:00 and 6:00 A.M., 9:00 A.M. and 4:00 P.M., and 6:00 and 8:00 P.M. Clock C covers the afternoon drive—4:00 to 6:00 P.M. Courtesy WTCM.

Figure 9.2 Country station bumper sticker. Courtesy WTCM.

"Because of our slower record rotation, there is less listener burnout with a song and, hopefully, less dial jumping. At KSDY the criterion is hits, but in moderation to keep the listener longer. This requires a somewhat more expansive playlist. We often dip back into the hits of the 1960s and 1970s to round out our sound."

Announcing

Depending on their programming formula, Country stations might either emphasize or deemphasize personalities. For example, full-service Country stations are more likely to go heavier into personalities, says Gary DeMaroney, program director at KROW-AM in Reno, Nevada. "We're very much a foreground service, so personalities assume high visibility."

Country radio personalities must first and foremost convey down-to-earth friendliness and warmth, says WTCM's Ryan Dobry. "Our goal is to be a friend of the listener. Personalities have to be able to relate one-on-one in this format."

WRRZ's C. David Denton agrees: "Our deejays are instructed to listen to their listeners, their callers, and to place things on a personal basis. When one of the Double R Country jocks walks down the street, he is recognized as being another human being, not someone who is supposed to be placed on a pedestal. If they can speak first, they do it. People love it, and that makes them want to tune 880 AM. They know that a *person* is talking on the air, not a superjock."

Stations airing Traditional Country are especially inclined to create an atmosphere of neighborliness on the air, notes KSDY's Edward McIntosh. "Traditional Country music fans, in particular, enjoy the feeling of kinship with their announcer. It is a delicate relationship. A lack of honesty or candor is quickly detected. Traditional personalities have to be real and warm above all else."

Humor has always been a staple of the Country personality, contends KROW's Gary DeMaroney. "Country jocks have to be able to evoke a chuckle and a sense of fun. Most of the really successful Country personalities have a tremendous capacity for humor and wit."

Not all Country stations encourage their deejays to be funny. "We want our announcers to be friendly without trying to be funny," WITL's John Austin says. "If a humorous observation happens in a spontaneous way, okay, but no contrived or rehearsed humor. Not here, anyway."

A knowledge of music is a must for Country personalities. "Announcers who know their music make the station sound believable," WDLC's Bruce Allen notes. "Country fans are a bit like Classical fans. They know their artists and songs and resent it when the jock doesn't."

Country outlets that stress music, as in other more-music formats, downplay the announcer's role. "KEIN takes the position that the music should carry the weight. The personalities are there but within well-specified limits," Skip Walters says.

The "Billy-Bob," "country-cousin" personality style is almost extinct in the 1980s, and southern drawls are nearly taboo on the air, even south of the Mason-Dixon line. Today Country personalities are best characterized by their sophistication and warmth. The country bumpkin style of announcing belongs to another era.

News

Country outlets that take a full-service approach offer extended news coverage, whereas Country stations deemphasizing nonmusic elements take the opposite path. According to WITL's John Austin, news is a key programming

> **AMID ALL THE TALK ABOUT COUNTRY SHARES GOING DOWN, ED SHANE WANTS TO TALK ABOUT TWO THAT DIDN'T**
>
> The two are KILT-FM, Houston, and WIRE-AM, Indianapolis. Each has dedicated management who demand commitment, integrity and success. Each has a consulting agreement with Shane Media Services. Because of the unique situations at each station, that's where the similiarities end.
>
> **NARROWING THE GAP**
>
> KILT-FM is one of two country FM's in Houston. When they went into the format they took the city by storm. More recently, the other guys have had an edge. That's where we came into the picture with a project that began with listener research, a competitive overview, and our Management Advisory Plan.
>
> In the spring of this year, our role expanded to add programming consultation for the station, and I'm pleased to report the results:
>
> KILT-FM 4.3 - 4.7
>
> The other guys went *down* a full share point. But that's the 12+ share. To get a better feel for the advances that KILT-FM made, look at Women 25-54:
>
> KILT-FM 3.5 - 6.0
>
> The other guys lost almost a full share point in Women 25-54 and were down two in Men 25-54.
>
> The other guys are still ahead, but it's refreshing to narrow the gap in such a short time. It's also fun to hear the other guys react on the air each time KILT-FM makes an adjustment.
>
> **NO NEWS IS GOOD NEWS**
>
> The radio industry loves explosive advances in shares, so it's probably hard to believe that I'd spend good money on advertising a station that stayed *even*. Yet, I'm encouraged by exactly that at WIRE in Indianapolis.
>
> The station has been known as a country giant until the last few years when FM competition began to heat up. At the end of last year, we were engaged to offer programming direction and implementation.
>
> WIRE is on AM. WIRE plays country. The country competition in Indianapolis is on FM. WIRE's share remained steady while the other guy went down.
>
> Again, looking beyond the 12+ shares, Women 25-54 are up:
>
> WIRE 4.6 - 5.1
>
> That's a success story, if you ask me!
>
> **MORE THAN A FORMAT**
>
> At Shane Media Services, we apply multiformat experience to positioning challenges. I like to sell solutions, because that transcends format. That's why you find stations of all types in our client group – AC, Soft Rock, CHR, AOR, News and Talk, Country, and Physicians Radio Network, which serves 39 markets.
>
> In the last year, however, country radio has been characterized by words like "decline," "slump," and "depression." That's why I wanted to focus on country and say there are signs of life.
>
> The managements and staffs of KILT and WIRE have put in a lot of hard work. I'm proud to be associated with them.
>
> **AN UNABASHED PITCH**
>
> Understanding the changing nature of the country audience is but one dimension of our expertise at Shane Media Services. We offer Research Coordination and Execution, including meaningful Focus Research; Programming Concept and Execution; Personnel Training and Development; and our specifically tailored Management Advisory Program.
>
> Call me at 713-952-9221 and let me develop a program to meet your needs.
>
> **COMMITMENT, INTEGRITY, SUCCESS.**
>
> Arbitron information from Houston-Galveston Market Reports compare Winter '85 to Spring '85. Indianapolis compares Fall '84 to Spring '85
>
> **SHANE MEDIA SERVICES**
>
> 6405 RICHMOND AVE. SUITE 311
> HOUSTON, TX 77057
> 713/952-9221

Figure 9.3 Country radio consultant's promotional piece. Courtesy Shane Media Services.

element at the majority of Country stations. "We schedule an abundance of news, weather, and sports. Information programming has a real place in Country, regardless of individual station programming philosophy."

WDLC's Bruce Allen views things similarly: "We really stress news, especially the local variety, and community happenings in our coverage area. Our mobile news units give us high visibility and help foster a solid community service image, something that is important in this format. The Country audience has an interest in sports, so we air plenty of local and regional games.

Contests and Promotions

Country radio fans enjoy promotions and contests, so most stations invest considerable energy in this area. "This is an active, foreground format, so contests have to be meaningful to our particular clientele," Bruce Allen says. "Obviously you don't give away Pavarotti albums, but among the smaller prizes—movie and concert tickets, life-style clothing, dinners, and so on—you help increase attention and hold listeners. Bright, energetic promotions fit in well with the overall mood and sound of what we do."

The Organization of Country Radio Broadcasters regards their particular format as among the most promotion-minded in radio, and WCXI's Gregory Raab corroborates this: "I couldn't name another format that goes into promotions as much as Country. We do remotes, appearances, and whatever else it takes to get the word out. What it comes down to is that we're giving the audience what it wants."

Commercials

Because of the diversity of programming styles found in Country, both the spot set and random slot methods of commercial scheduling are common, but spot setting designed to enhance quarter-hour maintenance has gained wider acceptance since the 1970s. The placement of commercials is not likely to be left to the discretion of the deejay, even at those Country stations that feature heavy personality.

Jingles

Although the use of jingles seems to move in and out of favor in the industry—in the mid-1970s there was a trend away from the use of jingles—Country has almost always maintained its affinity for the tuneful promo. "I believe the well-produced jingle that really captures a station's character and personality is a great asset," consultant Donna Halper says. "Jingles probably do more for Country than they do for other formats. Of course, the key rests in their application. Stations sometimes make the mistake of cluttering their airwaves with jingles, and no matter how good a jingle is, this will hurt the sound. Overairing a jingle is just plain damaging."

COMPETITION

The Adult Contemporary format is the most competitive with Country. "ACs seek a similar demographic and siphon listeners from us because so much of today's country music is crossing over onto the pop charts," WTCM's Ryan Dobry says.

WCXI's Raab holds a similar opinion: "AC playlists contain many popular Country artists, such as Kenny Rogers, Juice Newton, Willie Nelson, Dolly Parton, Ronnie Milsap, and Anne Murray, to name only a few. Our target audience is close to AC's, and what complicates things is the vast number of ACs out there. Sports events on other stations also cut into our number, since Country listeners are usually sports enthusiasts."

Top 40 or CHR stations also deflect listeners from Country. "Strangely enough, CHR can tug at our numbers," WITL's John Austin notes. "We share the bulk of our cumes with the number one station in the market, which happens to be CHR. The reasons are manifold: a. adults are often parents whose kids listen to CHR, so they do, too; b. some will listen to us for news and information and then go back to the CHR for music because they are not real hot on Country music; c. some regular CHR listeners get burned out on the tight rotation of hits, and they tune us for a day or so for something different to clean out their systems; and d. more and more adults who were raised in the late fifties and early sixties are appreciating some of the CHR music, and the oldies seem to appeal to them as well. So CHR is a prime competitor for a chunk of our demos."

WATN's Brad Peterson sees other contemporary formats as attracting some Country listeners. "There are so many contemporary music stations out there that all but the hard-core country traditionalists can relate to it to some degree."

News and Talk stations also have an impact on Country listenership, according to KROW's Gary DeMaroney. "The information and conversation stations catch some of our audience, especially the Talkers. Country music fans like relevant conversation and interview programs. They enjoy the involvement."

WDLC's Bruce Allen cites MOR and Nostalgia as being his prime competition. "Other broader and older music formats, with plenty of news and sports, pose obstacles for Country. The Soft or Lite Rockers can affect the Contemporary Country numbers, too."

FUTURE

The future looks good for Country, according to the Organization of Country Music Broadcasters. WCXI's Raab believes that the continuing effort to give Country listeners a solid product that is keyed to the times will ensure this. "Country music continues to evolve, so growing with it is the key. For us, this means dropping really dated Country products from the forties and fifties and retaining only superclassics and better produced, less dated material. We've also got to make a bona fide effort to recognize Country artists emerging from Adult Contemporary ranks, realizing that 'crossover' is not a dirty word."

WITL's Austin plans to concentrate his future efforts on refining his station's air product. "Production of country music out of Nashville is becoming more sophisticated and slicker sounding, so this helps us compete on a purely sound level with rock. More energy in the presentation, sharper jingles, and more up-tempo music are helping Country stations compete with CHRs. We dropped some news and talk programming when we were faced with a continuous Country FM station, and we put them out of business," Austin continues. "Basically, we try to anticipate what other stations may start doing and beat them to it. We also try to stay on top of the latest technology. Many Country AMs have converted to stereo. More will follow. That's a positive move. We do every Country HBO simulcast we can. WITL did 'Farm Aid' via satellite. We want our station to appear to audiophiles as the place to tune to hear what's new in electronics. However, CDs are not something we've gotten into yet, primarily due to the lack of product available in that form. No doubt this will change, and we'll be on it."

A more concentrated focus on the important 35- to 44-year-old Country cell and the creation of an attractive music alternative are goals established by WATN's Brad Peterson. "More research into our targeted demo is what will keep us strong and viable. We're also sharpening our playlists. It is a distillation process intended to make our sound leaner and more potent. We are striving to be a musical alternative."

According to Bruce Allen, WDLC is betting on its radio magazine approach to bring in the ratings numbers. "We feature a radio magazine type show that stresses senior citizen information, health and science features, self-help reports, consumer news, and local and regional service group activities. We keep our ears open for listener comments and suggestions on how to improve our service and take the necessary measures to incorporate them into our programming if deemed appropriate. However, we make no drastic changes quickly; rather we slowly blend new elements into our existing format. I do believe that the clue to the future is doing more for the audience and remaining versatile."

"Relatability" is the key to future success in Country, believes KSDY's Edward McIntosh. "An eye on the relatability barometer will certainly help keep the format in the clover. Everything should be designed for impact. Superfluous matter must be flushed. The music and personalities have to really gel and hit home. For example, we have found, like other formats, that the male with the heavy pipes is not the only announcer you can have on the air. Female announcers with pleasant voices work wonderfully in Country. The main criterion is how effectively a person relates to the listener. This is, and will continue to be, the most one-on-one format in the industry. Country stations that fail to realize this fact will find the going tough."

INDUSTRY NOTES

A consultant's Country personality critique:

This is the follow-up I promised in my last monitor regarding 65 Country morning man Marty Smithers. Believe me, I have tried my damnedest to like him, but, alas, I cannot, and to be honest, I do not see how your audience can either (your recent numbers indicate a falling out of love). Marty has gone stale. There is no joie de vivre. No blip on the screen. Sadly he has become a flat line. Let me explain:

1. Between 6:00 and 7:00 A.M., he is nearly nonverbal, and when he is, he sounds nearly comatose. Almost without exception (Tuesday A.M. he sounded somewhat enthusiastic—why?), Marty came across as apathetic and bored. As the morning proceeded, he seemed to wake up. From 6:30 to 6:55, he went straight "seguey city." No chatter ("good morning world . . . rise and shine"), sports, teasers, or weather. To paraphrase a popular song, "Kiss your audience good-bye and forget about good numbers." Even the music was out of whack for the daypart. In sum, 6:00 to 7:00 A.M. on 65 Country could be promoted as the "Dead Zone." Excuse the sarcasm, but you've got problems here.

2. Marty made several inane attempts at "good ol' boy" humor, but

he fell flat on his face. Correct me if I'm wrong, but isn't 65 Country trying to put to rest the "redneck," "gunrack in pickup truck" image? Well, MS is doing nothing to let the proverbial sleeping dog . . .

3. During Wednesday's morning show, MS must have been suffering from apoplexy. On four different occasions he stomped on carted tag lines. Aren't tags noted on cart labels? Sloppy! What happened to the slick professional we once knew and loved? This kind of thing reflects badly on the station.

4. I know, and the whole world knows, that Marty once saw Hank Williams in person, but he boasts that fact so often that, if it hasn't already, it is verging on becoming a joke. I can hear what is left of your audience chuckling sarcastically—"Did you know that Marty Smithers saw Hank Williams?" During the week of my October 20 monitor, he alluded to the cherished event no less than eight times. 65 Country is a *hot* contemporary? Not with an ongoing homage to a centuries-dead Country artist—wonderful as he was.

5. If I were relying on 65 Country to keep me on schedule, I'd be in real trouble. Marty mentioned the time once in a fifty-five minute period. (This is not a morning service station from where I sit.) During this same period, MS gave one mini forecast that didn't even include the current temp. Have you tuned your competition recently? Country 104 is doing an exceptional job servicing your demos. This spells trouble. Recall the last book?

6. The interaction between MS and his newsman, Bud Clark, is another sore spot. It must be obvious to the listener that neither Smithers nor Clark really have anything to say to one another. The discourse between the two is redundant and dull. Examples (7:59, 8:59, and 9:59 A.M., October 20): MS: "So Bud, what about those Redskins, yesterday. BC: "Something, eh? A look at sports in a few minutes, but first in the news . . ." Now there is some sparkling conversation for you. The camaraderie is infectious. Did MS and BC have a falling out or what? There used to be some genuine warmth and friendliness between those two. No more! Neither Smithers nor Clark referred to the previous day's big local game during their perfunctory exchange. The game was on everyone's mind but not on everyone's radio, at least not on 65 Country's morning show.

7. Suggest a rotation check be undertaken during A.M. daypart. Heard Willie Nelson's "On the Road Again" on two consecutive mornings between 7:30 and 7:45. Would you believe both times Smithers referred to Nelson as "that great Country King of the Road, Willie." Didn't he recall playing the song and saying the exact same thing the day before?

Let me cease this sad chronicle. If by now it is not amply clear that I feel 65 Country is in need of new blood in the morning slot, then I have understated my case. This must be the primary topic of our lunch meeting next Thursday.

10

Vintage

Nostalgia is a mass appeal format; many limit their success by programming to older listeners.

—Jay Williams, Jr.
Broadcasting Unlimited

One man's oldie is another's contemporary hit. "Oldie" is a relative term. To be sure, an oldie is a song that evokes memories of the distant, or not too distant, past.

—Carl Z. Harney
H.Z. and Associates Consultancy

Oldies, its offshoot Classic Hits, and Nostalgia are distinct format genres collectively referred to as Vintage and sharing an affinity for the hits of the past. Whereas Oldies stations base their playlists on the chart toppers of the late 1950s and 1960s, Classic Hits stations draw from the 1960s and 1970s (Classic Hits also has been described as the "Big Chill" format after the movie whose central characters listened to rock music from that period). Nostalgia goes back even further, focusing on the popular tunes of the 1940s and 1950s. Early rock 'n' roll songs by artists such as the Everly Brothers, Jerry Lee Lewis, Elvis Presley, the Beach Boys, Chuck Berry, and Paul Anka are the meat and potatoes of Oldies stations, while Classic Hits outlets find Creedence Clearwater Revival, the Monkees, Three Dog Night, the Eagles, the Temptations, James Taylor, Simon and Garfunkel, and the Rolling Stones appropriate material. Big Band constitutes one of the more prevalent music forms aired by Nostalgia stations, which present performers such as Glen Miller, Frank Sinatra, Peggy Lee, Tommy Dorsey, Bing Crosby, and Harry James.

Oldies stations have been in existence since the 1960s and were the inspiration of programmers such as Bill Drake and Chuck Blore. In 1962 Los Angeles station KFBW-AM offered listeners lengthy blocks of vintage hits, but in 1965 KWIZ-AM in Santa Ana, California, went total Oldies. Other stations around that time also instituted the Oldies format—a format that has attracted listeners from the 25- to 40-year-old demographic. According to the Radio Information Center, more than 168 stations, mainly AMs, now program "golden oldies." The Classic Hits approach is most in evidence on FM.

Nostalgia radio, the creation of programmer Al Ham, is a more recent innovation. Nostalgia (also called Big Band) was introduced in the late 1970s and has helped the failing AM band retain some music listeners. Like Oldies, Nostalgia is a predominantly AM format, although both have made some inroads into FM in the 1980s.

Nostalgia demos are skewed toward the forty-plus age group, but some stations claiming to be Nostalgia have attracted a slightly younger crowd by occasionally mixing in contemporary artists who blend well with the traditional playlist. The Nostalgia format claims about the same number of outlets as Oldies. In the first half of the 1980s, Nostalgia broadcasters claimed a 4.5 percent share of the radio listening audience.

According to the National Association of Broadcasters' audience research report, "Radio W.A.R.S.," which constructs psychological profiles of listeners in nine major formats, the Nostalgia radio fan considers himself or herself a music expert and tunes in the format to recapture memories. The report holds that Nostalgia listeners are loyal and want to be stimulated rather than sedated.

Figure 10.1 A representative Classic Hits playlist. The Classic Hits format emerged in the mid-1980s to fill a void left by Oldies and CHR. Another Vintage variation, Classic Rock, also surfaced during the same period in response to a desire for AOR-based classics. Courtesy WKLH-FM.

7:00 A.M.

Doobie Bros	Listen to the Music
Zombies	She's Not There
Fleetwood Mac	Hold Me
10CC	I'm Not in Love
Rolling Stones	No Satisfaction
Allman Bros	One Way Out
Turtles	It Ain't Me Babe
Browne, Jackson	Running on Empty
Beatles	She Loves You
Creedence Clearwater	Hey Tonight
Eagles	One of These Nights
Rundgren, Todd	I Saw the Light

8:00 A.M.

Who	The Real Me
McCartney, Paul	Maybe I'm Amazed
Davis, Spencer Group	Gimme Some Lovin'
Crosby, Stills, Nash	Ohio
Guess Who	Hand Me Down World
Cochran, Eddie	Summertime Blues
Moody Blues	Ride My See-Saw
Beatles	Magical Mystery Tour
Led Zeppelin	All My Love
Kinks	Lola
Fleetwood Mac	Second Hand News
Bad Company	Shooting Star

FORMAT CHARACTERISTICS

Music

As stated previously, Oldies stations base their playlists on vintage hits that occupied the music charts as far back as the 1950s. Today many Oldies stations also incorporate more recent chart toppers into their rotations in the hopes of expanding their audience base.

"Our image phrase here at WTRY is 'Classic hits of the sixties, seventies, and eighties,' and that means exactly what it says," program director John Gabriel says. "By hit music, we are describing songs that are tested to be hits from the Top 10. Any song that does not reach the number ten position or better does not get played on our station. We play off the heritage of WTRY, a long-standing hit radio station since the mid-1950s. We highlight the music of the station's heyday, plus the best of the more contemporary music charts, in order to form our music rotation."

Saginaw, Michigan, AM station WSAM also combines the new with the old. "Our format is distinctive in that we play the current hits and the best of yesterday," program director Dave Winston says. "In other words, today most CHRs play the Top 20 songs over and over. If they play gold, it's from the past three or four years only. Many CHRs do not play hits prior to the early 1980s. 14WSAM plays the hits of today plus the top songs from the 1950s to the present. For example, how many CHR stations play 'Won't Get Fooled Again' by The Who or Bachmann Turner Overdrive cuts? Our research shows that people respond well to those songs, yet most CHRs don't air them. We do."

A greater number of Oldies outlets take a more purist approach, confining playlists to hits of rock's early days—the mid-1950s and early 1960s. "We focus primarily on the genuine oldies of rock's first generation," says Fleet Gruver, program director at WQXI-FM in Atlanta.

KRLA in Pasadena, California, does the same thing. "We program 'all the Oldies, all the time,' which means 1954 through 1970," program director Mike Wagner notes.

At Nostalgia station KORK-AM in Las Vegas, the music reaches as far back as the 1930s. "We're known as 'Original Hits,'" program director Jim Austin says. "We air the hits by the original artists from the 1930s onward. The music flow is carefully researched for maximum effectiveness, with the aim toward variety and entertainment."

Nostalgia stations commonly use syndicated programming and frequently are automated, in contrast to Oldies operations, which more often than not originate their own broadcasts.

Announcing

Vintage format approaches are inclined toward personalities, although many automated Nostalgia operations reduce announcer presence in favor of more music. At KORK announcers play an integral role in on-air programming and are expected to possess a considerable knowledge of the music they play. "Our air staff not only remembers the hits but spends hours preparing and researching our musical history to come up with timely bits of trivia," Jim Austin says. "We believe in Nostalgia and deliver the most entertainment

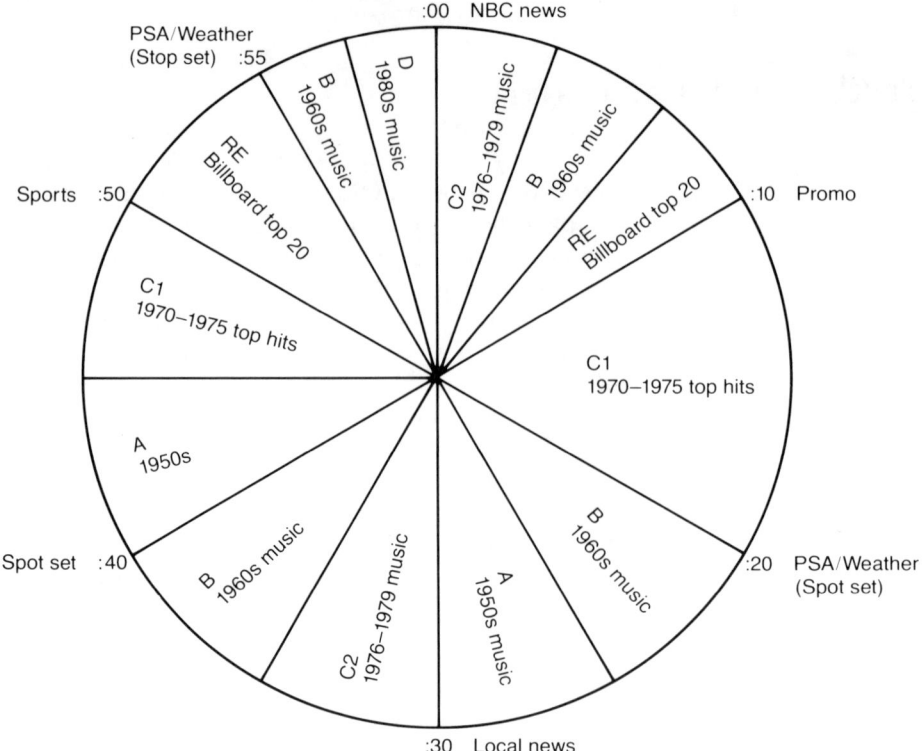

Figure 10.2 An Oldies/Contemporary clock reflecting the broad period from which it derives its music. Courtesy WSAN-AM.

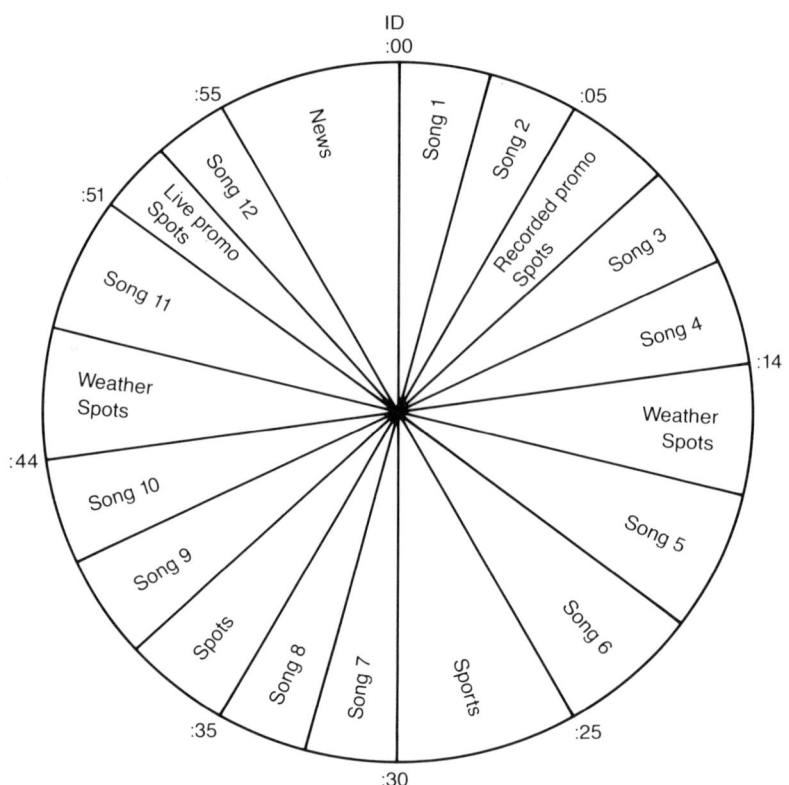

Figure 10.3 An Oldies morning drive clock. Notice that there are positions for twelve songs, as well as ten minutes allocated for news and sports. Courtesy KRLA-AM.

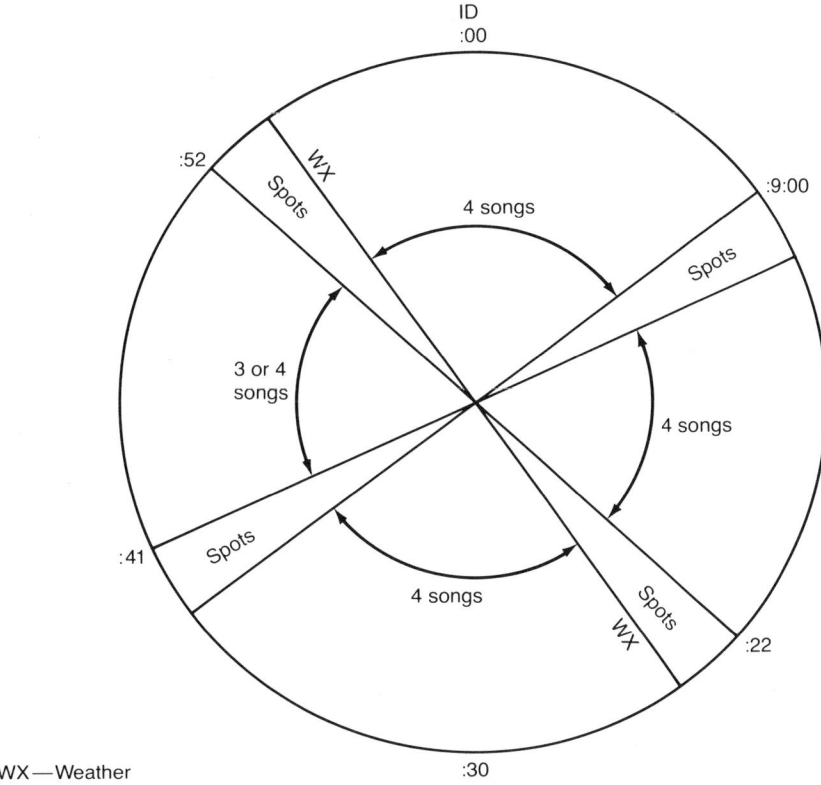

Figure 10.4 An Oldies midday clock employing the sweep and spot set programming schematic. Up to sixteen songs are aired hourly. Courtesy WQXI-FM.

every hour, every day. Personalities are central to our air product. We must be doing it right, because KORK has been enjoying the number one position in AM radio in this market since 1982."

Oldies stations have long been pro-personality and have, at times, mirrored the high-intensity jocks found in Top 40. WSAM's Dave Winston claims that Oldies deejays must bring more to the air than strictly a good voice and the ability to hype. "14WSAM is a bright-sounding station with personalities who talk to you rather than announcers who just read to you," he notes.

KRLA's Mike Wagner hires evolved personalities who possess qualities germane to the Oldies sound. "In other words, our jocks complement our music. They have the 1960s feel about them, although they are very much 1980s. It's not a question of sounding old-fashioned but rather sounding a part of the era from which the music is taken. I guess it's just being nostalgic."

Humor also is important in the Oldies format, says WQXI's Fleet Gruver. "More than anything, this is a good-time format. Deejays with a good, solid comic sense really enhance the sound."

News

News and information programming are important to Vintage radio listeners, and most Vintage formats are likely to be service-oriented. More than half of all Vintage stations air network news or wire service audio. "The Oldies listener is more mature and sensitive to world events than are listeners of many other formats, so we program service features around the clock and heavy-up in drive periods, when we offer more in-depth news and comprehensive weather and traffic coverage," Dave Winston says.

WTRY does the same. "If you don't program an appropriate amount of news and information, the Oldies listener will look for it elsewhere," John Gabriel notes. "That you can't afford."

To be successful in Oldies, a station must be more than a jukebox, contends KORK's Austin. "The folks who listen to this format also are tuned into the world around them. They're not kids or rocking chair occupants. KORK has a commitment to total community involvement. This includes, among a host of other things, constant weather updates, sports, and entertainment news—this is Vegas, remember. We also keep our doors open to community service groups and cover special events better than anyone."

Features

Features are popular with vintage music fans. For example, theme weekends, such as "Beach Music Party," and "Saturday Nite Rock Hop," create a festive, fun atmosphere on Oldies stations, while captivating the interest and attention of the audience. Nostalgia stations frequently air musical retrospectives of artists popular during the Big Band era—"An evening with the Dorsey Brothers, featuring the vocals of Frank Sinatra." "Features that connect with the mood, sentiments, and attitudes of the vintage music fan heighten the impact of the overall product," Austin notes. "They deepen the image in a nice, positive way."

Contests and Promotions

Oldies stations favor contests and promotions to a slightly greater extent than do Nostalgia outlets. Since the objective of Oldies stations is to convey an atmosphere of fun, entertaining contests have become a prominent programming ingredient over the years.

"Contests are an ongoing part of what Oldies give their listeners, and they respond very favorably to good ones," consultant Dick Ellis says. "There's a considerable range in what you can do and give away, anything from a 1950s T-Bird to trips to Fort Lauderdale. Although Oldies' demos target twenty-eight to forty-two-year-olds—from young to middle-age adults—you maintain a youthfulness in promotions, keeping in mind that the music you're playing was popular with the forty-year-old when he or she was a teen or young adult."

WSAM has tested numerous contests and finds that their Oldies audience is most responsive to cash giveaways. "We give away money all year long in the form of 'Cash Call,'" Dave Winston says. "We call listeners out of the phone book, and if they know the amount in our cash call jackpot, they win. Simple, but effective. We also do an abundance of other types of promotions throughout the year. This is one format where good contests, ones that bear relevance to the format's theme, strengthen market position."

Figure 10.5 Promotions play a major role at Oldies stations, as these pieces illustrate. Courtesy WHK-AM.

Public Affairs

Vintage music stations air public affairs features in proportions comparable to other adult stations. Oldies programming usually includes a modicum of community issues programs. "Oldies listeners are community-minded and are receptive to PA features when they touch upon aspects of their lives," KRLA's Mike Wagner notes.

Commercials

Like other adult music formats, Oldies and Nostalgia have embraced the spot set method for airing commercials. Since both formats emphasize music, sweeping is prevalent and clustering spots is the natural option.

Jingles

Oldies stations continue to be heavy users of jingles. "This is a jingle format," Dave Winston notes. "They were an integral part of the pop radio medium in the 1950s and 1960s, so they work well with the sound today. 14WSAM uses jingles for the weather and sports, in addition to the standard ID jingles."

Consultant Jeff Pollack takes the opposite position on jingles, contending that they date the format too much. He perceives the use of jingles in Oldies radio as forced nostalgia, which often causes burnout and tune-out.

Nostalgia stations use jingles that capture the feel of the period from which they draw their playlists, but generally they do not use jingles to the extent that their Vintage radio cousins do.

COMPETITION

A host of formats tap essentially the same cells that Vintage stations pursue. WSAM's Winston assesses competition on two levels: "There are two types of competition—vertical diffusion and horizontal diffusion. Let me explain. Vertical diffusion occurs when a station's sought after demographic splits and listens to another station that has a different format. Horizontal diffusion occurs when listeners leave your station for one offering the same format. 14WSAM does not suffer from horizontal diffusion since there is no other 'gold' in the market. We do tend to lose some ground against a CHR station. Those listeners go for more hits and less gold, so we do tend to suffer a bit from vertical diffusion within the demographic."

Adult Contemporary stations have the greatest impact on Vintage stations. "The 'brite' ACs that have a high mix of Oldies cause some erosion in our numbers," admits WQXI's Fleet Gruver.

WTRY's John Gabriel concurs: "Our greatest competition comes from AC outlets, and there is a legion of them out there on both bands."

West Coast Oldies station KRLA also regards AOR as a prime competitor. "Album Rock stations that program a lot of 1960s music skim listeners, as do Adult Contemporary stations that play a substantial amount of Oldies," Mike Wagner says.

Las Vegas Easy Listening station KXTZ is KORK's most prominent competitor, according to Jim Austin. "When our listeners float, they tend to show up at the local EL. Both our audiences are into the older tunes, and we dip way back, as does KXTZ, so there's some drifting."

Few Vintage stations find News or Talk outlets troublesome, since they commonly schedule an abundance of news and information features themselves to satisfy the needs of their listeners.

FUTURE

As long as listeners want to recapture the good old days through musical memories, Oldies and Nostalgia stations will enjoy a following. To stay competitive in an ever-expanding market, however, Vintage outlets must constantly freshen their playlists. "It may sound like a non sequitur, but 'new' oldies have to be added because emphasis on certain eras change year-to-year," WQXI's Gruver says. "You can't become a moldie-oldie station. It's a misnomer to think that a Vintage station doesn't have to be progressive. You have to keep up on trends in the marketplace like any other station."

Playlist sharpening goes on constantly at Oldies station WSAM as a means of retaining a vital sound. "Oldies stations shouldn't sound old," Dave Winston says. "Our gold is always being evaluated as to which songs should stay and which should be removed. When we first went gold, we played a lot of 1950s and 1960s music. This was back in 1981. As the format grew and evolved, we dropped the amount of 1950s music and increased our 1960s playlist.

"As an Adult Contemporary station in the market increased its 1960s output, we adjusted and added more 1970s gold. Currently we're playing more current product. We play less 1950s music and limit it to mornings and middays. We play more 1970s music, such as 'Lola' by the Kinks, 'Play That Funky Music' by Wild Cherry, and so forth. Just look at *Billboard*'s top hits from 1971 through 1979, and chances are we play them.

"In the future I'm sure that will be skewed upward. In some cases, just airing the top twenty hits of the week is enough. In our particular case, a one-thousand-watt AM stereo station, the Gold/CHR mix, fills a void in the marketplace and works for us and the listener."

Maintaining a firm grasp of what motivates the Vintage audience will keep stations viable, notes KORK's Jim Austin. "Our research department is constantly updating our format with special attention to the changes in audience age and other demographic as well as psychographic characteristics."

For KRLA, preparing for the future means returning to the basics. "We're not changing with the times," Mike Wagner notes. "As a matter of fact, we've gone back in time to bring back some very basic radio programming philosophies and techniques. We are forced to reset promotionally to a very competitive and active marketplace."

The market for the Oldies format became particularly bullish in the mid-1980s, leading some consultants specializing in the format to predict a meteoric rise (from 168 to 500) in the number of Oldies stations. AM broadcasters, in particular, looked to these prophesies with renewed hope of regaining some of AM's lost music audience. While the number of Oldies

RADIO PROGRAMMING

outlets has increased since these projections, as of this writing the figure remains far short of what was expected by some format experts.

INDUSTRY NOTES

What follows are some thoughts by a national consultant pertaining to the presentation of his company's own unique hybrid approach to Nostalgia.

We specialize in what I prefer to call MOR/Nostalgia, rather than isolating it to a strictly Nostalgia format. The reasons are twofold: First, a truly Nostalgia only format (and I don't know of any successful ones) is too restrictive. Every day that music is getting older and, almost by definition, less relevant. Secondly, Nostalgia might be better defined (along with MOR) as "nonrock" or a phrase that we and others have used—"unrock." Here, as with Beautiful Music/Easy Listening, are formats that appeal to people who did not grow up with rock 'n' roll or who simply want relief from it. Our definition of the music then includes everything from the Big Bands through the present—"What's New" by Linda Ronstadt/Nelson Riddle or "Hello" by Lionel Richie. Our MOR/Nostalgia format is thus alive because it is current while possessing songs that bring back memories.

Regarding music rotations and playlists, hits are hits, at least from our perspective. There are hit artists and hit songs, and they basically must rotate faster than medium hits. As with any format, covers should be avoided whenever possible. Most of our client stations play two currents (records within the last two or three years) an hour. One record per hour of the Swing era would be included (Big Bands). The rest of the clock is filled with music from the past thirty-five years, concentrating on established nonrock artists: Patti Page, Frank Sinatra, Perry Como, Andy Williams, the Andrews Sisters, the Lennon Sisters, etc. Although the mix is heavier in the 1950s, and much less so from the 1970s when many of the nonrock recording artists couldn't get a contract, all of these artists are played. Major hits such as Frank Sinatra's "New York, New York" are in fairly high gold rotation. Other records, especially novelty records such as "Doggie in the Window," are either never played or are aired only on special occasions. Novelty can easily be renamed "irritant" if it is heard by the listener too often, especially when it's old. The record library can easily contain up to 1,000 selections, although about 600 of these, the biggest hits by the biggest artists, form the basis of the active playlist.

Concerning personalities, except for morning drive, we recommend very little talk on our MOR/Nostalgia stations. Contrary to some syndicators and consultants (for example, Al Ham), we believe an active, involved, news-oriented morning show is a plus to our type operation. Personality here should be warm and friendly, and it should sound very today. The music should be presented as if it were the music of today—fresh and new even if it is a 40-year-old selection.

Listeners in the morning are insecure, regardless of what format they tune. They want to know the weather, time, sports scores, and the news that can affect their lives. We recommend a good solid news image for any Nostalgia station, but the key is a warm, mature-sounding personality who can communicate well with the listener. Brief telephone conversations, polls about some local activity or issue, and all the vitality you would expect from a traditional Middle-of-the-Road station can be effectively and easily introduced into a Nostalgia type format.

But beyond 9:00 A.M., personalities should take a back seat to the music. Announcers should present the music conversationally and enthusiastically, yet in a relaxed manner. Our research confirms that MOR/Nostalgia is used after 9:00 A.M. as a relax format. That is what the listener apparently tunes for. With that fact in mind, the music can do the talking. It's also very important that announcers sound like 1987 announcers; they shouldn't sound dated. They should avoid old-time radio clichés, such as "the clock on the wall says it's . . . ," and give the time the way normal people do. In fact, all announcer talk should be unaffected and very brief outside of morning drive. The presentation should not be unlike that of a bright Easy Listening station.

Although we alluded to the news and information presentation in the previous paragraph and in prior memos, one thing should be made clear. The adult who is tuned to us is typically above average in education and in discretionary income, and unlike younger listeners, he tends to be more interested in news. Paralleling newspaper readership and television news viewing, older radio listeners tend to appreciate more news programming.

As is true in most formats, we prefer to see the emphasis placed on local news. If an image network is used (a good idea), such as NBC, MBS, CBS, or ABC with Paul Harvey, then we recommend that clients use a wrap around their network news by providing a local news lead-in, go directly to the newsperson without a network logo, and out with local news following the top-of-the-hour network news. This is especially applicable mornings. News in midday can be limited to as little as three minutes at the hour's top. During afternoon drive five minutes is acceptable. News in the evening should be brief, headlines only. The news presentation can be more authoritative than in many other formats, but it still should be very relevant to the local person and should clearly explain how the news event will affect the listener. Cause and effect relationships should be clear in the story. If no cause and effect relationship can be shown in the story (in other words, the listener can't be affected by what happened), the story should not be used unless it is a particularly spectacular tragic event, in which case it is relevant to everyone.

MOR/Nostalgia programming, particularly after morning drive, tends to have a high TSL (time spent listening). Unlike rock stations, which must be particularly sensitive to the times of stop sets, MOR/Nostalgia programming, as with Beautiful Music, can be less sensitive to scheduling spots because of potential tune-out. Because of the flow of the music, it is much easier to program quarter hours, but the problem of having spots appear near quarter hours is really not much of a concern. It is when the traditional listener expects a break (particularly at the top and bottom of the hour) and is not really a problem. We do recommend, however, that spot sets be filled counterclockwise, starting from the hour's top. That is to say, the :58 be filled first, the :45 second, and so forth.

Regarding promotions, we suggested in a previous memo that promotions be life-style-oriented. If not life-style, we recommend cash. Simple promotions involving trips, vacations, and quality prizes are especially appealing to an MOR/Nostalgia audience. Surprisingly, things such as Big Band nights are not as appealing. They appeal more to an EL audience. The night out dancing and nightclubbing type of promotion does have great appeal. Cash, as with other formats, is the winner in MOR/Nostalgia. Our company does direct mail promotions, and we have found that lottery promotions and winning check promotions do well with vintage music audiences.

Now let me review what we feel should not be done in Nostalgia formats.

1. Don't treat the listener as old. Nobody wants to be considered old except the very old, and the very old aren't listeners who buy anything. Further, by appealing to the very old you drive off most who do not want to feel or think old. That's the vast majority of us.
2. Don't create fear. Funeral home commercials create fear. News broadcasts that talk about sharp interest declines create fear. Keep the mood positive and relaxing. Air constructive features, not those that deal with prophesies of doom and gloom. News features on money management, discussions on how to plan vacation travel, and so forth are always positive for Nostalgia audiences.
3. Do not let announcers go cliché crazy. Have them communicate on a one-to-one basis. For example, weather forecasts should not sound like this: "Variable cloudiness with a fifty percent chance of precipitation." This would sound more personal: "Lots of clouds today with a good chance of rain." Talk the way people talk, not the way radio announcers think they should talk.
4. Keep announcer chatter down, and keep them from repeating. Announcers do both, and listeners hate it.
5. Don't think MOR/Nostalgia is a specialty format. Our station in Smithdale is the number one Nostalgia radio station in the country with a 10.1 share. We believe everyone listens to Nostalgia, and we treat our listeners as if they're listening to the number one radio station, period. If they don't believe they're listening to the best and biggest radio station, they subconsciously will want to find one that is.

11

Urban Contemporary

It is not realistic for UC managers to expect a half-white/half-black audience. Such a balance is rarely attainable. The black demo is UC's prime market. Rather than adding white songs in the hope of expanding the white cell, UCs should concentrate on airing danceable and familiar songs to a general audience.
—Bob Laurence
Drake-Chenault Programming Consultants

This is the proverbial "melting pot" format. Urban Contemporary (UC) attracts substantial numbers of black, Hispanic, and white listeners. No other music format can claim such a diverse ethnic demographic. UC was born out of the short-lived Disco format of the late 1970s. In 1978 the hottest format in radio was Disco. Some metro markets had as many as three Disco outlets. By 1980, however, the enthusiasm for disco music had fallen off significantly, and many Disco stations abandoned the format. Those that did not chose to inject the ailing sound with hits from the pop charts, while maintaining a decidedly dance bias.

UC stations can give a CHR impression because of their fast-paced pop sound. Nonetheless, UC is a distinct format that has made substantial strides in the 1980s. The Radio Information Center estimates that a hundred stations across the country consider themselves to be UC outlets, and many of these stations operate in large markets.

UC is strong among teens and young adults and is particularly effective in attracting females. Although primarily an FM format, many AM stations do extremely well airing UC. The UC sound can be described as trendy, energetic, and festive. UC fans like the party and romantic ambience of the format. The desire to have fun is what bonds listeners with UC stations.

FORMAT CHARACTERISTICS

Music

UC stations borrow from the Dance, Black, and Top 40 music charts. Depending on the market, UC stations might skew their playlists toward a particular hit chart and even incorporate jazz and rhythm and blues (R and B) tunes into the rotation. "The Urban Contemporary format is best described as a mixture of dance music, rhythm and blues, and pop chart rock that is danceable or has a soulful flavor," says Al Parker, program director of WKKY in Pascagoula, Mississippi. "This format is the hottest in radio today, growing in popularity because the white listeners, some being exposed to R and B on an extensive level for the first time, find they like the music as much as pop and rock, which have been the white listener's (18-35 demo) primary preference. Of course, the black listener, in general, listens because Urban is the type of music he has always liked.

"Generally speaking, I think the key thing that distinguishes UC from the rest is our presentation of extended and album versions of songs, which tend to be longer than the average CHR song. TM Communications Incorporated, a major syndicator, provides a music service for our station. We use this as a base supply of music, and as a result of street and phone research, we insert music locally that we feel deserves airplay. This is a successful formula for us."

Black artists get more exposure on UC outlets than they do at other contemporary music stations. "Urban Contemporary is a dance music format combining the best black performers with a mixture of pop songs from the beat charts," notes W. G. Lynch, program director of KTIZ-FM in Alexandria, Louisiana.

Like WKKY, KTIZ also works with TM's Urban One format. "We air TM's Urban format and add to it such groups as we see fit. We play the cream of black music and the best of white, but we steer clear of blues, jazz, and street rap," Lynch says.

Boston's WILD-AM also focuses on black artists while incorporating compatible white performers from the hit charts. "WILD became more popular citywide when black artists gained greater acceptance on a mass appeal level, " says Angela Thomas, music director and assistant program director. "Our format is unique because of its rich diversity. While we are Urban and, therefore, dance-oriented, we air a fairly eclectic blend of good beat, rock, soul, and reggae. White artists are added to the rotation as they fit the sound. We're fairly sophisticated, but we do air familiars, even though the marketplace has become more knowledgeable of urban music."

Announcing

UC personalities resemble CHR's. They are hip, friendly, and highly energetic. "We use the basic CHR programming philosophy in UC," WKKY's Al Parker says. "We have white and black announcers with bright deliveries and hip personalities. We try to have as broad appeal as possible. We do everything that CHR stations do. We just play a different mix of music. We already have our black listener, and by projecting a contemporary image, the white listener, at times, doesn't even realize he's tuned to an Urban Contemporary station. We win."

URBAN CONTEMPORARY

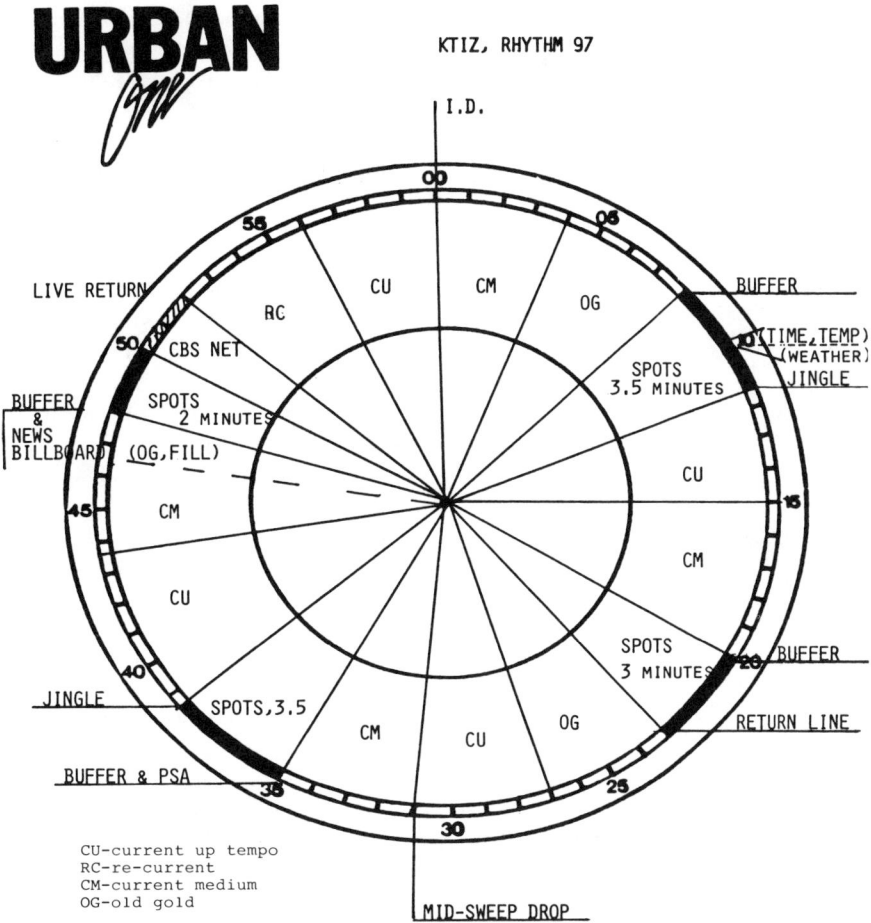

Figure 11.1 Characteristic Urban Contemporary clock with twelve minutes set aside for commercial matter. Courtesy KTIZ-FM.

In addition to a high-energy, up-tempo delivery, UC deejays must convey a genuine affinity and appreciation for the music programmed. "UC jocks must be credible—convincing," KTIZ's W. G. Lynch notes. "They have to know the music and be familiar with the artists the station airs. Relevant ad lib and with-it wit are indigenous to the format, too."

UC stations often allow their deejays more latitude than do the more structured CHR outlets, although UC stations with syndicated programming tend to reduce deejay presence.

News

The quantity of airtime devoted to news varies from market to market. Some UC stations have a more full-service slant and offer comprehensive news coverage around the clock. The far more prevalent method involves scheduling news in proportions similar to those at CHR outlets. "WILD goes expanded coverage during drive periods and backs way off during the remaining broadcast day," Angela Thomas says. "News is important at this UC station."

Many UC stations choose to rely on networks to enhance their news product. "We carry a rock news network feed, which gives us more succinct appeal," Al Parker notes. "The production value of the network's news really works with the sound we are after."

Features and Public Affairs

Music features, remote broadcasts from dance clubs, and special community events are a standard part of UC programming. "On weekends, especially Sundays, we schedule several special features of a musical nature, including gospel, Caribbean, Top 30 countdowns, and more," Thomas notes. "On Saturdays, we air a show called the 'Time Tunnel,' which focuses on an influential artist or group."

As a rule, UC stations are very community-minded and air an impressive schedule of public affairs programs usually dealing with issues confronting the urban area. "Since we appeal to such an ethnically diverse listenership, much of which resides in the inner city, public affairs programming remains an important factor," Thomas says.

Commercials

Commercials are most typically aired in spot sets at UC outlets (see Figure 11.1). Due to the lengthier nature of many songs aired in the format, however, scheduling commercial matter can be a concern. "Since we frequently play the long versions of songs, we are faced with some interesting programming problems," WKKY's Parker says. "What it comes down to essentially is reducing the number of songs presented between spot sets so that we can maintain clock."

COMPETITION

UC stations perceive the CHR format as their greatest competitor, although many programmers believe that UC is without a direct rival. "Actually, there isn't a format, per se, that poses a direct competitive threat to us," Parker contends. "Generally speaking, the black listener who likes Urban Contemporary will not tune other formats, and we actually pull listeners away from CHRs. In that respect, CHR has to compete with us, but they seldom pose a competitive threat to Urban. We have the black audience, and due to Urban's growing appeal, we pick up new white listeners every day."

Angela Thomas concurs: "There are no commercial formats that go head-on with us. In our market, another UC, KISS 108, is our main concern."

In certain major markets, the all-black and Spanish formats have diluted the UC audience pool, but UC poses more of an obstacle to these formats than they do to UC.

FUTURE

The UC format will continue to evolve to a point where it will be more mainstream, predicts KTIZ's W. G. Lynch. "We began as a black station five years ago. We are now Urban with white artist add-ons. Our on-air staff is now two-fifths white and the remaining black. Soon that figure will be more evenly balanced. We are, as are many UCs, becoming more mainstream contemporary. The line between Urban Contemporary and Contemporary Hit is growing vaguer."

WKKY's Parker sees UC retaining its distinctiveness while appealing to a larger audience: "Like the Country format some years back, today Urban Contemporary is the fastest growing format. Urban did not really exist a few years ago. R and B, pop, and rock were all being played on Top 40 stations. By applying CHR programming philosophy to Urban, the appeal will continue to expand. Our market has two Urban stations. Prior to 1981 there were none. Advertisers continue to be impressed by the format's growth, and they are seeing that they get real results with the dollars they place on Urban radio. UC is changing the market. It is competing monetarily with established formats."

INDUSTRY NOTES

A how-to memo from a UC consultant to client stations:

Do:
Talk naturally. You don't have to sound like a professor, but you don't have to sound like a dropout. Just talk to the audience the way you would talk to a dear friend. When giving the time, for example, ask yourself how you would tell your friend the time—do you normally say "It's ten before the hour of six"? Or would you usually say "It's ten before six"? Would you say "The probability of precipitation is ninety percent"? Wouldn't people understand you better if you said "There's a ninety percent chance of rain"? The point is to be a friend and companion to the listener, to give him or her the music and information that relates and will be most useful and enjoyable. So please look through your own habits and see where you might be able to talk more conversationally.

Years ago radio was an educational medium where we were all like teachers. Today the audience does not want to be educated. Whether we agree with this or not is not what matters, but are we willing to make the audience feel comfortable with us? We want to convey respect for listeners, but we always want to be careful not to sound as if we think our job is to educate. Our job is to entertain. If we can also give them some good information, that is fine, but our first job is to entertain the audience. Entertaining doesn't mean telling jokes or acting like a clown, but it does mean being friendly and human.

That even means when you are reading the news. Today's news is read in a human way, too. Notice on the networks how the famous newscasters have dropped that old serious style and have changed to a somewhat more friendly style. Again, friendly does not mean happy talk or sounding like everything is a joke. But it does not mean that you have to sound like you're teaching a class. Read the news as if you had a friend asking you for information. Avoid either extreme in reading news. Avoid sounding too light and fluffy, but also avoid sounding like the prophet of doom. Just be you. That is, in fact, the biggest "do" of all today. Radio voices and phony images no longer work for the audience. It wants you, as you really are, a friendly person who loves radio and enjoys entertaining. So do be yourself!

Don't:
Be stuck in the past. Just because you did it this way for fifteen years doesn't mean it works for today's audience. Don't be afraid to try new ways of being on the air. While basic rules of radio never change (do say the call letters every break, for example), the way we communicate does change. Radio today is a lot smoother and a lot more professional. Where years ago black stations often were regarded as second-class citizens, today's Urban stations often are number one in their market and enjoyed by people of all races. True, many successful black stations are on FM and call themselves Urban, but what is Urban really? It's just a name. The listeners don't know and care what we call ourselves so long as we meet their needs.

I can name you many AM stations that are getting good ratings, too, so don't believe that you can't compete because you're on AM—you can and you will. Listeners today are button pushers because they have so much more choice. They switch around a lot, and they don't care if it's AM or FM, if it sounds good. So don't worry. There are plenty of people ready and willing to switch over (or back) to WTTT. All we have to do is give them a reason to listen.

So let's sum all this up. *Do* entertain the audience. *Don't* teach them. *Do* be friendly and conversational. *Don't* sound very serious or formal. *Do* be yourself, as if you were with a good friend. *Don't* put on a phony voice or phony style. *Do* give your audience the information it needs. *Don't* bog down with difficult to understand or confusing communication. One more very important *Do* and *Don't* deserves its own paragraph:

Do follow the format. *Don't* let the actives run your show. Let me explain. There are, as you know, two basic types of listeners. One is the actives. These are the people who know a lot about music, have very definite opinions, write letters, complain, make requests, and give you a lot of feedback about what they like and what they want. Some of them will call you every day. The only problem is that actives only make up about 5 percent of your audience, but because they make so much noise, some announcers think there are a lot of them. Remember, if you don't get a lot of phone calls, it doesn't mean you are doing a bad show. Why not? Because most of your listening audience is made up of passives.

Passives are good people, but they listen to radio more as a background activity than the actives do. Actives are always listening very closely, and if you make a mistake, they'll call to correct you. But passives don't listen for mistakes. They listen to hear the hits. Passives never call. They want to, they mean to, but they just never do it. They don't enter contests; they don't know who Peabo Bryson is or who sang that last song. But they know what they like, and they like comfortable, familiar music—namely hits. So if you are being yourself, having fun on the radio, and playing the hits, don't be shocked if nobody calls. It just means the passives are happy and the actives have nothing to complain about. As for following the format, of course you do, but what I mean is that actives are always calling up asking for obscure and unfamiliar songs, and if you aren't careful, they'll take over the show. So do be friendly when an active calls, but don't feel badly if you can't always play what they want to hear. Requests are a nice bonus for the actives, but don't ever let the audience be more than one song away from a major hit. Your job is to keep the passives happy.

That leads me to one more *Don't. Don't* let yourself get interrupted while you are on the air. Today's radio requires lots of concentration. We can't sound sloppy or unprepared. If you are talking to somebody on the phone and then you jump back to talk on the radio, you will sound unprepared, believe me. So keep phone calls brief, don't encourage visitors in the studio (even other staff members), and keep your mind on what you plan to say to the audience. Don't open the mike if you have no idea what to say. Plan ahead. Sloppy radio doesn't work anymore. Not in UC or any other format.

On another subject, I know many of you do a lot of reading, but I don't know how much research you see, so let me share some with you. This is research done in a number of cities by my company and by another consultancy firm. The data is just another example of the way people's tastes and needs have changed. Here are some things that you might find interesting:

1. Among 18 to 34-year-olds (both black and white), the word "news" has very bad connotations. People associate it with wars, deaths, and tragedies. On the other hand, when asked if they like to know what's going on, most people are very concerned with being up-to-date or informed. So at many stations where they want to attract the young adult audience, news is no longer referred to as "news." Instead it is euphemistically called "information." Thus, people still get to hear about what happened in the world, but they don't turn off the moment they hear that scary word "news." At many major stations, they introduce their news as "Here's a W--- Information Update." Or they'll say "It's 11:00 A.M. and time for another W--- Information Update." You get the idea. While it may seem like a small point to you, if it makes the listener feel better, isn't it worth the energy to give them what makes them comfortable?

Also, 18 to 34-year-old adults have been shown to have a very short attention span. While those of us who are educated may feel that this is a shame, it is again a fact. So we have to deal with it. Research shows repeatedly that after two to three minutes of any one thing (except music), listeners get restless. Therefore, respected networks, including CBS, have designed shorter and more direct newscasts for the young adult listener. These newscasts are never more than two and a half minutes long and are written in a very easy to understand style. No, they aren't written in baby talk, but neither are they written in journalese. Keep in mind that most wire copy is written for newspapers, and when you read it aloud, it is often difficult to read and even more difficult to understand. The trend in news today is to write the stories the same way you would tell somebody some information, rather than writing them for an audience of professors.

Young adults do not want five-minute newscasts today, even in the morning drive. This is a fact that UCs must keep in mind. Older adults always want a lot of news, but on a music station it is very important that we keep things moving. Our listeners do not want long newscasts or long features or long anything that takes them away from music. Does that mean that we can't do the famous features we've done for so many years? No, but on the other hand, we need to reevaluate each feature and make sure that while we serve our audience's need to know, we do it in a way that makes them comfortable. Like it or not, research shows repeatedly that today's young adults want their information to be direct, to the point, understandable, and useful. But above all, they want it to be shorter than the audiences of perhaps twenty years ago. Like it or not, the successful Urban stations have all had to adjust to this reality. So keep being true to your news commitment, but change the way it is presented so that it fits today's adults and their needs.

2. Regarding music: Sixty-eight percent of black adults surveyed last year by a major firm said they like some oldies, they love the hits, they like some new music, but over and over they said it was the music that really mattered most to them about what made a station their favorite. They also said they considered their favorite station like a friend and they trusted it. They like friendly announcers, but they don't like a lot of talk. Even AM listeners said they listen to hear their favorite music. For these people, radio sets a mood. It cheers them up and keeps them company. This was especially true for the 25 to 44-year-old adults surveyed. The 18 to 24-year-olds mainly wanted the hits and nothing but the hits, while the 25 to 44-year-olds also wanted some information, life-style features (health, fashion, consumer tips, even horoscopes), and interviews with famous people (but short interviews mixed with music). Without exception, however, everyone was motivated to tune in by a desire for music and to be entertained.

Listeners want to hear the best of the old songs and the new songs, but they never want to be too far away from a hit. Actives will complain because they get sick of hits fast (they listen longer), but when actives are sick of a song, that is when passives are just becoming familiar with it. So again, don't worry when actives call to complain. Keep the passives happy and play lots of hit songs.

12

Middle-of-the-Road

MOR is keeping AM radio alive today. It attracts tremendous cumes and shares in many major markets because it provides an essential service. Due to its longevity as a format, people have come to believe and trust in it.

—Donna Halper, Consultant

The Middle-of-the-Road (MOR) format has been around longer than its counterparts and has its origins in the pretelevision era. Today several hundred stations, mostly AM, broadcast MOR programming, or variations of the format known as Full-Service, Variety, Diversity, and Block (Variety/Block). In the early 1950s, as radio sought an antedote to the eviscerating effects of television, stations filled schedules vacated by the networks with recorded music, news, and sports. Attempting to draw the largest audience, the majority of stations programmed mainstream artists with broad public appeal. Nothing too unconventional, avant-garde, or innovative was aired in an effort to retain the wide demographics targeted. Therefore, country, jazz, classical, R and B, and other forms of music were excluded from MOR playlists in favor of mass appeal pop standards. The idea was to satisfy as many listeners as possible. The concept of specialization had not yet taken root.

  The MOR programming approach was adopted by the many newly licensed small market stations that found their way onto the air as a result of the FCC's move to localize the medium. Numerous towns that had hitherto been without a radio outlet got one in the 1950s. These stations found that MOR generated the greatest listener and advertiser interest. In rural areas served by one or two stations, young as well as older adults found the format listenable if not captivating.

  By the mid-1950s MOR stations dominated the radio programming landscape as the phenomenon called rock 'n' roll made its auspicious debut. It would launch the true age of broadcast specialization and finally provide younger people with a listening alternative. Soon Top 40 stations were attracting those advertisers seeking a youth market. Sponsors who were investing in MOR in an attempt to reach younger listeners opted for the format that specifically targeted youth. As Top 40 stations drew more and more of the under-twenty-five audience, MOR stations adjusted their playlists to appeal more directly to older adults.

Further fragmentation of the MOR listenership occurred in the late 1950s as the Beautiful Music format was introduced. Again MOR witnessed an erosion of its numbers as the over-fifty audience gravitated to the soft, lush sounds of this newest entry into the radio programming arena.

The proliferation of station programming in the 1960s weakened the format's drawing power even further, although MOR stations continued to top the ratings in cities throughout the country. MOR stations felt the growing presence of Top 40, Beautiful Music, News, Talk, Oldies, and Country, however, and the competition would take its toll, especially in metropolitan areas. The MOR format would continue to be a mainstay of most small market AM stations.

The 1970s would have its own effect on the format, namely in the form of FM, which ascended to glory after an inauspicious start. A host of FM formats began to chip away at the younger end of MOR's traditional demographics. Mellow Rock and other contemporary easy listening formats attracted the 25- to 40-year-old listener. Gradually, MOR found its listenership skewed to those over forty-five. Many MOR outlets attempted to stem this tide by updating playlists. By the late 1970s, however, the AM band was no longer the preference of the majority of music listeners, and many MOR stations resorted to adding additional nonmusic programming elements to keep listeners tuned. According to a mid-1980s Arbitron share trends report, the MOR format ranked second in listenership on the AM band, while it fell to eleventh among twelve formats ranked on FM.

Today the MOR format is less definable and more hybrid than ever before. Some programmers would argue that the term "MOR" is no longer relevant, and some would go as far as to say that MOR no longer exists, having been replaced by Adult Contemporary and myriad other programming formulas. But several hundred stations still call themselves MOR, and they usually can be divided into three fairly distinct categories.

FORMAT CHARACTERISTICS

Middle-of-the-Road

Old-line or traditional MOR stations walk the line musically, avoiding anything too old, too new, too upbeat, or too solemn. "Our format airs nonrock standards—the best of American popular music by classic pop vocalists such as Ella Fitzgerald, Frank Sinatra, Rosemary Clooney, and Tony Bennett; Big Bands such as Benny Goodman, Glen Miller, and Count Basie; and some more recent artists such as Linda Ronstadt and Manhattan Transfer," says Janet Bailey, program director at WKBR-AM in Manchester, New Hampshire. "Our music is targeted at thirty-five- to sixty-four-year-old adults and is selected on the basis of sound, not chart position. We program songs with broad appeal. In deciding to air a song, we look at its artist, arrangement, message, and history. Because we do not have an infusion of new music like current—AC, CHR—formats, we keep the music fresh by periodically resting music."

Many MOR stations subscribe to music services, such as Al Ham's "Music of Your Life" and Satellite Music Network's (SMN) "Stardust." In 1986 SMN claimed more than seven hundred affiliates and was the largest satellite-driven supplier of MOR programming to stations in this country.

WASR-AM in Wolfeboro, New Hampshire, uses syndicated music for its polish and execution. "We've been subscribers to the Satellite Music Network's 'Stardust' format for about two years and have found it very effective," program director Peter B. Eckhoff says. "Along with the MOR music, the format offers a generous mix of talk and features that are very listenable and demographically keyed for our area."

Announcers usually play a key role on mainstream MOR stations. This is particularly true in metro markets. Small market stations, especially those using syndicators, sometimes pare down announcer presence in dayparts outside of drive times.

News also plays a central role in traditional MOR. "What makes our format distinctive and successful is our strong commitment to local news," Eckhoff notes. "Television is not a factor here, nor is the local newspaper, which is a weekly. So local news is one of our major strengths. We present three major blocks of news each day—from 6:35 to 8:40 A.M., noon to 12:35 P.M., and 5:00 to 5:40 P.M.."

Local sporting events and major league games of interest to area listeners are common fare, too, along with relevant community service features. "We embrace the listeners through public affairs shows, events calendars, bulletin boards, and the like," Eckhoff says. "'Local' is the access code around here."

Both Eckhoff and Bailey consider the Easy Listening, Adult Contemporary, News, and Talk formats to be MOR's most formidable competition. "Our primary adversaries are other nonrock formats," Bailey says. "We differentiate our format by positioning as foreground rather than background programming. This is achieved through a variety of methods, including promotions keyed specifically to our music, such as concerts. Our secondary competition comes from News/Talk because it's aimed at a similar demo. Rather than compete directly with this format, we try to emphasize drive-time information in order to cut down on the quarter hours we share with them."

Although the old-line MOR approach has lost some ground to other programming formulas in recent years, its proponents feel that with certain adjustments, it can remain viable. "This format is becoming more aggressive and educated," Bailey notes. "In order to attain and hold listeners, more creativity is necessary to add fresh music to rotations. Aggressive promotion is needed, not only from a programming perspective but also from sales. More live music and community activities get the juices flowing and keep the format vital, too."

WASR's Eckhoff concurs: "You have to beef up the music on an ongoing basis so that it doesn't become dormant. MOR does have to keep pace with the changing tastes and preferences of its public without sacrificing

RADIO PROGRAMMING

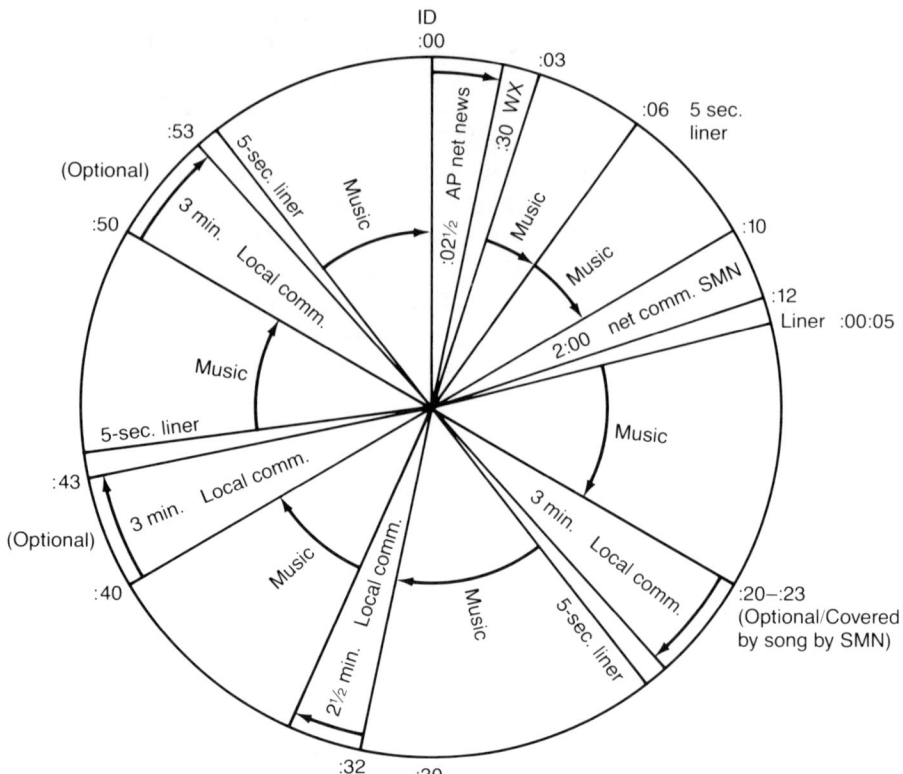

Figure 12.1 Non-drive-time MOR clock. Courtesy WASR-AM.

its basic integrity. More stimulating and engaging contests, such as our 'Club Car' giveaway, keep listeners interested. MOR hasn't been aggressive enough in the promotional area."

Full-Service

This is the most community-oriented of the three MOR format categories. Its heavy local emphasis is its primary selling point. While music is a fundamental element, it is less of a factor in drawing listeners than are its variety of features. "On an average day we'll run at least ten minutes of local and national news and several minutes of weather and business information each hour," comments Al Thurley, program director at KWNO-AM in Winona, Minnesota.

Full-Service MOR's approach to music is not unlike traditional MOR in that it sticks to well-established artists and songs. Unlike traditional MOR, Full-Service occasionally airs disparate kinds of music in blocks in hopes of attracting a broader audience. This is particularly true in small markets where certain formats are not available. For example, on Saturdays, oldies might be broadcast between 9:00 P.M. and midnight. The idea behind Full-Service is to satisfy the needs of the many—the "many" generally meaning those over forty-five.

MIDDLE-OF-THE-ROAD

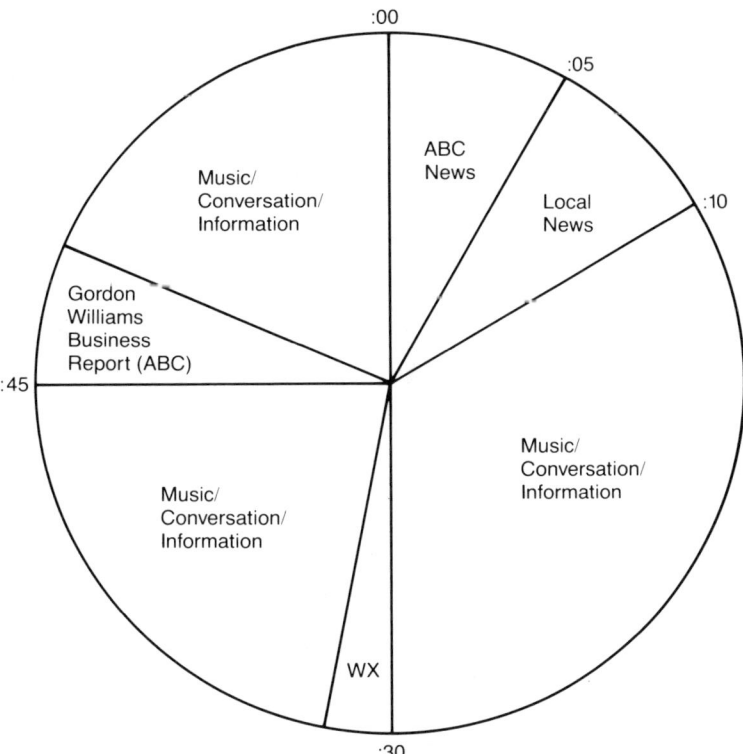

Figure 12.2 Midday Full-Service MOR clock. Note that the hour begins with ten minutes of news. Courtesy KWNO-AM.

Regardless of the size of the market in which Full-Service stations broadcast, air personalities invariably constitute a key element of programming. "A warm, funny, yet inoffensive personality works best here," says Brian Bruns, program director at KODY-AM in North Platte, Nebraska. "The announcer must be someone who genuinely relates to the listener—a friend. We tried the straight announcer style once, but it didn't work in our brand of MOR. It was simply too dry. The Full-Service format is too ingredient rich to low-profile announcing. We're live, not automated. The op-assist approach is incompatible here."

Listeners tune in Full-Service stations for companionship more than they do most formats, with the exception of Talk. Personalities are a main attraction and, in some markets, have kept AM stations on top of the ratings.

News programming is strong in Full-Service MOR. The audience expects extensive news coverage and gets it. "KODY is big on news, especially local," Bruns notes. "In fact, we offer more news and information than any other station in the market."

Informational programs dealing with a variety of topics, including health, finance, and others, appeal to the Full-Service audience. "In the 1980s, to keep pace with our listeners, we've added, among other things, business and financial news," Bruns says. "A program offering financial advice, called 'Talknet'—which we pick up from NBC—is quite popular."

A typical Full-Service hour might include ten to fifteen minutes of news, along with another quarter hour of life-style and public affairs features. Full-Service listeners enjoy music, but they want to be talked to and kept abreast of local and national events and issues.

While spot setting is evident in Full-Service, it is much less prevalent than in most formats, including traditional MOR. Commercials are aired in a somewhat more random style, based on where they fit most naturally in the flow of elements.

Other MOR format variations, as well as Adult Contemporary, pose the most substantial competitive threat to Full-Service. News and Talk formats also present some competition. In large metro areas, listeners often alternate between Full-Service MOR stations and News or Talk. To assuage this problem, many Full-Service operations offer listeners two-way talk programs, especially in the evening and overnight. This is less of a problem for small market Full-Service stations, since News and Talk stations usually are not available because of the expense of running strictly nonmusic formats.

"An All-News format would hurt us in Winona, but it's not a threat because no one could afford to do it here," KWNO's Al Thurley says. "News is big market, and even then it can be touch and go."

The age group most sought after by Full-Service stations is 39–54, although it tends to attract more listeners at the upper end of that age range. Dick Ellis, a former program director for several northeastern stations and programmer for Peters Productions, contends that traditional MOR and Full-Service stations attract an older listenership than they would care to admit. "MOR is basically a fifty-plus format and has been for several years," he says. "Of course, sports features bring in younger numbers, as do other special features Full-Service is more and more interested in offering."

The future for Full-Service appears solid, as its diverse offerings make it especially appealing. News, sports, and talk features, along with strong, locally oriented air personalities, are the lifeblood of Full-Service stations and their main attraction. Despite the continuing proliferation of specialized formats and the practice of narrow casting, Full Service stations should continue to hold a respectable share of the radio audience.

Block/Variety

In many respects, Block/Variety (Diversified) is a nonformat. It does not focus on any one thing long enough to be categorized as a primary format, per se. Because of this, Block/Variety has become known as "smorgasbord radio" in some circles. While some stations taking this approach call themselves Block, others feel more comfortable referring to themselves as Variety. Whatever it might be called, this is the "all things to all people" format.

Block/Variety stations are listed in the MOR column more because they attempt to satisfy the listening desires of a broader demographic than because they stick to the musical center of the road by playing established standards. Few stations take this programming approach. In fact, "magazine" programming, as it is also called, is relatively rare among commercial stations, although it is quite common among noncommercial educational stations.

Market conditions must be exactly right for the implementation of this format. Block/Variety seldom does well in a small market, unless the population is demographically diverse. For instance, WXXX's rationale for offering Variety is based on the fact that the competition, which consists of three other stations, programs conventional contemporary and easy listening music in an area that is dominated by a university that has no broadcast facility. WXXX has ascertained that a significant segment of the listening audience is not served by the existing stations. It also concludes that one type of programming would not attract a substantial enough piece of the audience to justify exclusivity. Thus, it chooses to program several types of music in blocked segments throughout the broadcast day.

Block/Variety stations emphasize music in general rather than a particular genre. "The sole criterion is that the music be good," says Jerome Gillman, general manager of WDST-FM in Woodstock, New York (the only station to win *Billboard*'s Station of the Year Award three times). "Our format is very distinctive and unique in this market. WDST programs jazz, rock, classical, country, R and B, and talk, as well as reading, comedy, and children's programs. We're very eclectic."

Depending on the station, news may or may not play a huge role in this format, although public affairs and issues-oriented features generally are accorded ample airtime. Announcers usually serve as hosts to the various programs and frequently enjoy personality status. Announcers are chosen on the basis of their knowledge of the particular music being presented. For

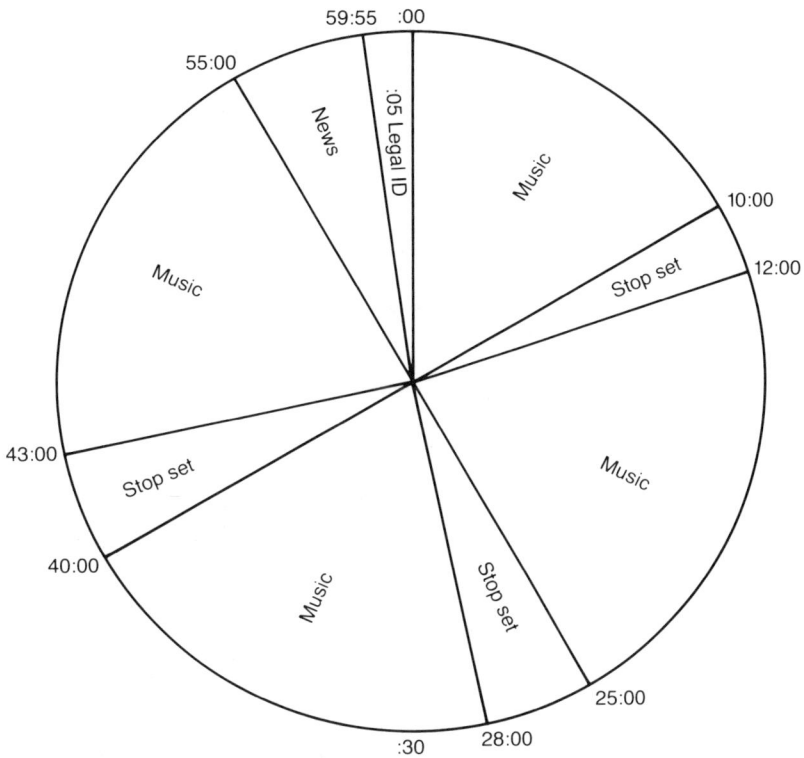

Figure 12.3 WDST's clock. Within each sweep a diverse mix of music, such as jazz, classical, rock, and so forth, is aired. Courtesy WDST-FM.

example, the host of the classical block would be expected to possess more than a neophyte's insight into that type of music. The hosts of programs on Block/Variety stations are considered authorities on the music they air rather than just announcers.

According to Gillman, Block/Variety stations do not regard their formatted broadcast brethren as competition. "There are no formats, as such, that compete with WDST's brand of programming, and that is pretty much true of other stations taking our programming approach."

In fact, Block/Variety stations often perceive themselves as the only legitimate commercial alternative to formula radio. "We are not conformists," Gillman says. "We dare to be unconventional, and the audience responds."

Gillman also believes that Variety programming is gaining greater acceptance by commercial stations around the country. "Because of our success, we're being duplicated by GMs who realize that you don't have to restrict yourself to a single musical form to attract listeners. We believe that people have more range in their musical tastes and will tune a station that reflects that range."

INDUSTRY NOTES

Consultant's MOR station monitor:

The following is based on approximately three hours of monitoring—11:00 A.M. to about 2:00 P.M. The monitor was done for the most part in my car while driving in and around the Middleton/Seymour area, several weeks ago. First the positives:

1. The morning announcer was personable and professional.
2. The morning announcer seemed to have excellent rapport with the jock who came on after him.
3. Both announcers utilized an adult-style presentation, being neither too hyped nor too laid-back.
4. In general, the station was technically acceptable and as loud as competitive stations in and around the target area.

There were, however, some problems that I was able to discern:

1. From 11:00 A.M. until 11:30 A.M. (when the morning announcer had to leave early to do a remote or make an appearance), the call letters were not said at all. Songs were back-announced and commercials run, but absolutely no call letters, even in one of those breaks. This, of course, is not a good practice in a market with other stations.
2. On the opposite end of this, we have the midday announcer, who, during one period (1:34 P.M. through 1:36 P.M.) gave the time *three* times. He also gave the time at three out of five back-announces. Does he have a clock fetish? I don't know if this was in fact the regular midday announcer, so perhaps whoever it was just was

having a tough day. In general, the time is only critical to adults during morning and afternoon drive. At other times, it can be given perhaps twice an hour, usually attached to some piece of information (bulletin board, events calendar, etc.).

3. Never, never, never go directly from a spot set into music without, at least, saying the call letters. I heard this several times, and it's just not a wise move to fail to remind the listener that he/she is with WZZZ after a prolonged nonmusic interruption. If you don't have a jingle to play out of spots, then have the jock come in and front-announce a record or something, but make sure you reestablish contact after your commercial breaks. Call letters should be included somewhere in every break. After four of five spots, some stations even pause to have the announcer come in and billboard the upcoming song just so that the listener is aware that the music will start up again soon. Human touch is very important and helps reduce the perception that the station is too cluttered. More on that later.

4. From about 1:40 to about 1:53 P.M. I heard five songs in a row segued. Research has indicated that you can segue two songs in an adult format, perhaps even three, but more than that is not comfortable for the average adult. Was the microphone broken, or is it part of the format to play long, unannounced sweeps of music, followed by long clusters of commercials? It creates a perception of being automated when too many songs are segued.

5. Along that line, it is also not a good idea to play so many songs and not tell the audience what any of them was. The announcer only gave the name of the fifth song in the set and none of the others. Since adults are usually musically unsophisticated, this can cause some confusion. While you need not do a full artist/title back-announce of every song you play, it is wise to at least give one or the other—"That was the new song by Juice Newton on WZZZ. Before that we had Andy Williams, and we started with the Beatles and "Good Day Sunshine."

6. I don't mean to seem overly critical of the midday announcer, but often when he did open the mike, he seemed very unprepared. How much other stuff does he have to do while he is on the air? Is something interfering with his concentration, or did I just happen to listen on a day when there were technical problems? He let the records fade virtually to dead air several times. While I am not saying we should be so tight that we sound teen Top 40, to be too sloppy sounds like bad Album Rock.

7. The newscasts I heard sounded very rip-and-read, even though there was a newsperson on duty. For example, in one case, he read about a "male subject." Did he mean a "male suspect," or did he read it directly from the wire in police lingo? Also, I heard no actualities [taped reports] at all in the entire cast. Several of the stories were very dry and dull as it was, so a piece of sound from another voice would have picked up the pacing considerably. Does the newsroom have the capacity to tape phoned-in interviews to be inserted into the news?

8. What I heard from 2:00 to 2:15 was very cluttered. It seemed like spot after spot after spot. While a news block is important, keeping the listener away from music for so long, even in MOR, is not wise or efficient, especially since we had just experienced a period of five songs in a row with no announcer interaction at all. This is either caused by tech problems requiring a lot of make-goods [rescheduled spots] on that day, or scheduling of spots should be juggled in such a way that after national news comes three minutes of local (you can do more in drive, but by and large, in small markets there isn't enough to fill up more than three minutes), a couple of spots, and then back to music. Research has revealed that five-minute spot clusters are a problem anyway. Could you do three minutes, play a record or two, and then come back with three more spots? The idea is to minimize clutter whenever possible.

   Fifteen minutes of nonmusic, especially when large amounts of it are commercials, is not easy to listen to and could cause people to tune elsewhere. Contrary to stereotypes about adults, most perceive themselves as music lovers, and they want to hear music more often than not. Yes, in morning things are different, but by and large, adults like to hear their favorite songs as much as teens do. The musical tastes may differ, but an adult station should still strive to be listenable.

9. The station seems to have a slight image problem. "The BBC Rock Hour" on an adult station? Also, based on what I heard, a number of songs that aren't hits are being played. On what is the WZZZ music policy based? I heard lots and lots of country crossovers. While country may be big in the market, too much of anything can confuse the listener. If WZZZ isn't a Country station, it should treat country crossovers the same as any other type of record. A balanced and varied music policy based on hits is the best course. More needs to be said on this. Let's discuss this in person.

13

Ethnic and Religious

Evil communications corrupt good manners.

— 1 Corinthians

ETHNIC

Radio stations have been broadcasting ethnic or foreign language features practically from the medium's inception. This practice continues today at hundreds of radio stations airing primarily Anglo or general market formats. For example, a station in a market with a substantial ethnic population might program Adult Contemporary music throughout the majority of its broadcast week and on Sunday set aside three hours for Portuguese language programming or some other type of foreign language feature. Hundreds of other stations, primarily AM outlets, devote themselves exclusively to a particular ethnic demographic.

Black

Of those formats classified as Ethnic, the Black format, which caters primarily to the interests, tastes, and desires of Afro-Americans, is the most widely offered. The Radio Information Center claims that approximately 175 radio stations regard themselves as Black. This number is down from 1978, when more than 200 stations presented the Black format. The rise of other formats, in particular Urban Contemporary, has resulted in the abandonment of the Black format approach by 12 percent of stations formerly classified as Black.

The Black format (called Negro prior to 1964) made its debut in 1947 at WDIA, Memphis, and then at WVON ("Voice of Negro Radio"), Chicago. The format originally aired a mix of rhythm and blues, gospel, and jazz. Old-line Black stations featured hip, jive-talking personalities and aired community-oriented promotions especially tailored to appeal to the interests of their particular following.

Initially advertisers were reluctant to spend money on a format targeting blacks, but by the late 1950s this attitude had largely dissipated as research bore out the fact that the buying power of blacks was formidable. Black stations could deliver the bulk of a specific demographic that constituted a substantial segment of the population. Advertiser skepticism ebbed.

The 1960s brought about significant changes in Black radio. As more and more black artists became known to the population at large, Black stations began to attract white listeners. To profit more fully from this occurrence, some Black stations dropped more traditional black music in favor of more mainstream programming. In addition, the crossover success of many black artists resulted in some audience erosion within the format. People who had typically tuned in Black radio also began to tune in pop stations, such as Top 40.

If the 1960s was a dramatic period in the evolution of the Black format, the 1970s was transforming. Black stations that had focused on a form of dance music called disco found their audience swelling. By the latter part of the decade, Disco had risen to national prominence and had become a bona fide radio format. Hundreds of stations nationwide went Disco, and in many metropolitan markets, as many as two or three stations programmed Disco full-time. Disco's effect on the Black format was at once interesting and disturbing.

Initially disco music drew listeners, especially younger people, to Black stations that emphasized the latest musical trend. As disco was embraced by the white audience, however, several non-Black stations converted to Disco, effectively fragmenting Black radio's listenership. This also resulted in the conversion of several Black stations to pure Disco. At the same time, many Black outlets that held fast to their traditional programming approach sought to deethnitize their sound in an effort to appeal to a more diverse demographic.

When the Disco flame flickered and faded, the Urban Contemporary format arose, and a substantial segment of the Black audience turned to it.

Today Progressive Black stations, such as New York's WBLS, not only are among the most successful within the format but also do exceptionally well in the overall ratings. While the more traditional, old-line Black format approach is very effective in attracting the over-forty demographic, the more contemporary sounding Progressive formula is very strong in the 18–34 cell and, moreover, can boast a more ethnically diversified audience than old-line.

Hispanic

Station KCOR-AM in San Antonio, Texas, first introduced Spanish radio in 1947, the same year Black radio premiered. By the 1950s dozens of stations, located primarily in large metropolitan areas and in the Southwest, catered exclusively to the listening needs of the Spanish-speaking audience.

Latin stations comprise the second largest block of radio stations in the Ethnic column. According to the Radio Information Center, there are about the same number of Spanish language stations as there are Black stations. Media experts predict that this will change, since Hispanics may become the largest racial minority in the United States by the latter part of the century.

Growth in the format was impressive during the 1960s and 1970s, as was the level of advertiser involvement. Advertisers found the format exceptionally effective in reaching the Hispanic community, where, according to recent statistics, more than 40 percent of the listening population tune in Spanish language radio. That computes to strong buying power, something advertisers keenly desire.

Hispanic stations, like general market stations, are interested in reaching a specific demographic within the Spanish listening community. Thus, many Hispanic stations choose to broadcast more traditional types of Latin music to lure the over-thirty crowd. "We program a variety of traditional Latin music that is representative of all Latin American countries, but we remain strictly Spanish in flavor," says Carlos D. Lopez, president of KNMX-AM in Las Vegas, New Mexico.

The full-service or diversified approach frequently is adopted by Hispanic outlets. "We have a Latin music orientation, but we incorporate oldies, new releases, inspirational, and some country into our rotation,"

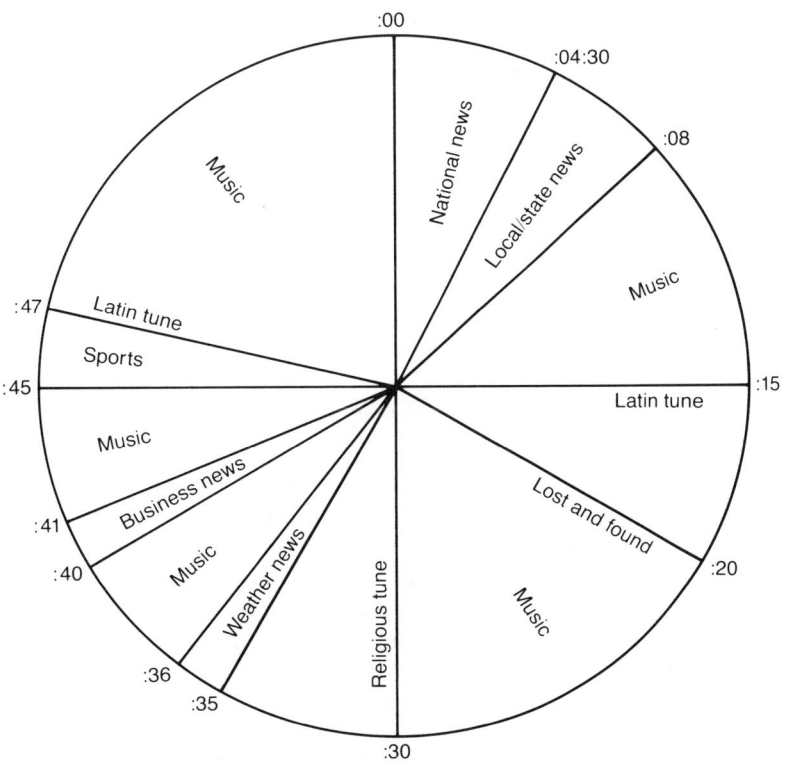

Figure 13.1 Diversified Hispanic format clock, mixing mainstream Latin tunes with inspirational music. Courtesy KCHS-AM.

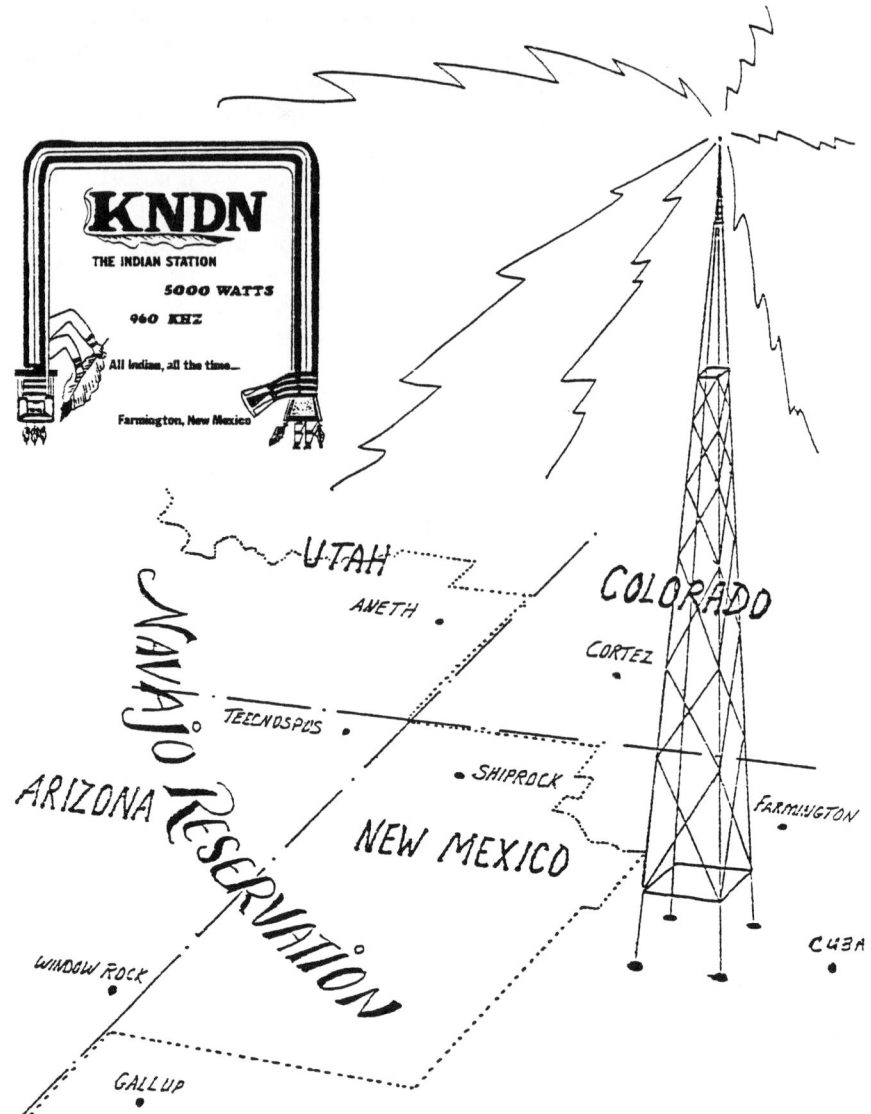

Figure 13.2 (A) Coverage maps and fact sheets of Indian station KNDN, whose slogan is "All Indian, all the time." Courtesy KNDN-AM.

notes Susan Baird, program director of KCHS-AM in Truth or Consequences, New Mexico. "We refer to our particular format as Town and Country rather than Ethnic or Spanish."

To attract the youth market, many Spanish stations tap the general market hit record charts, while still retaining their Hispanic identity. News, information, and public affairs features also are important to Hispanic broadcasters. "Along with an impressive schedule of news targeted to Spanish concerns, we program many educational features that have to do with cultural assimilation, health, religion, finances, language, herbs, poetry, and much more," KNMX's Lopez says. "We also run a forty-five-minute talk show mornings between eight and nine."

News is a central programming element in Spanish radio, notes Raul

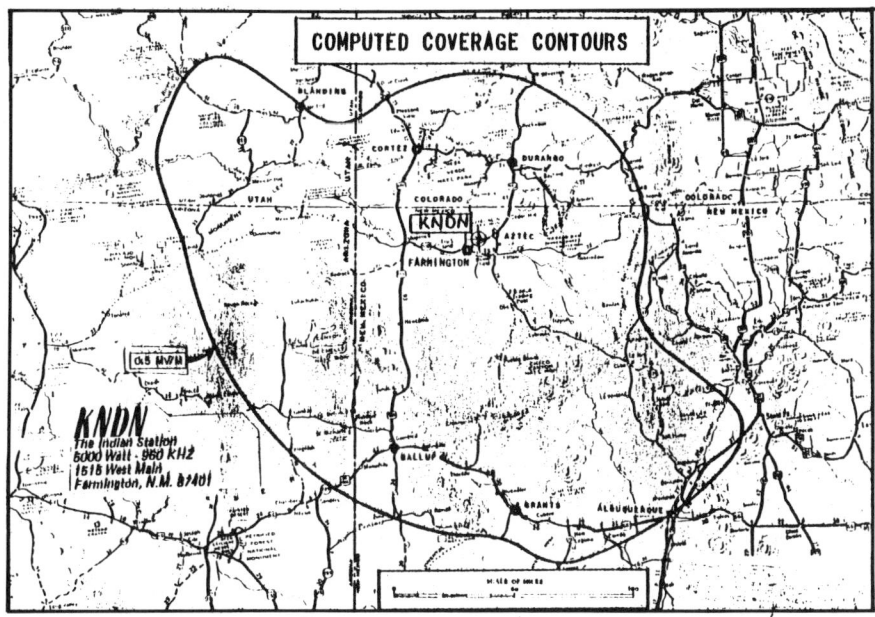

Figure 13.2 (B) *(Continued)*

Castro, program director at KRDD-AM in Roswell, New Mexico. "This is an audience that is often greatly affected by national and local news events. Our public wants news. They tune for news, and we give it to them. We also deal with civic issues through several nonmusic features, something of equal interest to listeners here."

The Spanish language format is little affected by general market stations seeking older demographics. "The older listener tends to be very loyal to Hispanic stations," Carlos Lopez says. But Urban Contemporary and CHR have had an impact on the younger Hispanic demographics.

According to KRDD's Castro, other all-Spanish stations pose the greatest competitive concern. "Anglo formats don't hurt us much. In fact, we pretty much stand alone and unscathed by other stations because of our very specialized nature. We literally talk our audience's language. About the only time things heat up is when there is another Hispanic outlet in the market, but we really face no competition in our particular signal area."

Since the number of Spanish language stations is predicted to increase significantly over the next decade, the level of competition within the format is likely to heat up also. To remain viable, Spanish stations will be forced to become more research-minded, KNMX's Lopez says. "The key to success in Spanish radio, as everywhere else in this day and age, is to stay relevant to the needs of the people who move the dial. Spanish language radio must continue to listen to its listeners. The future looks bright for us, but success never comes without hard work."

Other Ethnic

Although Black and Hispanic stations represent the majority of those classified as Ethnic, many stations broadcast exclusively to other minorities. On

KNDN
The Indian Station
5000 Watt - 960 KHZ
1515 West Main
Farmington, N.M. 87401

PERTINENT FACTS, KNDN RADIO

PROGRAMMING: ALL NAVAJO, 100% OF BROADCAST TIME, 7 DAYS PER WEEK. THIS IS A DAYLIGHT STATION

POWER: 5,000 WATTS, NON-DIRECTIONAL 960 KHZ

LOCATION: 1515 WEST MAIN, FARMINGTON, N. M. PHONE (505) 325-1996

BROADCAST AREA: APPROXIMATELY 130 - 150 MILE RADIUS (SEE MAP), OR ABOUT 80% OF ALL RESERVATIONS IN THE SOUTHWEST

ESTIMATED COVERAGE: BASED ON BIA CENSUS FIGURES OF 162,000 POPULATION, APPROXIMATELY 85,000 NAVAJO PEOPLE WITHIN THE KNDN COVERAGE AREA

* ABOUT 40% OF ALL RETAIL BUSINESS IN SAN JUAN COUNTY COMES DIRECTLY FROM THE NAVAJO.

* AVERAGE MILEAGE FIGURES FOR THE NAVAJO PEOPLE RANGES FROM 30,000 TO 100,000 PER YEAR PER VEHICLE. THE NAVAJO PEOPLE MUST TRAVEL LONG DISTANCES TO CONDUCT THEIR TRADE.

Figure 13.2 (C) (*Continued*)

the West Coast, stations program to Asian Americans, while some New England stations (such as WRCP, Providence, Rhode Island—"Radio Club Portugal") broadcast in Portuguese and other languages. In the West, especially in New Mexico and Arizona, more than two dozen stations direct programming to American Indians.

The programming at these Ethnic stations, although designed to appeal to a particular minority, often reflects general market formatting. "Our programming consists of information, news, public affairs, and entertainment geared to the likes of the Navajo Indian," says Dale Felkner, operations director at KNDN in Farmington, New Mexico. "We serve approximately half of the total population of the Navajo Indian reservation, the largest of all the U.S. reservations. A total land mass of twenty-five thousand square miles. KNDN serves about one-half the land area and one-half the population. All program elements—news, commercials, features—are done in native tongue."

ETHNIC AND RELIGIOUS

KNDN
The Indian Station
5000 Watt - 960 KHZ
1515 West Main
Farmington, N.M. 87401

SPECIAL PROGRAMMING INFORMATION, KNDN RADIO

LIVE REMOTE BROADCASTS AVAILABLE FOR BUSINESSES. ALL BROADCASTING FOR THESE REMOTE EVENTS IS DONE ON-SITE.

LIVE, ON-SITE BROADCASTS FOR MAJOR NAVAJO POLITICAL APPEARANCES, INDIAN RODEO EVENTS, AND OTHER EVENTS OF SPECIAL INTEREST TO THE NAVAJO PEOPLE.

DAILY CHAPTER HOUSE NEWS PROGRAMS.
DAILY*DINE SPEAK PROGRAM - THIS IS A PEOPLE'S FORUM TYPE PROGRAM, BROADCAST LIVE FROM THE SPONSOR'S BUSINESS ESTABLISHMENT. DAILY NAVAJO NATION NEWS PROGRAM BROADCAST DIRECT FROM WINDOW ROCK, ARIZONA (CAPITAL OF NAVAJO NATION). THIS PROGRAM IS BROADCAST BY AN AGENCY OF THE NAVAJO TRIBE, AND DEALS WITH POLITICAL, ECONOMIC, AND OTHER ISSUES OF IMPORTANCE TO THE TRIBE.

KNDN MAINTAINS AN OPEN MICROPHONE, MADE AVAILABLE DURING OUR BROADCAST HOURS FOR SOCIAL, ORGANIZATIONAL MESSAGES, LOST AND FOUND, AND OTHER MESSAGES IMPORTANT TO THE PEOPLE OF THE NAVAJO NATION.

KNDN HAS MANY OTHER SERVICES. WE ARE MORE THAN A SOURCE OF ENTERTAINMENT TO THE NAVAJO PEOPLE. WE ARE CONSIDERED A PRIMARY SOURCE OF NEWS AND INFORMATION, AND A MAJOR VEHICLE OF COMMUNICATION.

* Dine' - "The people" - pronounce: DaH-Ney

Figure 13.2 (D) *(Continued)*

The very specialized nature of KNDN's programming all but eliminates competition. "Some radio stations that 'ring' the reservation offer one hour to three hours daily of Navajo programming," Felkner says. "Stations in Gallup, Flagstaff, Holbrook, and Cortez block out portions of certain dayparts for the Navajo listener, but KNDN does so around the clock. We're pure-blood."

Some Ethnic radio experts anticipate a gradual decline in the all-Indian format in the future as Native Americans continue to be exposed to general market influences and as more Indian youths assimilate Anglo culture. Others, like Felkner, expect Indian radio to remain solid for many years to come. "Since the Navajo Indian is very traditional in his beliefs and slow to accept the white man's ways, the Indian format should remain workable for a long time," Felkner says. "Very little has changed in the many years we've aired Navajo, and there is no reason to believe that will suddenly change. We're a unique brand of radio."

RELIGIOUS

Like Ethnic stations, Religious outlets are more prevalent on the AM band, but more stations air religious programming than the number of Black and Hispanic stations combined. Today more than 450 stations deal with religion on a full-time basis.

Stations began broadcasting religion in the 1920s. Among the first to do so were KFOU, Clayton, Missouri; WMBI (Moody Bible Institute), Chicago; and KPBC, Pasadena, California. All were affiliated with religious organizations. While many of the full-time Religious stations today are owned and operated by fundamentalist Christian groups, others are the property of broadcasters who air religion primarily for its financial rewards.

Religious stations generally take one of two approaches. Some rely on music to fill their broadcast schedules, while others avoid music in deference to round-the-clock religious features.

Religious stations using the first technique typically concentrate on a particular brand of music, such as Rock, Adult Contemporary, or Country. Some religious music stations call themselves Christian (Jesus) Rock, Contemporary Christian or Inspirational, MOR Religious, and Southern Gospel, to name a few. One thing the overwhelming majority of Religious music stations share is a desire to air music that contains Christian values or life-affirming statements. Thus, records with lyrics that fall outside the boundaries of what might be regarded as morally prudent are not playlisted.

"The message in the music is very important on religious stations, so we go to great lengths to see that it conforms to the standards of our family-oriented audience," says Art Thompson, program director at WFME-FM in Newark, New Jersey. "Here at Family Radio WFME, the message of the song is more important than the artist or group."

Stations that do not program music primarily concentrate on features with a Christian or religious content. "Music plays little, if any, role outside of the regularly scheduled programs that present gospel singers or choirs," observes Bill Porter, program director at WROL-AM in Boston. "Occasionally soft inspirational music is used as a filler or bridge between our religious or informational programs."

Not all Religious stations air exclusively Christian programs. WROL is a good example of a Religious station that is nondenominational. The Boston station is one of the top-rated Religious outlets in the country, and it makes its airwaves available to all religious groups, regardless of their theological position. "Our daily broadcast schedule includes programs of a broad religious nature," Porter notes. "Although the majority of our programs are Christian, we also air Hebrew, Moslem, and other programs by divergent sects."

Many music-oriented Religious stations generate income by selling commercial airtime much like general format stations, while others depend on contributions by their listeners to sustain operations. "We're a listener-supported Christian station that doesn't go the commercial route," WFME's Art Thompson says. "We have periodic 'share-a-thons' to raise funds, somewhat like National Public Radio fund-raisers. Our fund-raisers are only one or two days long, as compared to the seven or nine days in National Public Radio."

WACE PROGRAM SCHEDULE

WACE/730
Chicopee/Springfield

MONDAY - FRIDAY

- 6:00 – Voice of Prophecy
- 6:15 – The Rosary
- 6:30 – Thru the Bible
- 7:00 – Songtime
- 8:00 – The Word for Today
- 8:30 – Listen to Jesus
- 8:45 – Shalom Fellowship
- 9:00 – Mission to Children
- 9:15 – Gospel Music
- 9:30 – Voice of Prophecy
- 9:45 – Believer's Voice/Copeland
- 10:00 – The Bible Speaks
- 11:00 – News/Gospel Music
- 11:30 – Focus on the Family
- 12:00 – Realities – M/W/F
- 12:00 – Gospel Music – T/Th
- 12:05 – The Don Wildmon Report
- 12:10 – Gospel Music
- 12:15 – Healing & Restoration Hour
- 12:30 – Old Time Gospel Hour
- 1:00 – World Missionary Evangelism
- 1:15 – Word of Life
- 1:30 – Gospel Music
- 2:00 – News on the Hour
- 2:03 – Yankee Kitchen/Saunders
- 3:00 – News on the Hour
- 3:03 – Yankee Kitchen/Saunders
- 4:00 – Roy Masters Program
- 5:00 – Faith Talk
- 5:02 – Peace, Poise & Power
- * 5:17 – Contact America
- 6:00 – Sign Off

* 5:17 – Dick Bragg's "Spell Like a Rabbit" Spell & Talk Show – Monday Only

- 6:30 – Sign Off/April
- 7:30 – Sign Off/April EDT

SATURDAY

- 6:00 – Better Days
- 6:15 – The Rosary
- 6:30 – Mission to Children
- 6:45 – American Indian Hour
- 7:00 – In the Public Interest
- 7:15 – Spotlight on Chicopee
- 7:30 – Chaplain Ray
- 8:00 – News/Gospel Music
- 8:30 – These Last Days
- 9:00 – News/Gospel Music
- 9:30 – Radio Bible Class
- 10:00 – The Bible Speaks
- 11:00 – Irish Hours/Jim Sullivan
- 1:00 – In Times Like These
- 1:05 – Irish Hit Parade/Latchford
- 2:00 – News on the Hour
- 2:05 – Irish Hit Parade
- 3:00 – The Larry Chesky Show
- 4:00 – News/Gospel Music
- 5:00 – Revival Time Telephone Hour
- 5:30 – Gospel Music
- 6:00 – Sign Off

SUNDAY

- 6:00 – Better Days
- 6:15 – The Rosary
- 6:30 – Gospel Music
- 7:00 – News on the Hour
- 7:05 – RBC - Sounds of the Times
- 7:15 – Sar Shalom
- 7:30 – Gospel Music
- 7:45 – Church in the Home
- 8:00 – That They Might See
- 8:30 – Radio Bible Class
- 9:00 – Word of Life
- 9:30 – Voice of Prophecy
- 10:00 – Park Street Church
- 10:30 – Prepare Ye The Way of the Lord
- 10:45 – Baptist Bible Broadcast
- 11:00 – Hour of Joy in New England
- 12:00 – Healing & Restoration Hour
- 12:30 – Gospel Music
- 1:00 – In Times Like These
- 1:05 – Hour of Decision/Graham
- 1:30 – Fr. Justin Rosary Hour
- 2:00 – Polish Melodies
- 5:00 – Daughters of St. Paul
- 5:20 – Amsterdam '86
- 5:30 – Gospel Music
- 6:00 – Sign Off

P.O. Box 1 • Springfield, Massachusetts 01101 • (413) 594-6654 or (413) 781-2240

Figure 13.3 Nonmusic Religious station program schedules. Courtesy WACE-AM and WROL-AM.

WROL
950 on your AM Radio dial
CATHOLIC PROGRAM GUIDE

MONDAY THROUGH FRIDAY

9:00 a.m.	THE ROSARY
9:15 a.m.	HEALING & RESTORATION HOUR Father Edward McDonough
11:45	IN SPIRIT & IN TRUTH Father Ed Serena & Jim Purtell
12:30	IN SEASON & OUT OF SEASON Father Tom Di Lorenzo & Father John Bertolucci
1:00	THE TRUTH WILL SET YOU FREE Father Ray Bourque
5:30	MISSION CHURCH NOVENA (Wednesday Only) Father Joseph Manton

SATURDAY

6:30 a.m.	THE ROSARY
8:00 a.m.	FATHER JOSEPH MANTON "MESSAGE"
8:30 a.m.	FATHER PHIL LaPLANTE PROGRAM
9:00 a.m.	DAUGHTERS OF ST. PAUL PROGRAM
9:15 a.m.	COME & WORSHIP PROGRAM with Father Michael McNamara
9:30 a.m.	GATES UNBARRED Rev. Mr. Buz & Mary Taylor
10:00 a.m.	A CATHOLIC SPEAKS OUT Harold McKinney
12:00 (Noon)	THE ANGELIS with Father Edward McDonough

SUNDAY

10:30 a.m.	THE LIGHT OF THE WORLD PROGRAM with Father Ed Serena
12:00 (Noon)	HEALING & RESTORATION HOUR with Father Edward McDonough
1:30 p.m.	WHERE CATHOLICS MEET

WROL/950 BOSTON

PROGRAM SCHEDULE (EFFECTIVE JUNE 1986)

(MONDAY THRU FRIDAY)

- 6:00 The Voice Of Prophecy
- 6:15 The King's Hour
- 6:30 Thru The Bible
- 7:00 Satellite News
- 7:02 Songtime
- 8:00 Back To The Bible
- 8:30 Messianic Vision
- 8:45 Prophecy For Today
- 9:00 The Rosary
- 9:15 Healing & Restoration Hour
- 9:30 The Voice of Prophecy
- 9:45 World Missions
- 10:00 Satellite News
- 10:05 Telephone Time Program
- (**) 11:00 TIDINGS FROM THE TEMPLE/CHARLES HENDRICKS
- 11:15 Listen To Jesus
- ** 11:30 HOUSE OF PRAYER PROGRAM
- ** 11:45 MIRACLE PROGRAM/POPOFF
- 12:00 The Restoration Revival Hour
- 12:15 Voice Of Power/R.W. Schambach
- 12:30 In Season & Out Of Season
- 1:00 The Truth Will Set You Free
- 1:15 The World Missionary Evang.
- 1:30 The Faith & Deliverance Hour
- 1:45 Country Gospel Music
- 1:57 Healthline/Dr. Joe Novello
- 2:00 Satellite News
- 2:03 The Yankee Kitchen/Gus Saunders
- 3:00 Satellite News
- 3:03 The Yankee Kitchen (cont.)
- 4:00 The Roy Masters Program
- ** 4:58 Faith Talk Feature
- ** 5:00 CONVERSATIONS WITH THE MONITOR
- ** 5:30 GETTING PERSONAL TALK PROGRAM
- ** 5:30 RADIO NOVENA (WED. ONLY)
- ** 6:00 SHERM FELLER PROGRAM
- 7:00 SONGTIME PM

(** PROGRAM CHANGE)

(SATURDAY)

- 6:00 God's News Behind The News
- ** 6:15 Sar Shalom Program
- 6:30 The Rosary
- 6:45 The American Indian Hour
- 7:00 Songtime Weekend
- 7:30 Chaplain Ray Program
- 8:00 Father Manton's Message
- ** 8:15 COUNTRY GOSPEL MUSIC
- 8:30 Father LaPlante Program
- ** 8:45 COUNTRY GOSPEL SOUNDS
- 9:00 Daughters Of Saint Paul Program
- 9:15 COME AND WORSHIP PROGRAM
- 9:30 Gates Unbarred Prison Ministry
- 10:00 A Catholic Speaks Out
- 10:30 The Irish Hit Parade

(SUNDAY)

- 6:00 The Voice Of Prophecy
- ** 6:15 Sar Shalom Program
- 6:30 The Full Gospel Hour
- ** 7:00 The Quiet Hour
- 7:30 Wings Of Healing
- 8:00 People's Gospel Hour
- 8:30 That They Might See
- 9:00 The Friendly Bible Hour
- 9:30 The Voice Of Prophecy
- 10:00 Trinity Pulpit
- 10:30 The Light Of The World
- 11:00 Tremont Temple Service
- 12:00 Healing & Restoration Hour
- ** 12:30 HOUR OF DELIVERANCE
- 1:00 Rev. Al Bates
- 1:05 The Hour Of Decision
- 1:30 Where Catholics Meet
- 1:45 Country Gospel Music
- 2:00 Father Keane Program
- 2:30 These Last Days
- 3:00 The Bishop Goodwin Program
- ** 4:00 The Irish Hit Parade

212 STUART STREET • BOSTON, MASSACHUSETTS 02116 • 617-423-0210

173

Still other Religious stations sell segments or blocks of time (fifteen, thirty, and sixty minutes) to clients, during which they can air their programs. "Clients base their buys on the donor response their features get on our station," Bill Porter reports. "WROL does extremely well for its clients and has a large donor pool."

The amount of news offered by Religious stations varies, but in the main it is less than that found on general market stations, although a small percentage of Religious outlets do place an equivalent emphasis on news programming. Network news services are prominent in this format.

Commercials are low-key and conservative in Religious radio. The use of harsh sound effects and elaborate bedding is rare, while announcers' deliveries are seldom done with high intensity. The friendly conversational announcer is the norm.

On those Religious stations featuring music, the sweep and spot set technique is most widely used. Nonmusic Religious stations that sell spot schedules insert commercial matter between features or within specially sponsored programs.

Religious broadcasters do not perceive other formats as competitive. "No other radio format competes with us," Art Thompson says. "People who want a Religious station know where to come. Ours is a very loyal audience. We offer a very specific service."

In larger markets two or more Religious stations might be broadcasting, but according to Bill Porter, the competitive climate is less heated than in general format situations. "Boston has two Religious stations, but we do not regard the other as direct competition," Porter says. "For one thing, they're a Christian music format, and we take the nonmusic feature approach. For another, they sell spots, and we market program slots. Rarely do Religious stations go head-to-head. I'm not saying that friendly competition doesn't exist; it does. But the nature of it is different from that in the general marketplace."

Religious stations have grown with the times and have exhibited a level of flexibility and market sensitivity that has impressed many, even general format broadcasters. There is no reason to suspect that the number of stations involved in airing religion will decline over the next decade. In fact, the National Religious Broadcasters Association predicts a very stable and healthy market for the format well into the foreseeable future.

INDUSTRY NOTES

Ken Carter, a nationally known religious broadcaster and owner of several stations employing the Religious format, conveys his sentiments about this unique programming service:

In previous years, the lazy man's format was the Religious format. The school of thought was "We've tried everything else, let's try Religion." The average Religious radio station owner or manager was known as Mr. Easy. He arrived late in the morning, was never available for telephone calls, and was home before the local banker.

That picture has changed. The Religious format is a very specialized format and must be treated in a professional manner by informed, energetic, and intelligent broadcasters. The Religious radio format today must present a diversity of religious and philosophical beliefs, as well as entertaining and informative programs.

The Religious station must appeal not only to the committed Christian believer but also to the noncommitted listener. Today the Religious radio station must perform a balanced format act. The station must cater to the Christian listener (not alienate him) and also must attract the new listener through its diversity of complementary programming.

Just as in any other radio format, the Religious format must be competitive. It must promote with one eye on religion and the other on radio. Management must remember that the radio station is in competition with every media outlet in the market. This is the key to success today and growth tomorrow.

14

Public and Noncommercial

Public radio is everything that commercial radio is not—and this is without those bothersome little spots that fill the ear like lint does the navel.

—Anonymous

Although the United States is the mecca of commercial radio in the free world, nearly one in six of all the nation's stations operate independently of advertiser support. Noncommercial stations date back to the medium's heyday when they provided an alternative form of broadcasting to a select group of listeners whose needs went relatively unfulfilled by conventional commercial radio programming.

Colleges and universities were among the first noncommercial broadcasters. In fact, the history of college radio actually predates that of commercial. During the medium's experimental phase, many institutions of higher learning constructed wireless stations. Among the pioneer noncoms were 3XJ at St. Joseph's College, Philadelphia (1912), and 9XM at the University of Wisconsin (1915). Most media historians regard WHA at the University of Wisconsin at Madison as the first noncommercial educational station. WHA began broadcasting in 1922 and remains one of the nation's foremost noncoms today.

The earliest noncommercial educational stations shared in common the Standard Broadcast Band (AM), although by the late 1930s, the majority had been pushed off the air by the proliferation of commercial stations. The number of AM noncoms peaked at just over two hundred between 1920 and 1935, but only a few remained in operation by 1940.

The first noncommercial FM station entered the airwaves in 1938, and with the allocation of twenty channels (88–92 MHz) for noncommercial broadcasting purposes on the newly reconstituted FM band (88–108 MHz) following the war, the medium slowly began to reassert itself.

In 1947 a dozen or so noncommercial stations were in operation. Around this time the FCC established a class (Class D) of noncommercial, low-power (ten-watt) stations, and many more colleges sought operating licenses. The lower cost of such operations was a prime motivator for schools looking to become involved with broadcasting.

Class D stations are less cost prohibitive because equipment for ten-watt stations is not as expensive as it is for those operating at more conventional levels of power. Another consideration has been the more relaxed operating strictures, especially concerning hours of operation. Until the late 1970s Class D stations enjoyed considerable latitude regarding the time they spent on the air, so staffing was not as problematical as at commercial outlets.

In 1979 the FCC, motivated by arguments presented by the Corporation for Public Broadcasting, implemented regulations that sought the more efficient use of noncommercial educational frequencies. This resulted in an extension of minimum operating hours and, when possible, the upgrading of station power. Today the number of Class D stations is small and getting smaller, since many college stations, as well as high school stations, have attained Class A status by cranking up their effective radiated power.

The growth of the noncommercial medium accelerated in the 1960s and 1970s. Currently more than eleven hundred stations fall into the non-com category. Several events contributed to the expansion of noncommercial radio. As already pointed out, the creation of twenty noncommercial channels following World War II provided the greatest impetus for the development of the noncommercial medium.

In 1967 the Public Broadcasting Act provided government funding for qualified noncommercial stations and gave birth to the Corporation for Public Broadcasting, which spawned National Public Radio (NPR) in 1970. More than 250 noncommercial stations are members of NPR, which provides funding and programming. Many NPR affiliates are licensed to colleges and universities, and others are owned by nonprofit public organizations. The eight hundred or so noncoms that are not eligible for government subsidy rely on their institutions of license for support or depend exclusively on public and private donations.

To be eligible for NPR monies, a noncom must operate with a minimum power of 3 kw and have at least one production studio and a separate on-air studio. NPR also requires that a station have five full-time employees and broadcast a minimum of eighteen hours a day. A total operating budget in excess of $80,000 is another stipulation. Consequently, 75 percent of existing noncommercial operations do not qualify because of power and staffing deficiencies. The majority of noncommercial stations are staffed by volunteers from the college or community.

Noncommercial stations can be divided into at least three categories: Public, College (noncommercial educational), and Community. A fourth category, noncommercial Religious stations, has been growing since the 1970s, and this growth shows no signs of abating in the immediate future.

PUBLIC RADIO PROGRAMMING

Classical music is a mainstay for most NPR-affiliated Public radio stations. Many Public radio stations are content to air classical music around the clock, while others choose to set aside portions of the broadcast day for classical programming. WGBH-FM in Boston has amassed a large and loyal following by broadcasting a program of classical music called "Morning Pro Musica" seven days a week. At noon the station shifts its focus to other forms of musical programming.

In contrast, KQED-FM in San Francisco airs classical music exclusively. "We're a fine music station first and last," program director Carol Pierson says. "The Bay area tunes KQED for the best in classical music. That is the primary reason people come to us, although we schedule an abundance of excellent news and information features, such as 'All Things Considered' and the 'MacNeil/Lehrer News Hour.'"

Public radio stations strive to provide listeners alternative forms of programming that typically are not addressed by commercial broadcasters, usually for reasons of economics. Whereas a commercial station might not perceive as viable a daily program of early American folk ballads, a Public station might consider it a perfect complement to its schedule.

WEDNESDAY, JANUARY 15, 1986

5:00 AM Morning Edition until 9AM
9:00 Symphonic Variations with Norm Howard. Torelli: Sinfonia a quattro in C, Maurice Andre, Bernard Soustrot, Thierry Caens and Jean-Paul Leroy, trumpets (Angel*). Mozart: Concerto No 2 in D, K314, Jean-Pierre Rampal, flute, Chamber Orchestra of the Jerusalem Music Centre, Isaac Stern, conductor (MHS). Byrd: Fantasy in three voices, Tom Pixton, harpsichord (Ti). Vorisek: Symphony in D, Philharmonia Orchestra, Michael Bialoguski, conductor (Uni). Chopin: Barcarolle, Op 60, Peter Serkin, piano (RCA). Bruch: Concerto No 1 in g, Itzhak Perlman, violin; Concertgebouw Orchestra Bernard Hartink, conductor (Angel*). Faure: Fantaisie, Op 79, Eugenia Zukerman, flute; Lisa Emenheiser, piano (Pro). Respighi: The Pines of Rome, Philadelphia Orchestra, Riccardo Muti, conductor (Angel*). Schubert, arr Liszt: Wanderer Fantasia, Ilan Rogoff, piano (Uni). Ireland: Concertino Pastorale, Westminster Cathedral String Orchestra, Colin Mawby, conductor (Uni).
12:00 NOON Forum. Call 415-553-2129 for details.
1:00 PM Just for the Record with Victor Ledin. Bomtempo's Requiem.
4:00 The MacNeil/Lehrer NewsHour
5:00 All Things Considered
6:30 MONITORADIO
7:00 A Musical Feast with Jerry Neuman. A dinner hour concert featuring a menu of tempting musical delights. Tonight's main course: Transcriptions. Bach: Sonata in g, BWV1020, Susanna Mildonian, harp; Maxence Larrieu, flute (Pavane).
8:00 KQED Presents: Pittsburgh Symphony Orchestra. Haydn: Piano Concerto in D. Mahler: Symphony No 5 in c-sharp, Ilse von Alpenheim, piano; Antal Dorati, conductor.
10:00 The Joyous Diversion with Jerry Neuman. Pipedreams: A.G.O. '84. An introduction to the 1984 National Biennial Convention of the American Guild of Organists, featuring digital tapes of concerts and recitals performed in and around San Francisco.

THURSDAY, JANUARY 16, 1986

5:00 AM Morning Edition until 9AM
9:00 Symphonic Variations with Norm Howard. Bach: Concerto in a, BWV1041, Anne-Sophie Mutter, violin; English Chamber Orchestra, Salvatore Accardo, conductor (Angel*). Foscarini: Sinfonia prima concertato and Sinfonia seconda pizigata, Catherine Strizich, lute; Robert Strizich, baroque guitar (Ti). Dvorak: Serenade in d, Op 44, Munchner Blaserakademie, Alexander Brezina, conductor (Orfeo*). Bizet: Suite "Jeux d'Enfants", Op 22, Orchestre National de France, Seiji Ozawa, conductor (Angel*). Brahms: Sonata No 3 in f, Op 5, Gerhard Oppitz, piano (Orfeo*). Smetana: "The Moldau", Cleveland Orchestra, George Szell, conductor (CBS). Strauss: Andante, Douglas Hill, horn; Karen Zaczek Hill, piano (Crys). Taneyev: Suite de Concert, Op 28, Christian Altenburger, violin; Vienna Symphony Orchestra, Yuri Ahronovitch, conductor (Pro*).

12:00 NOON Forum. Call 415-553-2129 for details.
1:00 PM Just for the Record with Victor Ledin. Unusual works by Liszt, Alyabyev and Grace Williams.
4:00 The MacNeil/Lehrer NewsHour
5:00 All Things Considered
6:30 MONITORADIO
7:00 A Musical Feast with Jerry Neuman. A dinner hour concert featuring a menu of tempting musical delights. Tonight's main course: New Releases.
8:00 KQED Presents: Saint Paul Chamber Orchestra. Daniel Shulman conducts Charles Rosen, guest pianist, and the Orchestra in an all-Elliott Carter program. The program includes commentary by Elliott Carter himself.
10:00 The Joyous Diversion: Chamber Music West. Wagner: Siegfried-Idyll. Schubert: Der Hirt dem Felsen, D965. J. Strauss II/arr Webern: Schatzwalzer. Mendelssohn: Octet in E-Flat, Op 20.

FRIDAY, JANUARY 17, 1986

5:00 AM Morning Edition until 9AM
9:00 Symphonic Variations with Norm Howard. Boyce: Symphony No 7 in B-flat, Bournemouth Sinfonietta, Ronald Thomas, conductor (CRD). Scarlatti: Sonatas, K501 & K502, Mark Kroll, harpsichord (Ti). Brahms: Sextet in B-flat, Op 18, Alberni Quartet; Roger Best, viola; Moray Welsh, cello (CRD). Ravel: Rapsodie Espagnole, Montreal Symphony Orchestra, Charles Dutoit, conductor (Lon) Vieuxtemps: Romance, Op 7, No 2 ("Despair"), Gidon Kremer, violin; Oleg Maisenberg, piano (Col). Tchaikovsky: Symphony No 2 in c, Op 17 ("Little Russian"), London Symphony Orchestra, Geoffrey Simon, conductor (Chandos*). Holecek: Smoke Rings, Josef Holecek, guitar (BIS). Taktakishvili: Concerto No 1 in c, Marina Mdivani, piano; U.S.S.R. Radio and T.V. Large Symphony Orchestra, Otar Taktakishvili, conductor (Mel).
12:00 NOON California Times. Call 415-553-2129 for details.
12:20 PM Commonwealth Club Live
1:30 Just for the Record with Victor Ledin. Andrei Eshpai's ballet A Circle....very eclectic!
4:00 The MacNeil/Lehrer NewsHour
5:00 All Things Considered
6:30 MONITORADIO
7:00 The Opera Box: My Best. The great singers captured in what they themselves considered their finest roles.
8:00 KQED Presents: Opera Around the World. Rossini's L'Italiana in Algeri. The cast features Marilyn Horne as Isabella, and Metropolitan Opera Music Director James Levine conducts this production by Jean-Pierre Ponnelle.
Simulcast with Channel 32

SATURDAY, JANUARY 18, 1986

6:00 AM Vintage Sounds. The music of the Big Bands with Bob Holmes from 6 to 10AM. Today: Swingin' Through Bandland, with the likes of Benny Goodman, Artie Shaw, Count Basie, Glen Gray, Gene Krupa, Charlie Barnet, Harry James, with a touch of Lunsford, Kenton and Miller.

Figure 14.1 Program listings for a Public radio station featuring a Classical format. Courtesy KQED-FM.

Public radio listeners expect more intellectually stimulating programming from their medium, observes KQED's Pierson. "Our listeners expect and get intelligent, in-depth information and music. Whether it is or is not commercially viable is not a criterion. We are not a Xerox machine or record player. We are responsive to our community of listeners. We inform, challenge, and entertain. In my opinion, the chief distinction between us and spot radio is the depth and variety of the music and news presented. When we do our job right, the audience responds. That is our goal. We work at satisfying the listener. Commercial stations also must please the advertiser."

In the future Public radio facilities might be confronted with an even steeper uphill climb to meet their financial needs. In the 1980s President Ronald Reagan's stand against federal funding for Public radio carried some negative economic implications for these stations. Although funding has continued, budgets have been pared. Future administrations will hold Public radio's fate in their hands. Should funding be withheld, the medium would have to rely more fully on user donations.

"Funding is, and I'm sure will remain, the foremost issue facing Public radio," Carol Pierson notes. "Raising the public's awareness of Public radio is also a challenge that must be met."

Since the late 1970s outside consultants have been used by an increasing number of Public radio stations, especially those located in large metro markets. "Consultants have been used fairly extensively in the area of audience and market research, but to a much lesser extent in the area of programming and formatics," says Ellen Kraft, program director at WGBH-FM in Boston. "The large commercial consultants, such as Burkhart/Abrams, are not usually contracted because they are cost prohibitive. Instead, programming professionals with backgrounds in Public radio are brought in. I haven't had an occasion to use a programming consultant here."

Kraft feels that the use of consultants is likely to increase in the future as the number of signals grows and competition intensifies.

KQED's Pierson perceives other Classical stations, including commercial stations airing classical music, as competition. "Being commercial-free places us at an advantage in that we have to contend with fewer interruptions," she says. "Jazz stations also tap into our target listenership. I'd have to acknowledge the existence of All-News stations, too. They can attract listeners in our demographic. We're fairly unique in what we do, so competition isn't the factor it is at other stations, particularly commercial stations."

COLLEGE (EDUCATIONAL) RADIO PROGRAMMING

According to the Intercollegiate Broadcasting System (IBS), more than 800 schools (high schools) and colleges hold noncommercial broadcast licenses, and 650 are members of its organization. IBS is a nonprofit association of student-staffed radio stations based at schools, colleges, and universities. The organization was founded in 1940 and functions as an informational resource center, as well as a source for consultation.

The majority of College stations operate at lower power, some as little as ten watts. Since the 1970s a large percentage have upgraded to a higher class, usually Class A, and radiate hundreds of watts. College stations serve as

PUBLIC AND NONCOMMERCIAL

training grounds for future broadcasters, while providing alternative programming to their listeners.

Rarely do College stations program a single or primary format. The overwhelming majority use block programming to provide options that might not be available in a particular market. For example, a College station might schedule two hours of Latin or reggae music to accommodate a segment of the population overlooked by the local radio media. See the Industry Notes section of this chapter for an insightful and informative essay by IBS president Jeff Tellis on the role of College radio.

COMMUNITY RADIO PROGRAMMING

The smallest category of noncoms is comprised of Community stations. Although few in number, these broadcast entities provide programming to hundreds of thousands of listeners.

Community stations are licensed to civic groups, foundations, and school boards, and an increasing number are operated by religious associa-

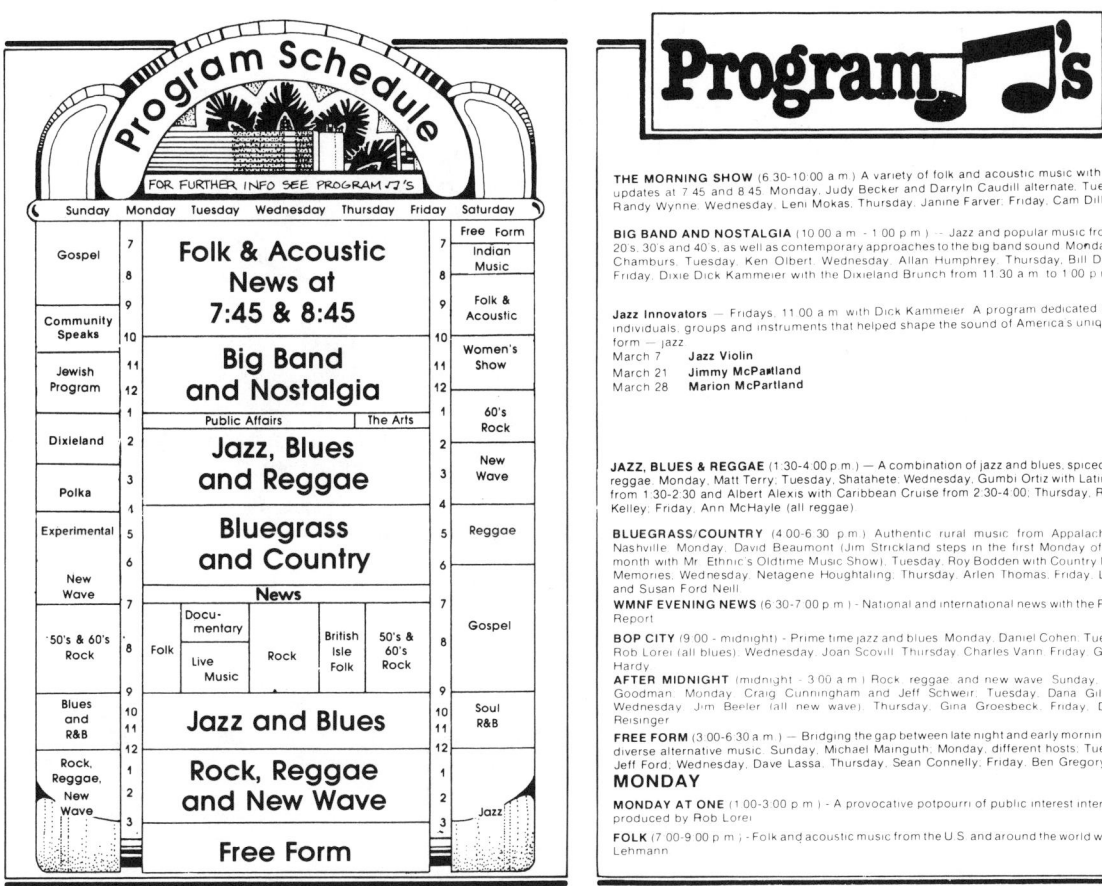

Figure 14.2 Community station program listing. Courtesy WMNF-FM.

tions. The majority of Community stations broadcast at low power, although some, such as WMNF-FM in Tampa, Florida (seventy thousand watts), are authorized to broadcast at very high power.

The block programming approach is most prevalent among Community stations. "Our listeners expect diversity," says Randall Wynne, program director at WMNF. "Included in our program schedule are folk, jazz, alternative rock, Big Band, bluegrass, blues, reggae, and so on. In other words, an eclectic potpourri of quality music. We also program to particular ethnic groups and offer substantial amounts of news and public affairs.

"Our goal is to be a genuine alternative to the other stations in this area. WMNF listeners expect programming with more integrity and imagination—a less commercial sound and a more aesthetic sensitivity when determining program content. I guess the real distinction between us and the commercial sector is our airing of music that is less popular and news that is more in-depth. We're a station with many formats. That is something you won't find in commercial radio."

Like Public radio stations, Community stations find funding a major challenge. "Unfortunately an uncertain funding base is leading to encroaching commercialism," Wynne says. "If this trend accelerates, it could pejoratively affect the nature of noncommercial radio."

As a consequence of tighter government funding, some noncoms have begun more overt experiments in the area of indirect advertising, and the FCC has allowed for lengthier on-air acknowledgments for program underwriters. "I think the future is a bit shaky for stations that rely on generous government funding, but I think enough people have grown to appreciate and depend on the noncommercial medium to secure its future," Wynne says.

Figure 14.3 While not as promotion-oriented as commercial outlets, noncoms are aware of the benefits to be gained by keeping their name before the public. Courtesy WERS-FM and Oregon Public Broadcasting.

INDUSTRY NOTES

Ellen Kraft, program director of WGBH-FM in Boston (one of the country's most successful Public radio operations), outlines her programming philosophy:

Radio is one person talking with another. When you strip away differences in format and approach, this is the one idea that holds true for all effective radio. It is also the basis of our program schedule and my programming philosophy.

I build on this concept of engaging personality and extend the approach to the station as a whole. In other words, the entire station has a distinctive personality and tone, which is an offshoot of the individual personalities of the hosts. This common thread gives a programmer the freedom to create program blocks of widely differing music forms to air on the same station successfully. Reggae is certainly a far cry from baroque music, but they can peacefully coexist if the presentational tone and style of the two hosts have elements that unite the sound.

Think of the station as one woven fabric. The colors may change from top to bottom, but the weave is the same—creating a whole piece of cloth.

Another important element in successful programming is affection for your audience. This sounds silly, but often programmers set out to try to change people's habits, to get them to do what programmers think they should be doing at a certain day and time. Instead, a more productive approach is to match the type of program content with the likely activity of your target audience at given periods.

Finally, know who you are talking to. Study your audience. Listen to them and avoid self-projection of taste or life-style. You aren't programming for yourself and your family. You're programming for your target.

One more note. I think the successful station should also leave room to violate all the rules every once in a while for well-reasoned specials. Times for extraordinary programming events that break format with unique content or circumstance should be accommodated. This will lend an element of excitement and freshness to the programming and keep the listener thinking and involved."

Jeff Tellis, president of the Intercollegiate Broadcasting System, defines the role of College radio:

For openers, the term "College radio" is an ambiguous one. While the outsider may see College radio as a single entity, it is anything but that. To some, it is a widely encompassing term that includes all radio stations based on college campuses. To others, it is a derogatory reference suggesting nothing more than an electronic playground. The most accurate, yet still practical, definition lies somewhere between these extremes.

In fact, the confusion probably results from the diversity of radio to be found on today's college campuses. These stations utilize different types of staff and any of several different methods of signal distribution, reach widely different numbers of people, and broadcast an almost infinite variety of programming.

Perhaps it is easier to draw the line between College radio and other campus-housed radio on the basis of staffing. There are a number of stations based on college campuses whose staffs consist primarily of full- and part-time paid professionals. The student role at these stations is most often as an intern. The station budgets usually exceed $130,000 per year, and they are typically affiliated with National Public Radio and qualified to receive funding support from the Corporation for Public Broadcasting (CPB). Their programming is often tilted toward classical music and fine arts, appealing to a generally older, more affluent audience. Most of these stations would never call themselves a College radio station. They would consider that a derogatory characterization. They are part of Public radio, thank you. Their affiliation with the college is often a marriage of the convenience and sometimes necessity, providing some security of funding, access to academic and cultural resources, and a location for studios and offices.

College radio stations, on the other hand, utilize a staff primarily consisting of students, often supplemented by community volunteers. Paid professionals are very much in the minority here, although one or two may not be unusual. In recognition of their increased operational complexities and responsibilities, more college stations are looking toward a paid professional to serve as general manager. Still, these stations strive to retain direct student involvement regarding day-to-day operations, programming, planning, and development—albeit with the added benefits of professional help and guidance.

Most students serve these stations on a voluntary basis, although some do receive academic credit through a practicum or a small stipend. This volunteerism engenders the kind of motivation that other stations simply cannot inspire. Staff people are there because they really want to be and not because they have to be. It's not just a job or another academic requirement.

Certainly the predominance of student staff has an important effect on the kinds of programming broadcast by College radio stations. But there are still other factors involved as well.

College radio stations typically operate with miniscule budgets in comparison to their counterparts in both commercial and Public radio. Again, diversity is the most appropriate description, with annual operating budgets ranging from under $1,000 to something approaching $100,000 per year. Funding comes from a variety of sources, including student activities funds, academic departments, the college itself, listener donations, local business donations and underwriting, and station fund-raising events. Because they do not meet the standards devised for CPB qualifications, specifically those relating to number of full-time professional staff and minimum annual operating budget, most College radio stations receive no federal funding whatsoever.

The different methods of signal distribution also contribute to the diversity of College radio. The smaller stations often use a closed-circuit or carrier-current system. Both terms mean the signal coverage is limited to certain defined areas. Closed-circuit stations are usually wired to amplified speakers in common areas, such as lobbies, lounges, and cafeterias, although they also can be wired to each room in a dormitory.

Carrier-current is a system originated on the campus of Brown University in 1940 by the founders of the Intercollegiate Broadcasting System. It utilizes one or more small transmitters, which broadcast their signal using the existing electrical wiring system of one or more buildings as an antenna. Reception is via conventional AM radios anywhere in the building(s) covered by the carrier-current system. In most cases, closed-circuit and carrier-current stations serve on-campus audiences exclusively and plan their programming accordingly. Neither of these types of stations requires an FCC license to operate. However, carrier-current stations must meet certain technical restrictions, including non-interference with licensed AM broadcast stations.

Cable radio represents the newest technology for College radio signal distribution. The station's signal is fed to the head of an existing cable TV system. From there, it is sent out over the system as a cable FM signal or as the audio portion of an automated video channel. A cable FM signal can be received by cable system subscribers who have connected their cable to an FM receiver. Cable FM can be mono or stereo, depending on the studio facilities at the station and the interconnection to the cable system. An audio signal on a video channel can be received by cable subscribers on their television sets when tuned to the automated channel involved, in most cases a continuous community bulletin board, newswire, or similar text service. Some closed-circuit and carrier-current stations have used cable radio as a growth path, providing a method of reaching beyond the campus, still without the need for an FCC license. The only required authorization is an agreement worked out with the local cable system operator. With cable radio, programming often changes to reflect the needs of a wider audience off-campus.

In terms of actual numbers, the largest group of college radio stations operate with noncommercial FM facilities. They are licensed by the FCC and operate within the commission's rules, regulations, and policies.

The smallest of these stations operate with a power output of ten watts. This translates to a coverage radius of some three to five miles or so, depending on antenna height, terrain, type of receiver, etc. The FCC is no longer accepting construction permit applications for new ten-watt noncommercial FM stations. It has allowed existing ten-watt stations to continue to renew their licenses, but on a secondary basis, receiving no protection against interference from new stations or from existing stations seeking power increases. Given the situation, most existing ten-watt stations chose to increase power to widen their coverage and maintain protection. There are relatively few ten-watt stations still on the air.

Most noncommercial FM College stations now operate with an effective radiated power (ERP) of one hundred watts or more. This is the minimum level now acceptable by the FCC for a new station application. You will find College radio stations operating with anywhere from one hundred watts to fifty thousand watts or more. In general, the more power (and antenna height) they have, the more coverage area they enjoy. That's just basic radio physics. Again programming does change to reflect the wider coverage and audience diversity.

As we've seen, College radio programming is in large part determined by the nature of its student staff, the budget and facility limitations of the station, the area covered by the station's signal, and the size and type(s) of listening audience within that area. Other factors may include the attitude and orientation of the college itself; geographic location; campus and community tastes, interests, needs, and problems; and what else may already be available on other area radio stations.

Unlike commercial radio, its prime motivation need not be attracting the largest number of listeners, which presumably translates into the most amount of advertising revenue. Unlike some Public radio, it does not necessarily tailor its programming to attract the largest amount of money from donors.

On College radio can be found virtually every type and kind of radio programming one can imagine, and probably a few that go well beyond those bounds. Whereas most commercial stations tend to have a single music format focused on constant repetition of a music playlist of one size or another, most college stations tend to play different kinds of music at different times of the week, many at different times of the day. The kinds of music may include everything from classics to contemporary, blues, rock, folk, jazz, progressive, eclectic, acoustic, heavy metal, old, new, and in-between.

These are stations that can afford to devote extended amounts of time to news, public affairs, and call-in programs at times when people actually do listen.

College radio constantly defies attempts to categorize its programming into neat little boxes like most other formats. That's part of what makes College stations exciting to work with and tune. They're often spontaneous and seemingly unplanned. You don't always know what's coming next.

Sure, there are some mistakes made, and things can sound a bit amateurish at times. After all, College radio is also a learning experience. But, in a world where conventional radio is often too perfect and sterile, it's refreshing to be taken by surprise now and then.

At its best, College radio is an alternative in the true sense of the word. It can and usually does provide another choice—something that isn't available elsewhere at all, or at least not in quite the same way.

It is interesting to note development of the evolutionary cycle in College radio programming. Originally, College radio took commercial radio as its role model and tried simply to imitate (a few stations still do). Then College radio became the proving ground for what was called underground or progressive radio. It started playing album music that ran well past the 2- to 3-minute maximum imposed by the then dominant Top 40 stations featuring hit singles. It started playing clusters of cuts that related musically, thematically, or otherwise, and the concept of sets developed. It gave the listener credit for some intelligence and reflected it in its programming.

The success of this alternative kind of programming was quickly noticed by commercial FM station programmers, and they adapted to suit their purposes. For a while this worked for them, but then the inevitable commercial pressures won out, and playlists were again tightened. This makes College radio today even more of an alternative than it was.

But now commercial radio programmers, unwilling to take chances on new artists and new music themselves, are listening to College radio to find out what is new. Today's College radio programmers are not afraid to experiment, to try out a new artist or some new music. They have become the cutting edge for independent record labels, an audience interested in more than just the hits, and commercial radio programmers looking for new ideas.

College radio is no longer simply an electronic playground, if indeed it ever was. Those who staff, program, and operate these stations take what they do seriously.

The medium is maturing. Its audience is growing as new stations come on the air and existing stations increase their power. Its graduates are going on to populate the professional broadcast industry. It's a place where exciting things are happening constantly. It is no longer a hidden medium. College radio is growing up.

Fran Berger, director of radio at Emerson College's WERS-FM, recounts her experiences when first assuming programming responsibilities for the station:

Coming from a commercial broadcast background, I had grown to know and respect the quality broadcasting in Boston, the nation's seventh largest radio market. I had lived, breathed, and worked with the best, and now I was faced with management responsibility of what most people referred to as the playpen.

It seemed there was an immediate assumption by both students and the audience that a college-staffed and -run station would be a place to go crazy, to play radio with little regard for quality programming. This is the image we set out to change.

First we needed to establish a programming philosophy. We started by deciding all our programming would offer an alternative to what you could find on other area stations. This was a departure from letting the students program what they knew best, which usually amounted to all day rock 'n' roll.

It was not easy at first finding the right students. However, there were one or two who appreciated jazz and were willing to learn, an occasional student with a passion for folk and acoustic music, and a few who were getting hooked on reggae.

Little by little we refined our air product. Our major departure from other noncom FMs was a decision to offer consistent programming Monday through Friday. Although the hosts would change, our listeners could always start their mornings with our acoustic program "Coffeehouse," which would always be followed by our "Jazzoasis," then our fusion show, and so on throughout the day.

The student programmers learned to work with clocks, a different one for each format. They learned the necessity of consistency, yet we still allowed room for personality and individual growth.

Many of our shows have had the same time slots for several years now and have a loyal and supportive audience. Above all they are patient and stick with us through each semester as we change our air staff and fluctuate in quality. The audience is also one of the best learning points for the students because they call in with constructive criticism, and when it's not constructive, the students need to learn how to deal with that as well.

The hardest part about managing a noncommercial, student-run station is the need to balance the learning experience with the desire to sound constantly professional. You have to allow the students to take risks, to make mistakes, but you also must impress upon them the power they possess with an open microphone.

Suggested Reading

Delong, Thomas A. *The Mighty Music Box*. Los Angeles: Amber Crest Books, 1980.
Eastman, Susan Tyler, et al., eds. *Broadcast Programming: Strategies for Winning Television and Radio Audiences*. Belmont, CA: Wadsworth Publishing, 1981.
Fornatale, Peter, and J. E. Mills. *Radio in the Television Age*. New York: Overlook Press, 1980.
Hall, Claude, and Barbara Hall. *This Business of Radio Programming*. New York: Billboard Publishing, 1978.
Keirstead, Phillip A. *All-News Radio*. Blue Ridge Summit, PA: Tab Books, 1980.
Keith, Michael C., and J. M. Krause. *The Radio Station*. Stoneham, MA: Focal Press, 1986.
MacFarland, David T. *The Development of the Top 40 Format*. New York: Arno Press, 1979.
McCavitt, William E., and P. K. Pringle. *Electronic Media Management*. Stoneham, MA: Focal Press, 1986.
National Association of Broadcasters. *Radio in Search of Excellence*. Washington, DC: NAB, 1985.
Routt, Ed, et al., *The Radio Format Conundrum*. New York: Hastings House, 1978.
Shane, Ed. *Programming Dynamics*. Overland Park, KS: Globecom, 1984.
Sklar, Rick. *Rocking America: How the All-Hit Radio Stations Took Over*. New York: St. Martin's Press, 1984.
Sterling, Christopher H. *Electronic Media*. New York: Praeger, 1984.

Index

Abrams, Lee, 89, 96
Acid Rock (Psychedelic) stations, 90
Adult Contemporary (AC), 45–58
  codification in, 21
  commercials on, 28
  as competition
    to Contemporary Hit Radio, 69
    to Country, 130
    to Easy Listening, 84
    to Middle-of-the-Road, 157
    to Vintage, 142
  competition against, 53
  drive-time format clock, 47
  format characteristics of, 46–53
  future of, 53–54
  industry notes on, 54–58
Advertisers, 167
Album-Oriented Rock (AOR), 89–97
  approach to news, 23–24
  as competition
    to Contemporary Hit Radio, 69
    to Vintage, 142
  competition against, 95
  format characteristics of, 91–95
  future of, 95–96

  industry notes on, 96–97
Allen, Bruce W., 125, 128, 129, 130, 131, 132
American Indian radio, 170–171
AM programming, 3, 6, 11
  dial position and, 14
  noncommercial, 177
  operating constraints and, 14
  stereo, 14
Announcing, 26–27
  on Adult Contemporary stations, 48–49
  on Album-Oriented Rock stations, 91–92
  on Classical stations, 116–117
  on Contemporary Hit Radio, 66–67
  on Country stations, 128
  on Easy Listening stations, 80–81
  on Middle-of-the-Road stations, 157, 159, 161–162
  on talk shows, 103
  on Urban Contemporary stations, 148–149
  on Vintage stations, 137–139
Arbitron, 5, 6
Artists, black, 148

Asian American radio, 170
Audience
  for classical music, 19
  for Middle-of-the-Road programs, 45–46
  targeting of, 18
Austin, Jim, 137–139, 142–143
Austin, John, 124, 128–131
Automation, 20, 49

Bailey, Janet, 156–157
Baird, Susan, 168
Beatles, 60
Beautiful Music (BM), 77–78, 156. *See also* Easy Listening (EL)
Begin, Gary, 26
Berger, Fran, 187–188
Big Band, 135–136. *See also* Vintage
"Big Chill" format, 135–136. *See also* Vintage
Black artists, 148
Black format, 165–166. *See also* Urban Contemporary (UC)
Block/Variety (Diversified), 160–162
Blore, Chuck, 135
Boston, 114

191

INDEX

Boulos, Andrea, 47, 49
Bronze records, 22
Browning, Paul, 91, 95
Bruns, Brian, 159

Cable radio, 185
Call letters, 30
Call out (telephone) research, 34
Carlin, George, 69
Carpenter, George, 48, 50, 52, 53
Carrier-current, 185
Carucci, John, 48
Caruso, Enrico, 113
Castro, Raul, 168–169
Chapman, Christopher, 50, 53, 54
Chicken Rock, 45
Clark, John, 46, 49
Class A stations, 178
Class D stations, 178
Classical, 113–121
    audience for, 19
    competition against, 119–120
    format characteristics of, 114–119
    future of, 120
    industry notes on, 120–121
Classic Hits, 135–136. *See also* Vintage
Codification of music, 21
College (educational) radio programming, 177, 180–181, 183–187
Commercials, 27–29
    on Adult Contemporary stations, 52–53
    on Album-Oriented Rock stations, 94
    on Classical stations, 119
    cluster or spot set method of presenting, 82
    on Contemporary Hit Radio, 68
    on Country stations, 130
    on Easy Listening stations, 82–83
    on Middle-of-the-Road stations, 160
    on News stations, 102
    on Religious stations, 174
    on Talk stations, 105
    on Urban Contemporary stations, 150
    on Vintage stations, 142
Community radio programming, 181–182
Competition
    to Adult Contemporary programming, 53
    to Album-Oriented Rock programming, 95
    to Classical programming, 119–120
    to Contemporary Hit programming, 69
    to Country programming, 130–131
    to Easy Listening programming, 84
    head-to-head, 20–21
    increase in, 3, 12
    market assessment and, 14
    to News and Talk programming, 107
    to Urban Contemporary programming, 150
    vertical and horizontal diffusion, 142
    to Vintage programming, 142–143
Computers in radio, 42–43
Consultants, 1–12
    directory, 8
    emergence of, 1–6
    future of, 11–12
    monitor sheets, 32
    obstacles faced by, 36–38
    research techniques, 33–36
    types of, 7–11
    See also Formatics; Industry notes; specific names
Contemporary country, 125
Contemporary Hit Radio (CHR), 59–75
    approach to news, 23–24
    commercials on, 28
    as competition
        to Adult Contemporary, 53
        to Album-Oriented Rock, 90, 95
        to Country, 130–131
        to Urban Contemporary, 150
        to Vintage, 142
    competition against, 69
    format characteristics of, 61–69
    future of, 69–70
    industry notes on, 70–75
    Oldies on, 61
Contests and promotions, 29–30
    on Adult Contemporary stations, 52
    on Album-Oriented Rock stations, 94–95
    on Classical stations, 119
    on Contemporary Hit Radio, 67–68
    on Country stations, 130
    on Easy Listening stations, 81
    on Talk stations, 104–105
    on Vintage stations, 140–141
Cooke, Holland, 101, 107, 108
Cost considerations, 20
Country programming, 123–133
    commercials in, 28
    as competition
        to Adult Contemporary, 53
        to Easy Listening, 84
        to News and Talk, 107
    competition against, 130–131
    format characteristics of, 124–130
    future of, 131–132
    industry notes on, 132–133
Critiquing time, methods and procedures, 31–38

Dayparts, announcing and, 27
DeDominicis, Enzo, 83
Dees, Rick, 26
DeMaroney, Gary, 128, 131
Denton, C. David, 124, 128
Dial position, AM programming and, 14
Diffusion, vertical and horizontal, 142
Directors, program, 11, 37
Directory, consultant, 8
Disc jockeys, 40. *See also* Announcing
Disco format, 147, 166
Dobry, Ryan, 125, 128, 130
Docket 80–90, 11
Douglas, Dwight, 90, 99
    on computers in radio, 42–43
Drake, Bill, 60, 66, 135
Drugs, mind-altering, 90

Easy Listening (EL), 77–87
    commercials on, 28
    as competition
        to Adult Contemporary, 53
        to Classical, 119–120
        to Middle-of-the-Road, 157
        to Vintage, 142
    competition against, 84

INDEX

format characteristics of, 78–84
future of, 85
industry notes on, 85–87
spot set, 29
Eckhoff, Peter B., 157–158
Edwards, Mike, 61, 66, 67, 68, 69–70, 102, 107, 108
Ellis, Dick, 80, 81, 140, 160
Ethnic and religious programming, 165–175
   Black format, 165–166
   cost considerations in, 20
   Hispanic format, 166–169
   industry notes on, 174–175

Facilitator, 33
Features, 31
   on Album-Oriented Rock stations, 93–94
   on Classical stations, 118
   on Contemporary Hit Radio, 67
   on Easy Listening stations, 81
   on News stations, 101–102
   on Religious stations, 172
   on Talk stations, 104
   on Urban Contemporary stations, 150
   on Vintage stations, 140
Federal Communications Commission (FCC), 2, 4, 11–12, 178
   on nonentertainment programming, 24–25
Felkner, Dale, 170–171
Fenning, Al, 79, 80
Fenstermacher, Peter, 28
FM programming, 3–4, 6
   Beautiful Music, 77–78
   Middle-of-the-Road format and, 156
   noncommercial, 178
   operating constraints and, 14
   Top 40 in, 60
FM station classifications, 11–12
Focus groups, 33–34, 35
Foreign language (Ethnic) format. *See* Ethnic and religious programming
Formatics, 13–43
   in Adult Contemporary programming, 46–53
   in Album-Oriented programming, 91–95
   announcing styles and, 27
   in Classical programming, 114–119
   in Contemporary Hit programming, 61–69
   in Country programming, 124–130
   critiquing time and, 31–38
   in Easy Listening programming, 78–84
   elements of programming and, 21–31
   in ethnic and religious programming, 165–169
   format selection, 13–21
      audience targeting and, 18
      case study of, 15–18
      cost considerations in, 20
      head-to-head competition and, 20–21
      income generation and, 18
      radio's popularity and, 18
   industry notes on, 38–43
   in Middle-of-the-Road programming, 156–162
      Block/Variety (Diversified), 160–162
      Full-Service, 158–160
      Middle-of-the-Road, 156–158
   in news programming, 100–102
   in news/talk and news plus programming, 105–107
   in talk programming, 102–105
   in Urban Contemporary programming, 148–150
   in Vintage programming, 137–142
Format sweep, 79
Frankel, Stuart, 71, 73
Full-Service, Variety, Diversity, and Block (Variety/Block) format, 155
Funding
   for community stations, 182
   for Public radio, 180
Furr, Jim, 78, 80, 81, 84

G-105-FM, 61, 66
Gabriel, John, 137, 140, 142
Gallagher, Brian, 48, 53
Gillman, Jerome, 161, 162
Gold records, 22
Gruver, Fleet, 137, 139, 142, 143

Haley, Bill, 2
Halper, Donna, 7, 8–9, 11, 18, 19, 31, 36–38, 69, 130, 155
Ham, Al, 136
Harney, Carl Z., 135
Harris, George, 35
Hayes, Jack, 125
Henabery, Robert E., 45
Hispanic format, 166–167
Hoffman, John, 107, 108
Holly, Gene, 107
Horton, Keith W., 77
Hot Adult, 46
Hotchkiss, Tom, 30

Imus, Don, 26
Income, generating, 18, 19
   through funding, 180, 182
   See also Commercials
Industry notes
   on Adult Contemporary programming, 54–58
   on Album-Oriented programming, 96–97
   on Classical programming, 120–121
   on Contemporary Hit programming, 70–75
   on Country programming, 132–133
   on Easy Listening programming, 85–87
   on ethnic and religious programming, 174–175
   on formatics, 38–43
   on Middle-of-the-Road programming, 162–164
   on News and Talk programming, 108–111
   on Urban Contemporary programming, 151–154
   on Vintage programming, 144–146
Informants, 33
Intercollegiate Broadcasting System (IBS), 180
Irmiter, Peter, 79, 81, 84

Jacobs, Karrie, 71
Jennings, Al, 85
Jingles, 30
   on Album-Oriented Rock stations, 94–95
   on Contemporary Hit Radio, 69

193

INDEX

on Country stations, 130
on Talk stations, 105
on Vintage stations, 142
Jocks. *See* Announcing; Disc jockeys
Johnson, Byron K., 107, 108
Joseph, Mike, 3, 4, 30, 33, 34, 60

KABC, 99
KAFY-AM, 125
KCAP, 49
KCOR-AM, 166
Keller, Eliot, 33, 37
KFOU, 172
KGO, 99
KGRC, 48, 49–50
KHFM, 118
KMPX-FM, 89
KNDN, 170–171
Kolodziej, Ann L., 48, 52
KORK-AM, 137–139, 140, 142–143
KPBC, 172
KQED-FM, 179
Kraft, Ellen, 180, 183
Krause, Joe, 28, 29
KRLA, 137
KSDY-FM, 125–127
KSYZ, 66
KTIZ, 148

Ladd, Craig, 102, 107, 108
Langner, Mike, 115, 117, 118, 120
Laurence, Bob, 147
Letters, call, 30
Lite (Soft) AC, 46
Lopez, Carlos D., 167, 168, 169
Lynch, W. G., 148, 149, 150–151

McGregor, Bruce, 91, 92–94, 95
McIntosh, Edward, 125–127, 128, 132
McLendon, Gordon, 3, 77, 99
McShay, Wes, 61
Maintenance, quarter-hour, 28
Male Adult Contemporary (MAC), 90
Management, 41–42
Market assessment, 14
Marshall, John, 91, 95, 96
Mellow Rock, 45–46
Michaels, Conrad, 105–106
Middle-of-the-Road (MOR), 155–164

approach to news, 24
audience for, 45–46
commercials on, 28
as competition to Country, 131
format characteristics of, 156–162
  Block/Variety (Diversified), 160–162
  Full-Service, 158–160
  Middle-of-the-Road, 156–158
industry notes on, 162–164
MOR Country, 125
Monitor sheets, 32
Mosley, Chip, 61, 66, 69
Music, 21
  Adult Contemporary, 46–48
  Album-Oriented Rock, 91
  charts, 36
  Classical, 114–116
  codification of, 21
  Contemporary Hit Radio, 61–66
  Country, 124–127
  Easy Listening, 78–80
  Middle-of-the-Road, 156, 158, 161
  National Public Radio, 179
  notation patterns for, 21–23
  playlist, 21
  Religious, 172
  syndicated, 9–11, 80, 148, 157
  testing, 35
  Urban Contemporary, 148
  Vintage, 137

National Association of Broadcasters (NAB), 28
National Public Radio (NPR), 178
Natural talent, xiii
Navajo Indian radio, 170–171
News, 23–25
  on Adult Contemporary stations, 49–51
  on Album-Oriented Rock stations, 92–93
  on Classical stations, 117
  on Contemporary Hit Radio, 67
  on Country stations, 128–129
  on Easy Listening stations, 81
  on Middle-of-the-Road stations, 157, 159–160
  on Religious stations, 174
  on Spanish stations, 168–169

on Talk stations, 104
on Urban Contemporary stations, 149–150
on Vintage stations, 139–140
News and Talk radio, 99–111
  as competition
    to Classical, 119–120
    to Country, 131
    to Easy Listening, 84
    to Middle-of-the-Road, 158
  competition against, 107
  future of, 107–108
  industry notes on, 108–111
  news characteristics and, 100–102
  News/Talk and News Plus characteristics and, 105–107
  Talk characteristics and, 102–105
Nostalgia, 135–136
  cost considerations in, 20
  See also Vintage

Odom, Homer, 79, 84, 85
Oliver, Denise, 53
O'Neil, Chuck, 80, 84

Parker, Al, 148, 150, 151
Pellegrini, Norman, 113
Personalities, 40. *See also* Announcing
Peterson, Brad H., 125, 131, 132
Pierson, Carol, 179, 180
Playlists, 21
  freshening of, 143
Pollack, Jeff, 142
Popularity of radio, 18
Porter, Bill, 172, 174
Portuguese radio, 170
Positioning, 15
Power cuts, 22
Presentation schema, 13
Presley, Elvis, 60
Princi, Carlo, 116–117
Program directors (PDs), 11, 37
Progressive (Free) Form, 89–90
Promotions. *See* Contests and promotions
Psychedelic (Acid Rock) stations, 90
Public Affairs, 25
  on Adult Contemporary stations, 52

194

INDEX

on Classical stations, 119
on Contemporary Hit Radio, 68
on Easy Listening stations, 82
on Urban Contemporary stations, 150
on Vintage stations, 142
Public and noncommercial programming, 177–188
  college (educational) radio, 177, 180–181, 183–187
  community radio, 181–182
  as competition to Classical, 114, 119
  industry notes on, 183–188
Public radio, 179–180
Publications, trade, 17
Public Broadcasting Act (1967), 178
Pyne, Joe, 103

Quarter-hour maintenance, 28

Raab, Gregory, 125, 130, 131
Rabb, Joel, 123
Radcliffe, Pru, 61, 67, 69
Radio and Records, 17
Radio and Television News Director's Association (RTNDA), 24–25
Reagan, Ronald, 180
"Rebel rock," 124
Recurrents, 22
Redo, Philip L., 48, 49, 54
Religious format, 172–174
Research Techniques, 33–36
Rock 'n' roll, 2, 123, 155–156
Rotations for playing music, 21–23

St. Pierre, Ron, 25, 26, 103
Sales, 40–41
Satellite Music Network (SMN), 157
Schema, presentation, 13
Scott, Dave, 9, 12
Segues, 46
Seymour, Steve, 71, 73, 74
Shane, Ed, 45
Sherman, Robert, 116–117
Signal coverage area, 5
Simon, Herbert, 41
Sklar, Rick, 7–8, 31, 33, 37, 59, 102
  article on, 71–75

Smith, Jim, 24–25, 31, 37
  critiquing approach of, 38–40
Soft Rock, 46
Spanish radio, 166–169
Specialization in radio programming, 12
Sports, 25–26, 157
Spots, 27–29. *See also* Commercials
Standard Broadcast Band. *See* AM programming
Stars, radio, 26–27
Stereo, 41, 113
Stewart, Bill, 59
Storz, Todd, 3, 59
Straus, Jeanne H., 102, 107, 108
Super cuts, 22
Superjocks, 26
Sweep format, 79
Syndicated music, 9–11, 80, 148, 157

Talent, natural, xiii
Targeting the audience, 18
Taylor, Marlin R., 22, 77
Teare, Paul, 117, 118, 119, 120
Telephone (call-out) research, 34
Telephone talk shows, 102
Television, 1–2
Tellis, Jeff, 181, 183–187
Terry, Bill, 66, 67, 69
Testing, music, 35
Thomas, Angela, 148, 149, 150
Thompson, Art, 172, 174
Thurley, Al, 158, 160
Time, critiquing, 31–38
TM Communications Incorporated, 148
Top 40 format, 2–3, 59–60, 156
Toscanini, Arturo, 113
Trade music charts, 36
Trade publications, 17
Traditional country, 124
Transistor, 2
Trembley, Mike, 48–49, 53
Tucker, David, 116–117
Two-way talk shows, 102

Underground rockers, 90
Urban Contemporary (UC), 147–154
  commercials on, 28
  as competition to Black format, 166

to Contemporary Hit Radio, 69
competition against, 150
format characteristics of, 148–150
future of, 150–151
industry notes on, 151–154

Vaneno, Dan, 101, 107, 108
Variety/Block, 155
Vasser, David L., 47, 48, 49, 53, 54
Vintage, 135–146
  competition against, 142–143
  format characteristics of, 137–142
  future of, 143–144
  industry notes on, 144–146

WABZ, 49
Wagner, Mike, 137, 139, 143
Walter, Skip, 125, 128
WAPP-FM, 28
WASR-AM, 157
"Watching a Radio Consultant Consult" (Jacobs), 71–75
WBCM-AM, 105–106
WBLI, 66
WDIA, 166
WDOK, 81
Weather, 26
WGBH, 114, 179
WGMS, 117, 118
WHA, 177
WHJJ-AM, 25
WHN-AM, 124
WILD-AM, 148
Williams, Jay, 8, 14, 18, 37, 135
  on aspects of radio station operation, 40–42
Wimmer, Ralph, 71, 74
WINS-AM, 99
Winston, Dave, 137, 139, 140, 142, 143
WKKY, 148
WLAM, 54
WLRS-FM, 61
WLTW, 47–48, 49
WMBI, 172
WMNF-FM, 182
WNWS, 99
WOR-FM, 89
WQXR-AM, 113
WROL, 172

INDEX

WRRZ, 124
WSAM, 137, 139, 140, 142
WSM, 123
WTCM, 125

WTOP-AM, 101
WTRY, 137, 140
WVON, 166
Wynne, Randall, 182

WZOZ, 52

XETRA, 99

Yates, Chuck, 48, 50, 52, 53

PN 1991.55 .K45 1987

	DATE DUE		
FEB 2 8 1991			
SEP 3 0 1991			
SEP 2 0 1993			

PN 1991 .55 .K45 1987